From Zero Waste to Material Closed Loop
The Way Towards Circular Economy

从零废弃到闭环物料
——通往循环经济之路

Jianming Yang

杨剑明 著

From Zero Waste to Material Closed Loop

The Way Towards Circular Economy

从零废弃到闭环物料

——通往循环经济之路

内容简介

本书是《从零废弃到闭环物料——通往循环经济之路》的英文版，共分14章，从废弃物的来源、形态、种类开始，介绍了其管理、转化和处理处置技术，在此基础上引入了"零废弃"的理论与实践，并进一步介绍了与零废弃相关的绿色设计、逆向物流和闭环物料。通过不同行业面临的零废弃机遇和挑战，阐述了循环经济这一重要发展概念，并从3个层面讨论了循环经济的标准与认证。最后从哲学与环境伦理学的角度对零废弃做了简单解读。书后附有美国、欧洲及中国颁布的废弃物相关标准列表，供读者参考。

本书内容丰富，涉及了零废弃的方方面面，语言流畅易懂，理论与实践并重。本书可供清洁生产、循环经济相关企事业单位中从事环境管理工作的专业人员参考，也可供高等学校环境类、生态类专业师生参阅。

图书在版编目(CIP)数据

从零废弃到闭环物料：通往循环经济之路 =From Zero Waste to Material Closed Loop: The Way Towards Circular Economy: 英文 / 杨剑明著. —北京：化学工业出版社，2022.8

ISBN 978-7-122-41168-6

Ⅰ.①从… Ⅱ.①杨… Ⅲ.①循环经济-研究-英文 Ⅳ.①F062.2

中国版本图书馆 CIP 数据核字（2022）第 062956 号

责任编辑：刘 婧 刘兴春　　　　　　　　　　装帧设计：韩 飞
责任校对：杜杏然

出版发行：化学工业出版社(北京市东城区青年湖南街13号　邮政编码100011)
印　　装：北京虎彩文化传播有限公司
710mm×1000mm　1/16　印张17¼　字数374千字　2022年8月北京第1版第1次印刷

购书咨询：010-64518888　　　　　　　　　　售后服务：010-64518899
网　　址：http://www.cip.com.cn
凡购买本书，如有缺损质量问题，本社销售中心负责调换。

定　　价：148.00元　　　　　　　　　　　　　　　　版权所有　违者必究

Für alle, die ich liebe und die mich lieben

Foreword

A lui seul le titre de ce livre «From Zero Waste to Material Closed Loop—The Way Towards Circular Economy» exprime très clairement l'immense domaine à traiter qui est tentaculaire avec des ramifications partout, dans tout l'ensemble de notre quotidien.

Le fil rouge de ce livre peut s'appuyer sur la citation d'Antoine-Laurent Lavoisier (1743–1794) : *Rien ne se perd, rien ne se crée: tout se transforme.*

Cette phrase reste très actuelle et se retrouve dans la suite du titre de ce livre «From Zero Waste to Material Closed Loop—the Way towards Circular Economy».

Les premières pollutions dues aux Hommes sont apparues lorsque ceux-ci ont accumulés de grandes quantités de déchets sur un même lieu ; c'est donc la sédentarisation (abandon du nomadisme et fixation en un lieu), il y a 11,000 ans et l'accroissement démographique que le phénomène de pollution est apparu.

Puis la révolution industrielle est le processus historique du XIXème siècle qui fait basculer une société à dominante agraire et artisanale vers une société commerciale et industrielle avec—(i) l'invention de la machine à vapeur,—(ii) l'apparition des chemins de fer et—(iii) l'accroissement démographique important. En conséquence de cette industrialisation, pollution des voies navigables, pollution de l'air par les fumées des usines de fabrications et pollution des sols par les résidus industriels.

Le réchauffement climatique a commencé vers 1830 concernant l'Arctique et les océans tropicaux. Les débuts de la dépollution ont apparu vers 1980; la première voiture équipée d'un pot catalytique fut une Opel en 1985. Il s'en est suivi une prise de conscience dès cette période et qui n'a fait que croitre depuis et de jeunes scientifiques ont pris à bras le corps cet immense problème comme le Dr. Jianming Yang.

Jianming Yang, après un cursus en «Environmental Engineering» en Chine à l'ECUST, il entreprit en France, dès 2001 des études d'ingénieur en environnement à l'ENSCMu de Mulhouse et poursuit un travail de thèse dans le laboratoire «Risque et Environnement»; thèse soutenue en 2008.

Reprenons un autre proverbe écrit vers 1672 par Jean de La Fontaine (1621–1693) dans la fable «le lièvre et la tortue»: *Rien ne sert de courir, il faut partir à point.*

La question qui en découle est: Sommes-nous partis à point?

Le Dr. Jianming Yang nous explique dès la lecture de la table des matières que son approche sera scientifique pour traiter se sujet concernant la «pollution», ce qui n'est que très rarement le cas. Ce thème est plutôt traité du côté sociologique, économique en mettant l'accent sur les contraintes à venir et en culpabilisant les populations précédentes.

Ce livre est une mine d'informations sur la situation actuelle et les chemins à suivre dès maintenant. Une vaste palette de domaines sont traités comme la thermodynamique de l'ensemble de la situation, les conventions internationales existantes, les lois nationales actuelles, les standards nationaux, les divers chemins à prendre pour le traitement des polluants, la chimie verte et le «zéro déchet», le recyclage, l'économie circulaire et les certifications à faire évoluer.

Le travail réalisé par le Dr. Jianming Yang est très important; il traite en profondeur ce sujet actuel qui nous touche tous et dont les effets à long terme sont dangereux pour le bien être.

Ce livre répond aux questions que l'on se pose actuellement:

- Comment faire pour éliminer les déchets actuels?
- Comment faire pour ne plus polluer?

L'analyse scientifique des causes et des remèdes liés à la pollution est très bien traitée et bien développée par le Dr. Jianming Yang. Ce livre est très didactique ce qui permet de comprendre la situation actuelle, de pouvoir y remédier et de voir le futur, pour nos enfants et petits enfants avec espoir et conscient que ce travail de dépollution en général, qui est entrepris va nous permettre de renouer plus efficacement avec la nature.

Août, 2021

Prof. Dr. François Garin
Directeur de Recherche émérite au CNRS
Ancien Secrétaire Général de la
Société Chimique de France (SCF)
Ancien Directeur du Laboratoire de
Catalyse, UMR 7515 du CNRS
Université de Strasbourg
Alsace, France

Preface

Circular economy is a hot topic.

The definition of circular economy is complicated, and the standards vary in different countries, regions and industries. But there is a relatively general and popular definition.

Circular economy is also known as "resource cycling economy". The economy development pattern features resource conservation and recycling, in order to stay in harmony with the environment. It emphasizes on organizing economic activities in a feedback process of "resources-product-renewable resources". Low exaction, high utilization and low discharge are the key. All materials and energy are reasonably and sustainably used in this ongoing cycle, keeping the impact of economic activities on environment to the smallest possible extent.

The way to a circular economy is also different from country to country, region to region or industry to industry. But, it always has to work for one's development. Many researches on this topic emerge in recent years, together with lots of theoretical books and practical thesis in China and overseas.

This book will start with the end of traditional economy—the waste. It goes from the compliance management of waste through material closed-loop material, threaded by waste diversion and utilization. This book will expound on the current inflection point of circular economy, explaining the opportunities and challenges of zero waste in different industries, and at the same time, points out a feasible roadmap to zero waste.

The waste discussed in this book, for the purpose of theoretical studies, refers to a broad sense of waste including solid, liquid and gas, etc.; but when dealing with various regulations and standards, unless otherwise specified, it only refers to a narrow sense of waste mainly in solid, as a common practice. This is in correspondence with the waste in material closed loop. Due to logistics challenge, liquid and gas are rarely discussed in material closed loop.

Moreover, this book uses entropy principle in traditional thermodynamics, from the perspective of mass balance and energy consumption, to analyse the most possible theoretical result of zero waste and material closed-loop strategy and development, as well as their influence on present society.

Last but not least, zero waste-related philosophy and ethics have also been discussed a little in this book.

Shanghai, China   Jianming Yang

Contents

1	**A Brief History on Waste**		1
2	**Waste Morphology and Types**		5
	2.1	Off-Gas	5
	2.2	Effluent	7
	2.3	Rubbish	8
3	**Thermodynamic Principle for Waste**		9
4	**Mass Balance and Unorganized Emission**		13
	4.1	Mass Balance	13
	4.2	Unorganized Discharge	16
5	**Waste Management**		19
	5.1	International Conventions	19
	5.2	International Standards	21
		5.2.1 ISO	22
		5.2.2 IEC	22
		5.2.3 ITU	23
	5.3	National Laws and International Organization Laws	23
		5.3.1 The United States	23
		5.3.2 The European Union	24
		5.3.3 China	24
	5.4	National Standards and International Organization Standards	26
		5.4.1 The United States	26
		5.4.2 The European Union	27
		5.4.3 China	28
	5.5	Industry Standards and Local Standards	28
6	**Waste Diversion**		31
	6.1	Diversion Strategy	31
	6.2	Diversion Method	32

		6.2.1	Landfill	32
		6.2.2	Incineration	35
		6.2.3	Elimination	37
		6.2.4	Reuse	38
		6.2.5	Reduction	39
		6.2.6	Recycling	39
		6.2.7	Aerobic Composting	41
		6.2.8	Anaerobic Digestion	42
		6.2.9	Biofuel	43
		6.2.10	Repairing	43
		6.2.11	Refurbishment	45
		6.2.12	Remanufacturing	46
		6.2.13	Conclusion	47
7	**Waste Treatment and Disposal Technology**			49
	7.1	Chemical Waste		49
		7.1.1	Inorganic Waste Compounds	50
		7.1.2	Organic Waste Compounds	54
	7.2	Construction Waste		58
		7.2.1	Management of Construction Waste	58
		7.2.2	Sources of Construction Waste	59
		7.2.3	Common Disposal Methods of Recyclable Materials	61
		7.2.4	Regulations and Examples of Construction Waste Recycling in Various Countries	63
	7.3	Electronic Waste		67
		7.3.1	The Hazardous Substances in E-Waste	67
		7.3.2	Treatment Technology of E-Waste	69
	7.4	Medical Waste		75
		7.4.1	Types and Hazards of Medical Waste	75
		7.4.2	Methods of Treatment and Disposal of Medical Waste	77
	7.5	Kitchen Waste		78
		7.5.1	Sources and Types of Kitchen Waste	78
		7.5.2	Oil and Water Separation	81
		7.5.3	Waste Water Treatment	82
		7.5.4	Off-Gas Treatment	82
		7.5.5	Solid Waste Treatment and Resource Recovery	83
	7.6	Laboratory Waste		84
		7.6.1	Laboratory Off-Gas	84
		7.6.2	Laboratory Waste Water	86
		7.6.3	Laboratory Solid Waste	87
	7.7	Secondary Waste		89
		7.7.1	Sources and Characteristics of Secondary Waste	89
		7.7.2	Municipal Sludge	90

8	**Zero Waste Theory and Practice**		103
	8.1	Chemical Industry	103
		8.1.1 Green Chemistry	103
		8.1.2 Treatment Process Selection	105
	8.2	Machinery Industry	107
		8.2.1 Industry Characteristics	107
		8.2.2 Corresponding Measures	108
	8.3	Automotive Industry	109
		8.3.1 Source of Generation	110
		8.3.2 Zero Waste Opportunities	112
	8.4	Consumer Electronic Industry	115
		8.4.1 Industry Characteristics	115
		8.4.2 Sources and Streams	116
		8.4.3 Stream Analysis	117
		8.4.4 Zero Waste Practices	121
	8.5	Retail Industry	123
		8.5.1 Industry Characteristics	124
		8.5.2 Zero Waste Practices	128
	8.6	Grand Event	133
		8.6.1 Characteristics of Grand Events and Their Waste Management	133
		8.6.2 Organizational Operations and Zero Waste	135
		8.6.3 Zero Waste Requirements at Different Stages	138
		8.6.4 Zero Waste Case Studies	139
	8.7	Property and City	143
		8.7.1 Unit Property	144
		8.7.2 Comprehensive Properties	145
		8.7.3 Zero Waste Cities (Waste-Free Cities)	150
		8.7.4 Nation-Wide Zero Waste	156
9	**Zero Waste and Eco-Design**		159
	9.1	Eco-Design System	159
	9.2	Design for Disassembly	160
		9.2.1 Dismantlable Design Definition	160
		9.2.2 Dismantlable Design Criteria	160
		9.2.3 Dismantlable Design Evaluation	162
	9.3	Design for Recycling	163
		9.3.1 Process and Principle of Material Selection	164
		9.3.2 Basic Requirements for Selection of Recyclable Materials	165
		9.3.3 General Methods for Selection of Recyclable Materials	165
		9.3.4 Calculation Method of Recyclability Rate	166
	9.4	Design for Maintenance/Repairing	167
		9.4.1 Several Definitions of Repairing	167

	9.4.2	Considerations in the Process of Repairable Design	167

9.5 Design for Remanufacturing 169
    9.5.1 From A to A 169
    9.5.2 From A to B 170
    9.5.3 Calculation of Remanufacturing Rate 172
9.6 Conclusion 173

10 Reverse Logistics 175
10.1 Definition and Category 175
10.2 Waste Logistics 176
10.3 Logistics Cost 178
    10.3.1 Cost Composition 178
    10.3.2 Costing 179
    10.3.3 Cost Analysis 179
    10.3.4 Cost Management 182
10.4 Drive and Development 183

11 Material Closed Loop 185
11.1 Recycling and Closed Loop 185
11.2 Regulatory Supervision 188
11.3 Material Identification 191
    11.3.1 Identification Procedures 191
    11.3.2 Technical Regulation 193
    11.3.3 Identification Standard 195
11.4 Economic Benefit and Environmental Benefit 196
11.5 Zero Waste, Carbon Neutral 198

12 On Circular Economy 201
12.1 Background and Support 201
12.2 Development Concept 203
12.3 Legal Difference 204
12.4 Innovation Model 206
    12.4.1 Commercial Leasing 206
    12.4.2 Sharing Economy 207
    12.4.3 Cloud Technology 210
    12.4.4 Blockchain Technology 212

13 Circular Economy Standard and Certification 215
13.1 Product Circularity 215
13.2 Facility Circularity 221
13.3 Corporate Circularity 222

14 Zero Waste Philosophy and Environmental Ethics 227
14.1 Zero Waste Philosophy 227
    14.1.1 Taoism 228
    14.1.2 Confucianism 229
    14.1.3 Marxist Philosophy 229

14.2	Environmental Ethics	230
	14.2.1 Environmental Ethics Principles	231
	14.2.2 The Content of Environmental Ethics	232
	14.2.3 Environmental Ethics and Environmental Legal System	233
	14.2.4 Case Studies	233
14.3	The Future of Humankind	237

Appendix 239

Epilogue 259

Chapter 1
A Brief History on Waste

Strictly speaking, the universe is a circular universe. Ever since the big bang, matter and energy emerges and disappears, transforming into each other. There are three popularly believed destinations of a stellar life in astronomy: for stars with relatively small masses, most of the material will return to cosmic space through red giant explosions or white dwarf explosions; for stars with relatively large masses, most of the material will return to cosmic space through supernova explosions (leaving behind neutron stars); for stars with extremely large masses, most of the material will go through the special phase of black holes, and, according to the speculations and predictions of Hawking's theory, will probably eventually return to cosmic space in the form of radiation or explosions.

Thus, there's no so-called waste in the universe—all materials in the universe are perfectly operating in a closed loop.

So, do we have waste on the Earth? Objectively speaking, no! From the birth of the Earth 4.6 billion years ago, every substance exists and transforms into different elements of different forms. All matter works in the same perfect closed loop in the atmosphere, the hydrosphere and the surface of the Earth's crust, like the nitrogen cycle in the early anaerobic era and the carbon cycle, which manifests itself in the form of life after aerobic times, although the Earth's mantle also occasionally replenish materials by volcanic eruptions from deep underground to the surface of the Earth.

Waste is actually a very objective matter and at the same time, a very subjective concept—the term "waste" is born with human consciousness, not produced by industrial civilization—industrial civilization only reinforced this consciousness.

Like all living species that exist and have existed on the Earth, human beings in early primitive societies sought carbon sources from nature to provide material and energy for their own reproduction. Even if there were fruit peels and crumbs, they were purely natural and not considered as waste. Humans, unlike animals, later invented working tools. And a tool must have a service life. Though discarded at the end of their service life, those tools still would return perfectly to the environment thanks to their natural nature (stone or wood until early pottery). Then the problem begins—the Earth does not consider these discarded tools as waste, it is the humans themselves regard the worn-out tools as "waste" and throw them away! But of course, the impact of these discarded tools on the natural environment should be none, no matter how one thinks of it.

However, men generated more ideas along the way from slave society through feudal society. Production and consumption began to differ by district or social stratum. This difference, in turn, led directly to the creation of surplus goods and surplus food. Part of the population started to own what they can't all use or use out. They then discarded what they own for the sake of having new ones. Food was not scarce to them anymore. Instead, there began to be food leftovers. But fortunately, almost all the man-made goods or food, though discarded or left over, were either natural or biodegradable, due to limited technology. Coupled with the fact that there were a rather smaller population worldwide at that time, the nature was able to digest all the human stuff without much effort. Waste, for humans at that time, was just a vague idea.

But civilization changed it all. Industrial civilization arrived as the definite product of any higher species' development. The First Industrial Revolution made it possible for humans to be truly aware of waste for two reasons. Firstly, the fast development of production technology gave men the opportunity to make lots of materials that would by no means be created naturally. Such materials, to meet the requirement of men's living and production (like durability), were made not to be easily decomposed or digested by nature in a short time. Secondly, production and consumption (supply and demand) were normally not synchronized or balanced. Newly created substance may be over demand in a region or during a certain time. The surplus ones would, as a result, be stored and accumulated in human society and in nature.

Unfortunately, it didn't occur to men at the early stage of industrial civilization that whether nature could take in and digest all the surplus materials, nor did it come to their mind what problems the accumulated materials would cause to nature, until the beginning of the Second Industrial Revolution.

The Second Industrial Revolution, has basically led humans to an electrical age, while also brought chemical industry into history. Chemical industry was built to create substances that do not exist in nature, in order to meet the growing needs of human society. The rapid development of chemical industry has resulted in the creation of a lot of new substances and the intermediate substance (e.g. catalyst) needed for industrial production. When humans used these industrial products and discarded them after they served their purpose, it became also clear that nature didn't seem to grow any likings for those artificial materials.

As a matter of fact, the nature can absorb them. It just takes time, and the time could be exponential of geological time scale in order to break down certain man-made material like polyvinyl chloride plastic. Besides, even if a few man-made substances could be degraded by nature in a short time, the cost would be environmental pollution in a given time and space, for instance the soluble organics discharged into water.

When industrial products, especially chemical industry products, became either hard to return to nature by degradation, or brought along with them local pollution, the concept of waste finally settled in human cognition—humans created them, but humans didn't like them! A new academic discipline thus emerged in the middle of twentieth century—environmental science. In this new discipline, science and technology related to waste treatment and disposal became a significant part.

In the past decades, humans have made enormous progress in waste treatment and disposal, led by the effort of worldwide environmental scientists and engineers. Most of the commonly seen waste can be treated and disposed in economical and non-hazardous ways.

We are facing new challenges now, however. The waste produced by human beings can't be 100% non-hazardous due to economic and geographical reasons. And a challenge even greater is that the scientific researches and engineering projects can't keep pace with the growth of waste produced, in terms of variety and volume. Waste will eventually and gradually be accumulated on the Earth, at its own pace.

In twenty-first century, humans finally come to the conclusion that it won't work like this. The ultimate or the fundamental solution to this problem, should not just be to deal with how to treat and dispose of waste. Rather, the concept of waste should be removed from our mind again—because it doesn't exist in the first place.

There are two ways to completely remove the concept of waste. One, by maximizing the utilization of materials so that the production process doesn't generate industrial waste (pre-consumer waste). Two, by reintroducing into raw materials the industrial waste which is unavoidable at current stage and the products at the end of their normal life cycle (post-consumer waste).

These two ways are indeed the theory of zero waste and material closed loop, which will be discussed in this book.

Chapter 2
Waste Morphology and Types

Simply speaking, any material that is produced by human activities but is no longer of use value to the owner thus neglected is called waste. In other words, anything that is produced during the course of construction, production, daily activities and other social activities of human beings, loses most or all of the use value within certain period of time and space, and can't be recycled or reused is waste.

Wastes are in essence substances; therefore, their forms and types shouldn't be different from those of other substances in nature. A substance in nature has three basic forms—solid, liquid and gas, though under certain conditions there can also be ionic and neutron states. As we are only discussing waste in the normal sense, we will adopt what is academically agreed of the waste forms, respectively gas, liquid and solid. They are also known as the "three kinds of waste", off-gas, effluent and rubbish.

2.1 Off-Gas

Off-gas has not been regarded as waste for a very long time, fundamentally because it can't be seen or touched, except for a few ones with color and odor. Yet off-gas has long played a part in history and has a huge impact on the fate of mankind.

There are two sources of off-gas. One is biological activities in nature, and the other is industrial emissions by human. Natural activities like volcanic eruptions will not be discussed in this book, simply because volcanic eruption is not caused by human activities and is in no ways controlled by human being. At the same time, volcanic eruption is part of the matter and energy cycle of the Earth. Gases emitted by volcano directly become part of the atmosphere and start circulation. They are not the off-gas we talk about here.

Then why the emission of biological activities in nature—mainly greenhouse gases like carbon dioxide and methane should be included in off-gas? Before there were ever human-kind on the Earth, carbon dioxide in nature was basically produced by the respiration of animals, and methane generated as a result of ruminant animals' digestion and metabolism (such as excrement). But since the advent of men, crop farming and livestock farming came into being, the domestic animals had greatly satisfied men's needs for meat and milk, whether they lived on natural grass or fed on planted fodder. Therefore, humans enlarged the livestock farming and protected the animals from carnivores. Those domestic animals multiplied, which in turn sped up the conversion of carbon in the plants into carbon dioxide and methane which then emitting into atmosphere. That's why we say, whether it's human beings or ruminants producing carbon dioxide, the living organism in nature is a source of off-gas (greenhouse gases).

The off-gas emitted by human industrial activities are more complicated in terms of types. Generally speaking, it refers to the gases with pollutants emitted into the air during the plant's fuel combustion and production process in the plant itself. These gases could be, in terms of substance types, carbon dioxide, carbon disulfide, hydrogen sulfide, fluoride, nitrogen oxides, chlorine, hydrogen chloride, carbon monoxide, sulfuric acid (fog), lead and mercury, beryllide, soot and production dust, etc. In terms of substance forms, the industrial off-gas can be divided into particulate exhaust and gaseous exhaust.

Particulate exhaust—these pollutants are mainly the polluting soot from the manufacturing process. It could come from cement plants, heavy industrial material manufacturing plants, heavy metal manufacturing plants and chemical plants. During their production, the raw materials need to be processed or purified, and the residue cannot be completely burned or decomposed, so they exist in the form of smoke and soot. If the plant facilities are not efficient enough to capture the smoke and soot particles, it will cause air pollution in the process of emission to the atmosphere.

Gaseous exhaust—these pollutants tend to be the most hazardous among all the industrial off-gases. The main gaseous exhaust currently includes nitrogenous off-gas, sulfuric off-gas and hydrocarbon off-gas.

Nitrogenous off-gas will damage the air's component and change the atmosphere's composition. Particularly, petroleum products contain large amount of nitride in it, while the combustion of petroleum products takes a significant part in industrial production, which means the off-gas will contain lots of nitrogen oxide. If emitted into air directly, it will increase the nitrogen oxide content, affecting the atmospheric circulation.

Sulfuric off-gas will cause damage to human life and environment directly. This is because it can combine with water in the air to form acid (sulfuric) rain. And acid rain will hurt plants, buildings and human health, especially human's respiratory system. Meanwhile, acid rain in earth and water will cause secondary pollution.

Hydrocarbon off-gases, collectively known as hydrocarbons, are organic compounds consisting mainly of carbon and hydrogen atoms. The diffusion of such gases into the atmosphere will cause damage to the ozone layer, which can lead to a series of problems in the long run. The destruction of the ozone layer increases the exposure to ultraviolet light, which can cause skin injury and health problems. Changes in ultraviolet radiation can also affect the ecosystem and the climate.

2.2 Effluent

Effluent can be classified into two kinds: organic and inorganic, which respectively refer to waste organics (commonly known as waste oil) and waste water (commonly known as sewage). Relatively speaking, mankind has the longest history, the most pains and the most experience in the treatment of waste water. But the treatment of waste organics only started within the last hundred years.

Looking back at human history, there was no man-made organics before industrial age, thus there was no waste organics (as used natural organic liquid can be easily degraded). When chemical industry bloomed, men found the organics can be widely applied as solvent, lubricant and others. On the other hand, the liquid organics are basically auxiliary in production and won't be made into the final product. That means they will be discharged as waste organics after they finish the auxiliary mission in the production process. Residual loss in containers during the production, storage and transportation process is another substantial source of waste organics.

Waste water usually refers to domestic sewage, industrial waste water and primary rainwater polluted by atmosphere or the surface.

Domestic sewage is discharged from residents' daily lives, mainly from residential buildings and public buildings, such as residences, institutions, schools, hospitals, shops, public places and toilets of industrial plants. The pollutants in domestic effluent are mainly organic substances (such as proteins, carbohydrates, fats, urea, ammonia, etc.) and a large number of pathogenic microorganisms (such as parasite eggs and intestinal infectious viruses). The organic substances living in domestic sewage are extremely unstable, easy to decompose and stink. Germs and pathogens can live on those organic substances in the domestic effluent and multiply rapidly, causing contagious diseases to spread among people.

Industrial waste water includes production waste water, manufacturing waste water and cooling water, referring to the waste water and other waste liquids produced during industrial production, which contain industrial raw materials, intermediate products, by-products and pollutants formed during the production process that are lost with the water. There are various types of industrial waste water with complex composition. To name just a few, mercury contained in electrolysis industrial waste water, lead and cadmium contained in heavy metal smelting industrial waste water, cyanide and chromium contained in electroplating industrial waste water, phenol contained in petrol refining industrial waste water and different pesticides in pesticide manufacturing industrial waste water.

Domestic sewage or industrial waste water in nature is the aqueous solution or hydrosol of various waste substances. It is human beings proactively using water as the vehicle to transport waste substances out of their residential and production area, and discharging the waste water directly or indirectly (through water treatment facilities) into natural waters. However, the polluting primary rainwater is formed by the pollutants on surface or atmosphere passively being taken into the aqueous solution or hydrosol by the effect of rain. It directly flows into (normally without any treatment) natural waters via surface runoff. Compared to domestic sewage and industrial waste water, primary rainwater, though containing limited volume of pollutants, can still exert hazardous effect to environment due to lack of effective treatment.

2.3 Rubbish

Rubbish is commonly known as waste solid, which as the name implies, refers to the solid or semi-solid waste produced by human in production, consumption, living and other activities, or more popularly called "garbage". Waste solid mainly includes ore particles, slag, sludge, discarded products, broken utensils, defective products, animal carcasses, spoiled food, human and animal waste, etc. In some countries, highly concentrated liquids such as waste acid, waste alkali, waste oil, and waste organic solvents are also classified as waste solid.

Waste solid is basically classified by its source, generally as domestic waste solid, industrial waste solid and agricultural waste solid. Domestic waste solid mainly refers to the solid waste produced in the process of urban livelihood or activities servicing urban livelihood, also known as urban domestic garbage. It includes the residents' living garbage, medical garbage, commercial garbage, construction garbage (spoil), etc. Industrial waste solid refers to the solid waste produced in the course of production, storage, logistic activities, also known as industrial rubbish or industrial garbage, including defective products, scraps, sludge and tailings. Agricultural waste solid is also called agricultural garbage, referring to the solid waste produced by agricultural actives (including scientific researches), including the waste produced by five agricultural industries, namely farming, forestry, livestock, fishery and agricultural sideline.

The influence of waste solid on nature and human beings is undoubtedly long-lasting and far-reaching, though only until recent decades it has been recognized as a problem.

Chapter 3
Thermodynamic Principle for Waste

In the previous chapter, the historical background and social conditions of waste generation are briefly described. From a more scientific point of view, we will discuss the thermodynamic principle of waste generation.

Thermodynamics is a subject that studies the thermal properties and laws of matter from the macroscopic aspect. Thermodynamics mainly studies the thermal properties of matter from the energy conversion. It points out the macroscopic law of energy conversion from one form to another, and summarizes the macroscopic phenomena of matter. Thermodynamics does not focus on the microstructure of a matter composed by a large number of micro particles, but only on the thermal phenomena and the fundamental laws that must be followed by the change and evolution of the system as a whole.

The first step to describe the state of a thermodynamic system, is to identify the scope of system. Thermodynamics defines systems into the following three categories: open system—there is energy and matter transfer between the system and the environment; closed system—there is only energy transfer and no matter transfer between the system and the environment; isolated system—there is neither energy transfer nor matter transfer between the system and the environment.

Since waste is mainly generated in the area of human activities on the Earth's surface, when we use thermodynamic principles to study waste diversion, we first define this area of human activity as a system. It is obvious that the biosphere in which human activities take place—the bottom of the atmosphere, most of the hydrosphere and the surface of the lithosphere—is an open system, since it not only transfers energy from solar radiation, but also transfers matter with the atmosphere, hydrosphere and lithosphere.

At present, the biosphere system of human activities on the Earth is in a thermodynamic stable state for a relatively short period (non-geological age). We can use entropy, one of the three basic state functions of thermodynamics, to analyze the evolution trend of the system.

Let's go back and look at the evolution of life. Biosphere system has already been in a relatively stable thermodynamic state before the emergence of life. Due to various uncertainties, the probability of inorganic molecules forming complex organic macromolecules by chance through various chemical reactions is very small. That is, the probability of occurrence is very low. According to the mathematical interpretation of the second law of thermodynamics, a system with a low incidence of a particular event has a higher entropy value. However, as solar radiation continues to energize this system, the entropy of the system decreases as it becomes ordered according to the physicochemical interpretation of the second law of thermodynamics. At first, it is only a small quantitative change, which may be a slight shift of chemical reaction equilibrium of water vapor, ammonia and other substances. But quantitative change leads to qualitative change. After amino acids are synthesized under the condition of lightning, an accidental phenomenon in the atmosphere, the initial elements of life appear, and the entropy decreasing is also accelerated. From amino acids to organic macromolecules to primitive single-cell life, a "frightening" property emerged, that is, a class of matter with DNA and RNA that could replicate itself. The significance of self-replication is that the cell can autonomously absorb and metabolize small molecules free from the external environment to obtain its own life continuity—to make order out of disorder. Life, at its very beginning, knows how to use external matters and energy to reduce entropy, the higher the degree of its evolution, the faster the rate of entropy reduction.

Humans, the highest level of living things on the Earth, appeared. Their wisdom to reproduce increases greatly, bringing about more significant entropy reduction to biosphere. But more entropy reduction means increased need of matters and energy. The amount of minerals that can be easily mined and processed every year is limited and the energy that solar radiation brings to biosphere in unit time is relatively constant. As a result, not only the surface mining is getting deeper, but a large number of continental shelf and seabed minerals are exploited; the fossil energy stored from the solar radiation of geological age is developed and used, together with the development of micro-scale thermonuclear. Furthermore, renewable energy such as solar energy and wind energy also come into sight of the human kind.

One of the results from humans reforming biosphere using matters and energy is that the system becomes highly organized thanks to the continuous entropy reduction, and the probability of elements returning to nature is greatly reduced. In other words, matters become more indecomposable, or the chances of natural degradation of man-made matters is getting much lower. As we mentioned earlier, industrial civilization will produce surplus materials, and those non-biodegradable surplus materials are the thermodynamic results of waste generated by entropy reduction of biosphere system!

By the way, does this entropy reduction have an end? Intelligent life can only reduce entropy to meet its various desires, so the human demand for matter and energy is endless. We all know that the minerals and energy on the Earth will be exhausted sooner or later. When the day comes, the mineral resources are completely exhausted and renewable energy can't meet the huge demand of human beings, the entropy reduction of the Earth's biosphere system will naturally end. In other words, the entropy reduction of biosphere system will reach a theoretical limit.

3 Thermodynamic Principle for Waste

What does the end of entropy reduction of the Earth's biosphere system mean? First of all, the smaller the entropy of the system, the more inevitability of the things in the system, and biodiversity will no longer exist. Furthermore, the time and space available for human survival are becoming more and more limited. In other words, human beings will not have too many choices and can only survive as simple as machines. Secondly, the universe is an isolated system, and it evolves in the direction of entropy increase. When a micro system in the universe goes against its way and keeps decreasing entropy, there will be a huge entropy difference around the system. According to the entropy flow theory of I. Prigogine, a Belgian scientist, the Earth biosphere system is a dissipative structure, which relies on the constant supply of matter and energy from the surroundings. That is to say, through the exchange of matter and energy, the Earth biosphere system can obtain negative entropy from the surrounding (giving entropy to the surroundings) so that it can be maintained and developed. Once the system can't gain constant and stable negative entropy from the surroundings, it tends to stagnate and die, and eventually becomes a disordered ruin, which we can call it entropy collapse.

Even for the dissipative structure, there's another problem in front of us. The dissipative structure must release the waste generated from the inside while receiving matter and energy from the outside. However, it is absolutely impossible for human beings to remove all wastes from the Earth's biosphere system on a large scale, which means that wastes will accumulate in the system. This accumulation process will further accelerate the evolution of dissipative structure, and the process of entropy collapse will come earlier than in theory.

If it is a social challenge to produce less waste, while it is a scientific challenge to divert waste as much as possible. There are many kinds of waste diversion technologies, but the goal is basically to decompose the waste into primary raw materials for human production, or to use the waste as energy directly or indirectly. The first scenario is the material recycling and material closed loop which we will discuss in detail later. We think that the partial replacement of the virgin mineral mining can effectively reduce the dependence on the external negative entropy, and also can partially inhibit the evolution process of the dissipative structure. The second scenario is more complex. On the one hand, as energy, waste can reduce the demand for external energy; on the other hand, it will inevitably continue to produce waste (whether residue or off-gas), and cannot be discharged from the system, which still needs external negative entropy. Whether the positive and negative effects can be offset depends on the waste composition and energy efficiency. In short, there is great uncertainty.

Therefore, since the evolution of higher life inevitably leads to the emergence of waste, only generating less waste and diverting waste as much as possible to partially replace the required external matters, the Earth biosphere system can maintain thermodynamic stability in a relatively long period of time (but not geological age), and various biological forms, including human society, can also have a sustainable development.

Of course, if human evolution can transcend the geological age and jump out of the constraints of the Earth, making use of the matter and energy of the solar system and even the whole universe, or can enter Planck scale to continue to reform our biosphere system with the matter and energy of the quantum world, it will be a different story, as it is not the simple space and time scope of the Earth biosphere system that we defined in the first place.

Chapter 4
Mass Balance and Unorganized Emission

With the understanding of the historical and social causes of waste generation, and the discussion of the thermodynamic principle of waste generation in mind, let's re-focus on human industrial civilization and see the actual situation of waste generation.

From the previous chapter on the morphology and types of waste, we can see that in fact, the waste can be simply divided into two categories: pre-consumer (or post-industry) waste and post-consumer waste. If the development of human industrial civilization makes it difficult to reduce or eliminate its own post-consumer waste, it's still hopeful to reduce (completely elimination is almost impossible) the generation of pre-consumer waste through process improvement. In fact, we should firstly talk about mass balance, whether the waste is pre-consumer or post-consumer.

The direct application of mass balance in environmental management is to calculate the unorganized emission of pollutants through the amount of organized emission of pollutants. This calculation has great significance for zero waste in industry and for environmental authority enforcement.

4.1 Mass Balance

We are all familiar with the law of mass conservation. The law of mass conservation means that the change of the mass of a system is always equal to the difference between the input and output masses of the system. The law of mass conservation is one of the fundamental laws in nature. It shows that mass will neither be created nor destroyed, but will only be transferred from one substance to another, and the total amount remains unchanged.

Mass balance is actually an industrial application of mass conservation. In a given space and time of production or consumption, the amount of material entering the system should be equal to the amount of material leaving the system. For the production system, if the input is greater than the output, the products cannot be sold, so the inventory will increase, resulting in the overstock of products; if the output exceeds the input, the production will be difficult to continue due to lack of raw materials, until the production is stopped. For the consumption system (household or individual), if the income is greater than the output, the house will be full of things, and people may get weight; if the income cannot cover the expenses, the family will not have enough to eat, and people may lose weight. In short, only dynamic mass balance is sustainable.

If we look at the production and operation of the factory which is most related to the waste topic, it is particularly important to maintain a good mass balance. This importance is not only reflected in the daily management of the factory, but also reflected in the economic and environmental benefits of the factory. But why? Let's take a look at the following examples.

There are two production lines HC-1 and HC-2 in HC workshop of a plastic manufacturing enterprise. The annual and monthly mass balance calculation (unit in kg) is carried out in one production cycle (12 months). It is not difficult to find that there is still a significant difference as "lost" between the general input and the product after eliminating the normal process loss and the diluent volatilization as organized emission and treatment.

For both matter annual and monthly calculation, the mass "lost rate" of HC-1 production line is not too high (within 1%), which may come from various errors. As shown in Figs. 4.1 and 4.2.

Relatively speaking, the mass "lost rate" of HC-2 production line is very unstable, and even approaches or exceeds 10% in two months. At the same time, there are two "negative" months, which means that there are more materials—this is not a simple error that can be explained, there must be other internal reasons. As shown in Figs. 4.3 and 4.4.

Although an accurate material balance is very important, it is not so easy to achieve. Firstly, we need to determine the space involved in this balance—we usually consider a complete and independent manufacturing unit, usually a workshop, as the smallest unit for calculating the mass balance. A workshop is the basic organizational

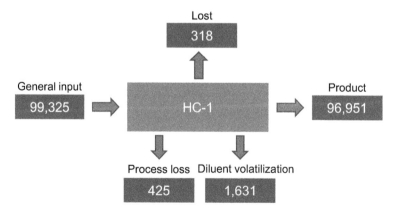

Fig. 4.1 Production line HC-1 annual mass balance

4.1 Mass Balance

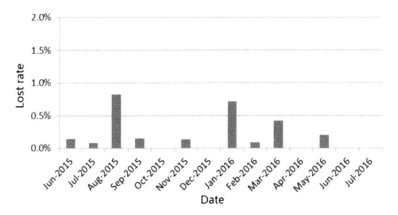

Fig. 4.2 Production line HC-1 monthly mass balance

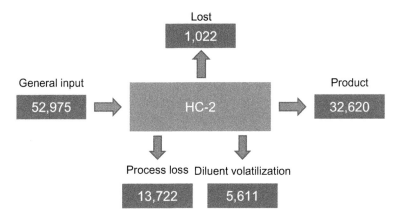

Fig. 4.3 Production line HC-2 annual mass balance

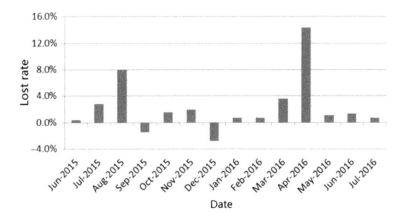

Fig. 4.4 Production line HC-2 monthly mass balance

form of most manufacturing enterprises, with the workshop director (or other titles) as the highest leader in the structure and regular feeding and output records of workers. It is relatively convenient to confirm the workflow or query the data source. Secondly, it is necessary to determine the time involved in this balance—as the materials may not enter and leave at the same time, the shorter the selected time range, the more difficult it is to balance. However, the longer the selected time range is, the more accurate it is, but the problems found will be less instructive. Manufacturing enterprises can take mass balance analysis on monthly basis, and a yearly analysis at the same time of year-end material inventory.

In the previous example, we can also see that the material in and out of the workshop is unbalanced. There is an obvious difference (lost) between input and output of the workshop, whether it is calculated by month or by year. This difference has two meanings: one is that there may be loopholes in the daily management of the workshop. Because of the negligence of subjective consciousness, the managers did not fully count all the incoming and outgoing materials; the other was that there might be technical defects in the workshop. Due to the limitation of objective conditions, the technicians would have large non-systematic errors in weighing and calculating materials. Whether subjective or objective, this "lost" part is completely different from the "loss" part—the loss material is caused by known management or process reasons, although it is a loss, it is still in the statistics; and the lost material has no exact source and destination, whereas comes from the mass balance calculation, its existence will certainly lead to two negative results: one is economic, which is equivalent to the increase of raw material cost; the other is environmental, which is called unorganized discharge (because it is not effectively collected and treated).

4.2 Unorganized Discharge

On the economic level, the inexplicable increase in the cost of raw materials is unacceptable to any enterprise. This is a basic management problem and will affect the efficiency of the enterprise. On the environmental level, the problem caused by the unorganized discharge is much more serious. It is a compliance problem, which will affect the image of the enterprise and even the survival of the enterprise.

Unorganized discharge is essentially different from organized discharge (discharge with treatment). The discharge with treatment refers to the collection of scraps, by-products or wastes by physical and chemical methods when the material efficiency is lower than 100% (a percentage that can be approached infinitely through all efforts but can never be achieved) due to technology limitations—after the treatment and meeting certain standards, they are discharged legally into the nature. Unorganized discharge refers to the uncontrollable discharge in an open process, that is, parts of the materials escape into the nature during raw material preparation, chemical reaction, finished product packaging, etc. It is obvious that the organized discharge is compliant and more environment-friendly, while any unorganized discharge is not in compliance and will pollute the environment.

4.2 Unorganized Discharge

Unorganized discharge is closely related to mass balance. In fact, the amount of organized emissions can generally be measured or calculated, while the amount of unorganized discharge cannot be measured (or not exact at all), and it needs to be calculated through an accurate mass balance. From the following example, we can understand the calculation and application of unorganized discharge.

Fatty amine is produced in a workshop of a chemical enterprise. We calculate the mass balance of nitrogen element (N) with "year" as the time unit (data from monthly material inventory, so the system error is minimized). As the only source of nitrogen, the liquid ammonia (NH_3) purchased by the workshop in one year contains 1,536 tons of nitrogen, and the nitrogen content of various fatty amine products is 1,193 tons. Meanwhile, 69 tons of nitrogen is contained in the by-products and waste amine residues (draffs) produced in the same period. A total of 63 tons of NH_3-N is collected and treated in waste water, and 121 tons of nitrogen is contained in the sell ammonia by recycling. As shown in Fig. 4.5.

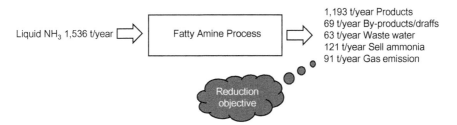

Fig. 4.5 Nitrogen balance in fatty amine workshop of a chemical enterprise

Through simple mass balance calculation, it is easy to find that 91 tons of nitrogen entering the workshop are lost in one year. In fact, the fate of these 91 tons is inevitable, that is, in the form of nitrogen compounds (N_2 will not be produced under the process) in various non-closed containers or operations, most of them escape into the atmosphere as gas emission which is a very typical pollutant discharge.

If we want to find out the exact sources of these pollutants and try to reduce them, we must further analyze how much they come from organized discharge and how much from unorganized discharge. By further combing and investigating the nitrogen footprint, we found that, 620 tons of nitrogen are discharged due to reactors deflation in a year, of which 540 tons are captured and absorbed into the liquid phase by the scrubbers, and 80 tons could not be intercepted due to the insufficient absorption capacity. Therefore, it is concluded that in 91 tons of nitrogen pollution discharge per year, 80 tons (about 88%) are organized discharge and 11 tons (about 12%) are unorganized discharge. As shown in Fig. 4.6.

This calculation is very meaningful. There are two obvious conclusions for the workshop to improve:

①   In theory, there is a gap of 13% (80 tons/620 tons) in the organized discharge part due to the insufficient treatment capacity of the scrubbers. It is necessary to install more scrubbers or increase the absorption efficiency of single scrubber.

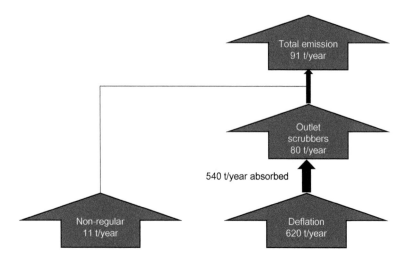

Fig. 4.6 Nitrogen discharge from fatty amine production workshop of a chemical enterprise

② It is necessary to find out all the unorganized discharge points (waste water pit, packaging line, etc.) and put all 11 tons of nitrogen into the scrubbers for recycling.

From the above example of the chemical enterprise, it can be seen that the analysis and elimination of unorganized discharge through mass balance, including the control of organized discharge, is the first step for enterprises to reduce pre-consumer waste and finally achieve zero waste.

Of course, not all material "lost" must be organized or unorganized discharge. When an enterprise finds there's something "suspicious" in a workshop after comprehensive and detailed mass balance calculation, people can take following actions immediately:

① Sort out all kinds of materials in and out of the workshop again to avoid omission of statistical items.
② Select another typical production and operation period to avoid the difference in material selection between different production plans.
③ Review the Standard Operation Process (SOP) to avoid the human error caused by different operators.
④ Calibrate measuring instruments to avoid weighing errors caused by instrument accuracy.
⑤ Education and training to eliminate possible violations of internal personnel.

Only if every enterprise takes mass balance seriously can the whole society have the opportunity to reduce the pre-consumer waste and then save more energy for post-consumer waste. This process involves all aspects of waste management, which is often ignored or despised by enterprises in the past. The following chapters will discuss about waste management step by step from various dimensions.

Chapter 5
Waste Management

As long as there is waste, no matter for what reasons, of what kind, or of what volume, the waste producing subject—manufacturers need to effectively manage it (Extended Producer Responsibility, EPR).

Technically, there are two kinds of waste management, compliance management and sustainability management. A manufacturing company, with the ambition of long-lasting development, must comply with relevant international conventions and standards, with national laws, regulations and standards of its located country and with the various industrial and locational standards and codes. This is compliance management. If this manufacturing company even aims at leading the industry and capturing good business opportunities, it is more important to have a good company image and corporate responsibilities. Sustainability management which is higher than compliance management, should come into place.

This chapter provides a general overview of international conventions, international standards and national laws, the details of which will be cited in subsequent chapters.

5.1 International Conventions

There are not many international conventions related to waste, notably the London Dumping Convention and the Basel Convention. But the contents, provisions, interpretation and enforcement of these conventions are extremely complex. A country making its commitment to and implementing the provisions of an international convention after it becomes the signatory, is compliance management.

Convention on the Prevention of Marine Pollution by Dumping of Wastes and Other Matter, referred to as the London Dumping Convention or the 1972 London Convention, is a convention for the protection of the marine environment, urging the nations across the world to work together and prevent pollution of the marine environment caused by dumping waste. The Convention, in the form of three annexes, enumerates in large details on "substances the dumping of which is prohibited at sea", "substances requiring a special permit for dumping" and "substances capable of being dumped by general permit". The Convention was signed by 80 States on 29 December, 1972 and entered into force on 30 August, 1975. As of the end of July 2014, there were 87 contracting States to the Convention. China acceded to the Convention on 15 November, 1985, and the Convention entered into force for China on 15 December of the same year. The 1996 Protocol to the Convention (hereinafter referred to as "the Protocol") is a supplement and amendment to the Convention. The Protocol imposes stricter controls on the dumping of wastes by permitting the dumping at sea of only those substances expressly listed in the annex to the Protocol, while requiring States to apply the relevant provisions of the Protocol to their internal waters or to adopt other effective permit systems to prevent the intentional dumping of wastes at sea or their incineration at sea. The Protocol was signed by 80 States, including China. The Protocol entered into force on 24 March, 2006. By the end of July 2014, 45 States had become contracting parties to the Protocol, which was ratified by China in 2006. The Protocol applies to the Hong Kong SAR and does not apply to the Macao SAR for the time being.

According to London Dumping Convention, it is of vital importance to recognize the need to protect marine environment and the life that depends on it, and it's in the interest of all people to ensure the environment is protected in such a way that its quality and resources aren't impaired; it should be noted that the capacity and capability of the seas to absorb and transform waste into harmless substances and to regenerate natural resources is not unlimited; the States, in accordance with United Nations Charter and the principles of international law can legitimately use resources pursuant to their national environmental policies and at the same time have the responsibility to ensure their activities within their jurisdiction do not cause damage to the environment of other States or of areas beyond their jurisdiction; and United Nations General Assembly resolution 2749 (XXV) on the Principles Governing the Seabed and Ocean Floor and the Subsoil Thereof beyond the Limits of National Jurisdiction; it should also be noted that marine pollution has many sources, such as the atmosphere, rivers, estuaries, sea ports and pipeline dumping and exhaust, and it's necessary for the States to take the most practicable actions to prevent such pollution and to develop products and processes which can reduce the volume of hazardous wastes to be disposed of; it's convinced that international actions to prevent and reduce pollution of the sea caused by dumping can and must be taken without delay, but that such action should not preclude the speedy discussion of measures to control other sources of marine pollution; it is desirable that the States of a certain geological region with common interest can contracting appropriate protocols as supplement to this Convention, in order to improve the protection of marine environment.

This Convention has provisions to limit the variety of waste to be dumped into the sea, and has very specific description of reducing hazardous waste. Our marine environment can only be effectively protected by global cooperation and collaboration.

Basel Convention on the Control of Transboundary Movements of Hazardous Wastes and Their Disposal, referred to as the Basel Convention, passed the International Environment Protection Meeting of United Nations Environment Program on 22 March, 1989 in Basel, Switzerland. It entered into force in May 1992. The Amendment to the Basel Convention was passed in Geneva on 22 September, 1995. There are already over 100 countries signed this convention and China signed it on 22 March, 1990.

The Basel Convention aims to curb the transboundary movement of hazardous wastes, especially their exporting and movement to developing countries. The Convention requires the States to reduce the volume of hazardous wastes to a minimum and to store and dispose of them as locally as possible in the most possible environment-friendly manner. The Convention clearly states that: if it is necessary for the transboundary movement of waste with respect to environmental protection, the country exporting hazardous wastes must first notify the importing country and concerning countries of the quantity and nature of the waste; when transporting hazardous waste across boundaries, the exporting country must have the written approval of the government of the importing country. The 1995 amendment to the Basel Convention prohibits developed countries from exporting hazardous wastes to developing countries for final disposal, and requires developed countries to stop exporting hazardous wastes for recycling and reuse to developing countries by the end of 1997.

The Basel Convention carries a significant meaning to contracting States. As the countries and regions across the world develops quite differently on their economics and industries, without the existence of this Convention, developed countries would, for the sake of economic interest, transport waste especially hazardous waste to underdeveloped or developing countries. This Convention, as a matter of fact, requires developed industrial countries to reduce as much as possible hazardous waste of low value and high disposal cost, and to dispose the waste locally.

5.2 International Standards

International standards are also worth mentioning. Companies follow those standards voluntarily. It's not against any rules not to follow them, but international business conducts may require it and companies not following them will probably lose some international business.

International standards related to waste can be divided into general international standards, mainly the ISO series, and professional standards related to different international industry associations, typically the IEC standards (product-based) of International Electrotechnical Commission (IEC) and ITU standards (technology-based) of the International Telecommunication Union. Those professional standards also have articles or chapters regarding waste management.

5.2.1 ISO

ISO 14000 environmental management series standard is another management system launched by the International Organization for Standardization (ISO) after the ISO 9000 system. The standard is developed by the Environmental Management Technical Committee of ISO/TC 207. There is a total of 100 numbers from 14001 to 14100, collectively known as the ISO 14000 series of standards. The significance of the standard is to urge companies to consider the impact on the environment in their production and business activities, and to reduce the load on environment; urge companies to strengthen environmental management, and to enhance the environmental awareness of employees; urge companies to consciously comply with environmental laws and regulations; establish corporate image so that companies can gain the "Green Pass" to the international market.

In ISO 14000 standards, waste reduction and recycling are essential in five main parts (environmental policy, planning, implementation and operation, inspection and corrective measures and management review). Those standards can also be divided into two categories in terms of functions. The first category is to evaluate organizations, to see if they have taken measures in waste management, including waste reduction and recycling. Another category evaluates the product from the life cycle perspective. It does not allow large volume of waste without recycling to be produced from the product design to manufacturing.

5.2.2 IEC

The International Electrotechnical Commission (IEC) was founded in 1906 with a history of more than 100 years. It is the world's first international electrotechnical standardization organization, responsible for international standardization work in the fields of electrical and electronic engineering. The IEC's objectives are: to meet the needs of the global marketplace effectively; to ensure that the usage of its standards and conformity assessment programs are prioritized and maximized worldwide; to evaluate and improve the quality of the products and services covered by its standards; to create conditions for the common use of complex systems; to advance the effectiveness of industrialization processes; to enhance human health and safety; and to protect the environment.

IEC standards are acknowledged worldwide. Every year, IEC holds over a hundred meetings about international standards development and revision, with nearly 100,000 experts from all over the world involved. There are 89 Technical Committees (TC) and 107 Sub Committees (SC) in IEC. The standards IEC developed increased rapidly in recent years. There are already 4,885 international standards developed by the end of 2000, while in 1963, there were only 120.

Some of the IEC TCs (e.g., Technical Committee TC 111 on Environmental Standardization of Electrical and Electronic Products and Systems) and SCs have set up special environment-related Working Groups (WG) to develop environment-related product standards. These related standards basically have requirements and elaborations for the life cycle assessment of electrical and electronic products, which also involve a lot of waste management requirements.

5.2.3 ITU

The International Telecommunication Union (ITU) is an important specialized agency of the United Nations and the longest-standing international organization among UN agencies. The ITU is responsible for information and communication technology, the allocation and management of global radio spectrum and satellite orbit resources, the development of global telecommunications standards, the provision of telecommunications assistance to developing countries, to promote the development of global telecommunications. As a worldwide link between governments and private companies, the ITU operates through the Telecommunication Standardization Sector (ITU-T), the Radiocommunication Sector (ITU-R) and the Telecommunication Development Sector (ITU-D) within its organizational structure.

There are 10 Study Groups (SG) in Telecommunication Standardization Sector (ITU-U), among which SG 5 is specialized in environment and climate change. SG 5 in ITU, similar to TC 111 in IEC, has developed and is developing standards that emphasizes and reinforces more and more frequently waste reduction and recycling in telecommunication products (including related services).

5.3 National Laws and International Organization Laws

Different sovereign countries and regions have also developed strict legislation, a whole set of administrative norms and implementing regulations for effective management of waste. The compliance with and implementing of laws and regulations are all called compliance management.

5.3.1 The United States

The Solid Waste Disposal Act (also known as the Resource Conservation and Recovery Act), enacted in 1976, was the first law to comprehensively control the pollution of U.S. land by solid waste. In 1984, the Solid Waste Disposal Act was revised by Congress to address problems encountered in its implementation and has been in use ever since. The legislation of Solid Waste Disposal Act was to promote the protection of public health and environment, and to conserve valuable materials and energy. The two basic policies about solid waste are: to reduce or eliminate the generation of hazardous waste as soon as practicable; to minimize the hazards to public health and environment caused by the storage, handling and disposal of solid waste.

5.3.2 The European Union

Waste management law (Directive) of the European Union is based on the existing solid waste laws of each sovereign state. In 1992, the Europe was united into one big market, and the EU members can interchange merchandise, personnel, capital and services ever since. As a result, waste management has been brought up to a strategic level by EU. European Union's Waste Strategy was enacted on 30 July, 1996 and it was revised on 21 December, 2005. This strategy has played a positive role in enhancing citizen's environmental awareness and guiding the effective disposal of waste.

At the same time, the EU gradually improved the waste directive at the regulatory level. 1998 saw the enactment of the Waste Framework Directive, which replaced the 1975 Directive 442 and the 1991 Directive 156. The directive provides the basic concepts and clear definitions related to waste management, such as the precise meaning of waste, reuse and recycling. The Directive establishes the basic principles of waste management: waste disposal should first of all not cause any adverse effect to health or to environment, especially not to water quality, air, soil, as well as the survival of plants and animals. Other principles also include "Polluter-pays Principle" and "Extended Producer Responsibility Principle". In 2008, the EU revised 1998 Waste Framework Directive, with revisions about the general principles of waste categorization, waste list and 15 hazardous characteristics that lead to hazardous waste. The revision, for the first time, introduced pyramid waste disposal priority, pointing out that landfill as the last treatment process to dispose waste, should only be taken when reuse or recycling can't be achieved with current technological efforts.

In addition to the main legislation of the Waste Framework Directive, the EU has also enacted the Landfill Directive, the Incineration Directive, and the Waste Shipment Regulation (2006), which provide specific rules for the treatment of waste oil, batteries and accumulators, end-of-life vehicles, packaging waste etc. Basically, there are special legal provisions governing the treatment of all waste categories in the Waste Framework Directive.

5.3.3 China

Law of the People's Republic of China on the Prevention and Control of Environmental Pollution by Solid Waste (referred to as Solid Waste Law) is developed for protecting environment from solid waste pollution, protecting human health, maintaining ecological safety and promoting sustainable development of society and economy. The law, containing 77 articles, was adopted at the Sixteenth Meeting of the Standing Committee of the Eighth National People's Congress on 30 October, 1995, and promulgated by Decree No. 58 of the President of the People's Republic of China on 30 October, 1995, and put into effect since 1 April, 1996. This law was later revised in 2004 and amended subsequently in 2013, 2015 and 2016, and then revised for the second time in 2020. The newly revised Solid Waste Law went into force on 1 September, 2020, with 126 articles in total.

The new revision of Solid Waste Law makes it the principle that solid waste should be reduced in quantity, reused and recycled as a resource and kept harmless. It also clearly sets the supervision and management responsibility of government and relevant departments, emphasizes the systems of target responsibility, credit record, joint prevention and control, whole process monitoring and information technology traceability, and the goal to gradually import zero solid waste for China.

The law has improved the system of environmental prevention and protection from industrial solid waste. Polluters' responsibility is emphasized, and mechanisms like discharge permission, management log and evaluation of comprehensive resource utilization are set up.

It's also clearly defined in the law that domestic waste classification system should be established and promoted. Environmental protection and prevention in urban and rural areas are to be planned as a whole. Local government can also develop customized management methods taking into account of the actual situation.

The law also improves on the environmental protection and prevention system of construction waste and agricultural solid waste. It establishes the construction waste classification system and whole process management system. It has also improved the environmental protection and prevention system from straw, waste agricultural film, livestock and poultry manure. It defines the extended producer responsibility of electrical and electronic, lead batteries, and automotive power batteries. Excessive packaging and plastic pollution will be put into more control efforts. Sludge treatment and laboratory solid waste management requirement is also clearly stated in the law.

The law has improved the system for the prevention and control of hazardous waste pollution, providing for the graded and classified management of hazardous waste, monitoring with information technology and building regional centralized disposal facilities. The management of cross-provincial transfer of hazardous waste should be strengthened through information technology means, transfer data and information sharing, and creating electronic transfer record. Hazardous waste transfer should be controlled with efficiency throughout the whole process.

In terms of legal liability, the law imposes severe penalties for violations, increases the amount of fines and the types of penalties, and takes the punishment to responsible individuals. At the same time, the law revision has supplemented a few legal liabilities for some violations.

5.4 National Standards and International Organization Standards

Apart from legal regulations, each country has its own system of national standards for waste management. National standards are usually divided into mandatory standards and voluntary (recommended) standards, and the implementation of these standards corresponds to compliance management and sustainability management respectively. Taking the United States, the European Union and China as examples, their standard systems are roughly as follows.

5.4.1 The United States

The pluralistic and liberalized state of American society has resulted in a uniquely decentralized standards system in the United States, with nearly 400 professional bodies, societies and associations developing and publishing standards in their respective areas of expertise. The U.S. national standards system is mainly composed of two sources, the American Society for Testing and Materials and the American National Standards Institute. The vast majority of the U.S. national standards related to environmental protection or waste management are developed and promulgated by these two organizations.

ASTM is short for American Society for Testing and Materials. It was previously the International Association for Testing Materials (IATM). ASTM is a non-profit organization and one of the largest to develop standards. It has nearly 34,000 members in ASTM, out of which 4,000 are from countries other than the U.S. ASTM has already developed over 10,000 standards, and over 100 of them are related to waste management. They mostly focus on the testing and analysis of waste materials from different industries (Refer to Appendix 1).

The American National Standards Institute (ANSI) was founded in 1918. Initially, the American Society for Testing and Materials (ASTM), the American Society of Mechanical Engineers (ASME), the American Society of Mining and Metallurgical Engineers (ASMME), the American Society of Civil Engineers (ASCE), the American Institute of Electrical Engineers (AIEE) and other organizations, together established the American Engineering Standards Committee (AESC). In 1928, the American Engineering Standards Committee was reorganized as the American Standards Association (ASA). In order to devote to the cause of international standardization and the standardization of consumer products, in August 1966, it was reorganized into the United States of America Standards Institute (USASI), and on 6 October, 1969, it was renamed into its current name: American National Standards Institute (ANSI). ANSI now has about 200 group members such as affiliated industrial societies and associations, and about 1,400 company (corporate) members. The staff of the National Bureau of Standards (NBS) and official representatives of many other U.S. government agencies also participate in the work of ANSI through various means.

5.4 National Standards and International Organization Standards

As a matter of fact, ANSI itself barely develops standards directly. The ANSI standards development are usually realized through the following three ways:

① Relevant organization will draft a standard, inviting experts or professional groups to vote. The voted result will be sent to the standard review committee for review and approval. This method is called voting-survey method.
② ANSI's technical committee and the representatives from other organizations' committee will draft a standard for all committee members to vote. The standard review committee will take the final review and approval. This is called committee method.
③ ANSI will also select from relatively well-developed standards by various professional societies and associations, which are relevant nation-wide. After being reviewed by ANSI's technical committees, the standard will be upgraded to national level and with ANSI's code and classification number, but at the same time retain its original standard code.

Therefore, ANSI's standards mostly come from different professional standards. Different professional societies and associations can also develop certain product standards based on existing national standards. But they can also develop their own association standards without referring to national standards. ANSI standards are voluntary—the U.S. believes that mandatory standards may limit the improvement of production efficiency. However, standards cited by law and government agencies are generally mandatory. There are about 20 ANSI standards related to waste, mainly focusing on waste management equipment, technology and practice (Refer to Appendix 2).

5.4.2 The European Union

The European Committee for Standardization (Comité Européen de Normalisation, CEN), founded in 1961, is head-quartered in Brussels, Belgium. It is a non-profit international standardization organization for science and technology, with members mostly from Western European countries and composed of national standardization bodies. The European Committee for Standardization (CEN), together with the European Committee for Electrotechnical Standardization (CENELEC) and the European Telecommunications Standards Institute (ETSI), form the three major European standardization organizations that support and complement each other.

Since CENELEC specializes in standardization in the field of electrical and electronic engineering, and ETSI in the field of communication technology and engineering, other areas and comprehensive standardization work are undertaken by CEN. As of 2010, CEN has published 1,090 documents, including EN standards (ENs), the European prestandards (ENVs), technical specifications (TSs), technical reports (TRs), CEN reports (CRs), CEN guides (CGs), and CEN working group agreements (CWAs). This naturally also includes more than 40 standards related to waste management and technology (Refer to Appendix 3).

Although not listed here at length, it is worth mentioning the BS standard (see Appendix 4) developed and published by the British Standards Institution (BSI), the DIN standard developed and published by the Deutsches Institut für Normung e.V. (see Appendix 5), and the NF standard (see Appendix 6) developed and published by the Association Française de Normalisation (AFNOR), are a few very early but independent and self-sufficient European standards. Among those standards, there are in total hundreds of articles about waste management and technology, comprehensive and in great details—many of them are also cross-referenced and cross-cited by other EU standards.

5.4.3 China

The State Administration for Market Regulation (SAMR) of the People's Republic of China, through State Standardization Administration of China (SAC), issues national standard plans, approves the issuance of national standards, reviews and promulgate standardization policies, management systems, plans, announcements and other important documents; carries out external notification for mandatory national standards implementation; coordinates, guides and supervises the work of industry, local, group and enterprise standards; represents the country in the International Organization for Standardization, the International Electrotechnical Commission and other international or regional standardization organizations; undertakes the signing of relevant international cooperation agreements work; undertakes day-to-day work of the State Council's standardization coordination mechanism.

In China's national standards system (as of 1 September, 2018), there are 41 mandatory standards (refer to Appendix 7) directly related to waste management, and all managed by Ministry of Ecology and Environment; 23 recommended standards (refer to Appendix 8), managed by Ministry of Ecology and Environment and other relevant ministries or professional standardization committees.

5.5 Industry Standards and Local Standards

Industry standards and local standards vary greatly from country to country, from industry to industry, and from region to region, so it is difficult to list them in detail for comparison. In China, for example, most of the mandatory standards are related to hazardous waste and medical waste management, and most of the voluntary standards are related to waste reduction and treatment or disposal technologies. As of 1 September, 2018, there are 72 industry standards directly related to waste available on the National Public Service Platform for Standards Information, basically developed and promulgated by various industry technical institutes or industry standardization technical committees; there are 23 local standards, all of which are managed by the environmental protection department of the government of the province, municipality or autonomous region to which they belong.

Chapter 6
Waste Diversion

There should always be a way out for waste, whether it's produced before consumption or inevitably generated after consumption. Any disposal method or process other than landfill is, in principle, waste diversion.

Waste diversion is strategically based on research and tactically depends on the right method. The strategy and tactics talked about here is regardless of waste components and sources.

6.1 Diversion Strategy

Off-gas diversion can only be achieved through technology—to increase the yield of the primary reaction, and to choose technology that can constrain the temperature and pressure condition under which gaseous substances occur. Once the off-gas is generated, capturing and treating it would be relatively difficult. To keep off-gas harmless is to remove substances that may be harmful to the atmosphere directly or indirectly before exhausting, except nitrogen, oxygen, carbon dioxide and water vapor. There are two directions to use off-gas as a resource. The first is to collect, concentrate and purify the harmful substances that can't be reduced and must be emitted, and to use it as raw materials for new industrial or agricultural production. The second is to liquefy essentially harmless substances into basic chemical raw materials (liquid nitrogen, dry ice, etc.) through process changes or equipment optimization. And of course, the appropriate use of the physical property of off-gas such as residual pressure or residual temperature is also a method of resource utilization.

The effluent diversion opportunities lie in the adoption of dry reaction as much as possible instead of water-based liquid phase reaction, and non-liquid phase off-gas absorption (most of the time off-gas is diverted into waste water after being absorbed by water). The way to keep effluent harmless is to use physical and chemical methods such as neutralization, filtration, coagulation, flocculation and sedimentation to separate hazardous substances from water, so that the industrial and agricultural effluent no longer has negative impact to the aquatic organism and aquatic ecology in natural waters. To use effluent as a resource is to further treat the harmless effluent emission and use it a second time or multiple times in industrial and agricultural production (reclaimed water). For instance, reclaimed water can be used as municipal water to cleanse roads or buildings, or to dredge rivers and to improve lake waters as landscape water.

However, it is a much more complicated story for solid waste diversion. Simply speaking, solid waste diversion depends entirely on the improvement of process technology and advanced management of materials—under the principle of mass balance, the higher yield of the primary reaction, the less the solid waste is produced. Meanwhile, it's relatively challenging to make solid waste harmless because hazardous substances, once mixed with solid phase materials, are difficult to be separated. Thermal treatment like incineration consumes energy and will add up to the risk of atmosphere pollution. In this case, not to be transformed into solid phase during manufacturing process in the first place is the key to keep solid waste harmless. Resource wise, solid waste can be used as raw materials or downgraded as auxiliary materials in other production industry, or be biodegraded or thermal treated to provide its calorific value directly or indirectly.

6.2 Diversion Method

For manufacturing companies, there are internal and external ways for waste diversion. Elimination, reuse and reduction can generally be realized by the company itself. However, recycling, aerobic composting, anaerobic digestion, biofuel and thermally processed with energy recovery (TWER), is usually achieved with the assistance of external organizations specialized in these professions.

On top of above mentioned, the hot topics of waste diversion in recent years are repairing, refurbishment and remanufacturing. But these three directions require the collaboration between the internal and external of a company, which means the manufacturing companies and their ultimate consumers collaborate under the guidance of market supervision department, so that waste is diverted from an opposite logistic direction.

6.2.1 Landfill

Let's first take a careful examination of landfill since waste diversion is all about avoiding landfill.

To throw away a product at its end of service life without any treatment, is discarding a waste; to collect all the thrown away waste and put at a specified location, or to guide people to throw away things at a given time and location, is called stacking; to bury all the stacked waste under the Earth surface (landfill site) in an organized and well planned way (even if it's leisurely organized or planned), or to bury the waste in areas with no human activities (desert or valley), is called landfill.

There is not a very definite classification of landfill internationally, but there are mainly three ways of landfill in terms of technology, as followed:

(1) Direct landfill

As explicit as it could be, direct landfill means to store waste directly at landfill sites without any treatment or protection, letting waste weather through storm or sunshine naturally. Also, as apparent as it could be, this method takes up precious land and damages ecology; furthermore, the odor generated by organic substance decomposing and the hazardous substances seeped into surface water or ground water, will take long-lasting and at the same time irreversible effect on the environment.

This primitive method once was dominant in history, but it is rarely seen nowadays in developed countries. As shown in Fig. 6.1.

(2) Segregated landfill

It is to segregate the landfill waste from the nature in a relatively closed system. The odor generated by the decomposition of organic matters can be effectively reduced by capping measure (in some cases by air extraction and purification), and the harmful substances can basically be prevented from leaching into soil and surface or ground water by water-proof material at the bottom (in some cases by leachate collection and treatment). But is landfill in this way a once-and-for-all thing?

Fig. 6.1 Landfill site in Colorado, the U.S

Apparently not. Similar to buildings in any other kind, segregated landfill site follows certain construction standards as well. And any building has its own protection level against the disaster risk level. It means a building can bear a certain level of natural disasters, like a three-year fire, a ten-year flood or a fifty-year earthquake. However, human history taught us that the savageness of natural or man-made disasters tend to exceed what a building is designed to bear—instances like the fire in Chernobyl and the tsunami in Fukushima are all living examples, not to mention uncontrollable events like war. As a matter of fact, no human buildings can withstand the attack from the weapons built by humans themselves. Thus, once those happen to segregated landfill sites, the closed system will possibly be damaged and the atmosphere as well as surface and ground water will undergo certain level of impact.

Even if a closed landfill is so well fortified that it couldn't be destroyed (not considering the cost), there could be a negative ecological impact given the considerable size of any landfill. Imagine there was a huge closed building somewhere. It would for sure block the nearby local ecosystem: the flow of the ground water would be blocked, and most likely the ground water level on one side of the landfill might fall and on the other side rise, affecting the local growth conditions for plants and animals. At the same time, the ground vegetation pathway might be blocked, leaving it impossible for the rabbit in the east mountain to find his mate in the west, therefore biodiversity affected, even natural evolution interrupted—especially for those species at danger.

In a nutshell, the more and larger the segregated landfills are, the worse and weaker the local ecosystem would be. For this reason, segregated landfill is not a desirable solution for waste in the long-run. As shown in Fig. 6.2.

(3) Degraded landfill

It is also called advanced landfill. Different from other landfill methods, advanced landfill does not only rely on natural decomposition of the waste. Instead, it will use multiple artificial interventions (mainly physical heating and pressurization and oxygenation, or the addition of trace chemicals, targeted introduction of degradation bacteria, etc.) to enhance and accelerate the degradation process of waste. It is somewhat developed in many countries, with obvious advantages and disadvantages.

Enhanced degradation can reduce the volume of the landfill relatively quickly to facilitate subsequent re-fill; it can also control and select the products of waste decomposition to avoid and reduce harmful substances generated in the process; furthermore, the landfill site may able to be reused for development if the site is assessed to be overall harmless in numbers of years.

But advanced landfill is still a way of landfilling. All negative impact of landfill still applies. Meanwhile, due to the limited choices of available technologies, it dictates a very limited variety of waste to be landfilled in this way. And base investment of advanced landfill will be relatively larger than others, plus there is long-term operational cost to be considered.

In light of above mentioned, even with the enhanced waste degradation, advanced landfill is still not a very effective diversion method.

6.2 Diversion Method

Fig. 6.2 Landfill site in Hangzhou, China

6.2.2 Incineration

Incineration, as the most mature and the most practical diversion technology, turns out to be the most controversial at the same time. Even if incineration could reduce the waste volume significantly, saving lands for landfill, eliminating various pathogen and turning toxic and hazardous substances into harmless substances, it is still a choice out of no choice when landfill is not desired and no other diversion methods can be found even when the most advanced technology is adopted.

Waste incineration is a process in which waste is reduced to residue or molten solids through appropriate thermal decomposition, combustion, and melting, resulting in oxidation at high temperatures. The core of the process is to destroy the carbon chains of organic compound by advanced oxidation, of which the fully oxidized part generates carbon dioxide into the atmosphere, and the part that cannot be fully oxidized forms other small molecule organic compounds into the atmosphere, or remains in the incineration residue. See Fig. 6.3.

The typical incineration technology usually has a controlled temperature higher than 850 °C inside the incinerator. The waste volume can be reduced by 50%~80% compared to its original size. Combustible waste that has been sorted can even be reduced by 90% of its volume after incineration. The final volume of the waste can be further reduced if incineration is combined with high temperature (1,650~1,800 °C) pyrolysis and melting treatment. In theory, incineration can convert the chemical energy of waste organics into thermal energy for recovery (energy recovery). However, this is subject to several limitations.

Fig. 6.3 Marchwood incineration plant in Hampshire, the UK

First of all, the net calorific value of waste itself can't always sustain the incineration temperature. Fuel, in this situation, needs to be unceasingly filled to boost combustion. It normally is petroleum-based products or natural gas, with too high the cost. Secondly, waste may need to be pre-treated due to high water content. But whether it's mechanical dehydration or thermal dehydration, they all require additional energy. Thirdly, the thermal energy recovering efficiency is hard to be guaranteed, and it requires stable operation of incineration power plant and single type of waste. Lastly, there are also engineering difficulties in connecting smaller power incineration plants to the grid, and a certain scale effect is needed to generate basic economic benefits.

Waste incineration technology still has some natural disadvantages even with all the above mentioned fixed.

First, mixed solid waste (like municipal waste) is rather complicated in composition. Nitrogen and sulfur could be oxidized as nitrogen oxide and sulfur oxide to contribute mainly to atmosphere pollution. Carbon elements that can't combust completely can also easily be turned into dioxin and other carcinogenic and teratogenic compounds. The fly ash from combustion and the fine materials that cannot be burned together become in turn the main source of particulate matter (like PM_{10}, $PM_{2.5}$ as smog triggers) in the atmosphere. In addition, since waste containing chlorine or other halogens can corrode the incinerator and other metal equipment under the high temperature in combustion, they must be removed as much as possible by pre-treatment. Finally, no matter how thorough and complete the incineration is, there will always be rubbish produced, and the substances that can't be oxidized still have to be landfilled, with leachability toxicology test done beforehand to ensure harmlessness.

The construction of an incineration project is so complicated that its environmental assessment is bound to be in the spotlight. The incinerator has to be the most advanced, equipped with off-gas and particulate matter capturing and treatment devices, as well as a nearby curing landfill site. Not only should 24 h automatic monitoring instrument for air and water be equipped, but also contingency plans should be fully prepared. As an environmental facility, the incinerator itself is subject to environmental monitoring, and also to the complaints from nearby residents—it may need to relocate constantly due to those complaints. It could then be concluded that incineration technology should not be the main diversion direction, rather, it should just be a supplement at the end of other diversion methodologies.

6.2.3 Elimination

The fundamental goal of elimination is to optimize the production process or management process so that no waste is generated during these processes. In other words, it is to eliminate the waste generating mechanism.

To find the elimination opportunities, each and every step in the production or management process need to be well understood. Though there's a saying that goes what is rational is actual and what is actual is rational, the rationality is still confined in certain time and space. A process might be a must in certain history or in certain countries and regions, it's still not needed everywhere all the time. The production or management process, if not being thought through before applying, may produce unnecessary waste.

An example is that the early production process of a daily chemical manufacture required the use of high-salt liquids, and the stainless-steel parts in its reactor had to be replaced periodically due to corrosive pitting and became waste metal; however, after they changed their production process to use only organic liquids, the original corrosive pitting situation no longer existed, and the stainless-steel parts could be used almost indefinitely. The waste metal generation mechanism was thus eliminated, and the metal waste is also completely eliminated here. Another example is a furniture manufacture that used double-layer plastic film inside the cardboard boxes of its export products for maritime moisture and corrosion protection, and the same for its domestic sales products—these plastic films were useless to consumers and were plastic waste. It was later found that in most of the market areas in northern China, the climate is dry with little rain—after eliminating the unnecessary plastic film, the furniture manufacture was able to eliminate plastic waste at the consumer end.

It can be seen that elimination is objectively driven by technological innovation. Whenever there's new technology emerged, certain waste could be eliminated. But it's also worth noting that the proactivity of human beings plays a very important role. Otherwise new technology may eliminate the existing waste, but at the same time bring new waste. Only when both the objective technology development and human beings' proactivity are in the same place can the elimination be truly realized.

6.2.4 Reuse

To reuse is to use the waste directly, and if necessary, only with simple treatment (excluding repairing, refurbishment and remanufacturing) as an equivalent product; in some cases, it also includes the use of all or part of the waste as the component of another product.

Reuse is a significant part of circular economy, with profound value. On the one hand, reuse has direct contribution to waste reduction; on the other hand, it indirectly reduces material and energy consumption in resources extraction and production.

In Chap. 1, the history of waste generation, we mentioned the product manufactured by humans in industrial societies has a relative durability for the sake of commercial competition—"relative" here means its physical life tends to outlive, even way too far, its economic life. When the commercial value or the economic life of a product ends, being abandoned and replaced by newer generations, its use value or physical life still remains intact and can continue to be used directly or indirectly.

The meaning of reuse is actually very clear to us. That's why it is applicable in many manufacturing companies. For instance, the depreciated equipment, if not affecting safety and product quality, will not be easily scrapped by manufactures. The key to the problem lies in consumer market. If the products are extensively reused at the end of their commercial value, it will for sure impact the market demand for newer iterations of the product, which any manufacturing company is unwilling to see. For individual consumers, reused product is in general unsightly and loss of face to many. As long as it's financially possible, consumers will choose new departments over second-hand ones, new cars over used ones. Even younger brothers will not want the old clothes from older brothers—if not driven by economic interest or social value, the living space of reuse is bound to be limited.

To encourage reuse, the states or corporates can drive its implementation and popularization from the perspective of economic interests and social values. Economically, the states can leverage tax and corporate finance to increase the competitiveness of reuse products, such as to raise tax on new products, or to subsidize on products which has not yet reached the end of their physical life. In terms of social value, the states can enhance education and promotion, and corporates can adopt reward and recognition to acknowledge individuals who reuse products, so as to help the public recognize and get used to reuse.

6.2.5 Reduction

Broadly speaking, waste reduction includes: to reduce the amount from the very beginning—namely to give sufficient consideration at the product design and manufacturing stage in order to reduce waste; to reduce the amount in the process—that is, divert as much waste as possible from the beginning of waste generation that can be used as a resource; to reduce the amount at the end of treatment—it is, in nature, to reduce waste to be directly landfilled.

As the broad definition of waste reduction overlaps with diversion methodology, we tend to use a narrow sense of reduction, that is when the waste generation mechanism can't be changed, and no appropriate diversion method can be found, waste generated should be as less as possible, in order to minimize the amount to be incinerated or landfilled.

Waste reduction is, relatively speaking, the most achievable and acceptable for manufacturers and residents. It is acceptable because waste is something that no one would want in sight. Waste reduction, either in volume or in mass, would always be a happy thing. At the same time, the reduction of waste also means the reduction of waste disposal expense, both environmentally and economically beneficial. It is achievable because there is no hard KPI (Key Performance Indicators) on reduction. Every little help, more or less it is still the performance; and if it's reduced to none, it's upgraded to elimination. Meanwhile, there are multiple ways to reduce waste. Environment management staffs or engineers can work their own ways to reduce waste in the long run.

This is why companies can create a clear environmental management program and set long-term goals for waste reduction, aiming to reduce a few percentage points per year; then seek concrete steps to reduce waste and implement them by setting up waste reduction action teams.

6.2.6 Recycling

Unlike "reuse", which is a simple, non-destructive treatment of waste, the process of "recycling" must include a very critical step, which is the physical and/or chemical transformation of the waste from the discarded "product" or "component" state to the original "raw material" state (if not transform to the original "raw material" state, it may be categorized as remanufacturing) so that it re-enters the manufacturing process. This type of physical and/or chemical method is generally difficult to be compatible with the processes and equipment of manufacturing companies, so this is why recycling generally requires the assistance of external companies specializing in these operations to complete.

In theory, all waste can be recycled, but in practice, only a few major categories of waste can be well sorted and recycled: metal, paper, plastic and glass. Why?

The value of metals is the highest, whether they are precious metals such as platinum, gold and silver, or common metals such as copper, iron and aluminum, or rare earth metals such as lanthanum, cerium and yttrium. The recycling of these metals is relatively more rewarding, the process is mature, and the recycling industry is rather complete. The core business of metal recycling is to dismantle or separate metals from the waste and pursuit the value of raw materials.

As one of the Four Great Inventions of ancient China, the process of paper making determines its recyclability: except for pretreatment, the subsequent process is almost identical! Mankind has even found that using used paper to make paper not only reduces deforestation, but even makes primary processing of used paper simpler compared to log processing—provided, of course, that the used paper for recycling is of a single type and contains no other impurities. In addition, because the plant fibers of recycled paper have been destroyed once or several times, its quality is usually not as good as that of virgin paper.

As a new material invented by man, the chemical structure of plastics allows a significant portion of them to be recycled. Similar to recycled paper, recycled plastics will be downgraded as well, meaning that each time they are recycled their quality decreases a little, i.e. their physical and chemical properties are not as good as those of virgin plastics. But unlike recycled paper, the market price of recycled plastics is more volatile and depends almost entirely on the price of crude oil on the international market—when oil is expensive, virgin plastics are expensive and the price of recycled plastics goes up; when oil is cheap, virgin plastics are cheap and the price of recycled plastics goes down.

The recycling situation of glass is relatively more complex. With the development of the contemporary silicate industry, a wide variety of glasses have been developed to suit different needs. The main chemical composition of ordinary glass is silicate, but there are also tinted glass mixed with oxides or salts of certain metals to reveal different colors, as well as tempered glass made by special physical and/or chemical methods. The recyclability of different glass products is different. There are several types of recycling of general glass products: as casting flux, transformation of building materials, and back to the furnace melt manufacturing (glass containers or glass fiber), etc., not all described here.

Wastes that cannot be recycled or are difficult to be recycled, in addition to the above-mentioned easy-to-recycle ones, are generally the following:

① Complex compounds whose various single substances are difficult to separate out by either mechanical or manual methods, or are too costly to separate out.
② Specially required materials at the end of their lives, as they are made of special raw materials through unusual chemical processing, they cannot be decomposed once their lives are completed.
③ Biochemical or radiation-contaminated waste, whether from laboratories for scientific research, medical institutions for clinical use, military exercises, or natural disasters, cannot be considered for recycling if it is chemically, bacteriologically or radiologically contaminated.

Generally speaking, there are two sources of recyclable waste, namely pre-consumer waste and post-consumer waste, which we mentioned earlier in Chap. 4. In comparison, pre-consumer waste is easier to recycle because it's essentially found at the manufacturing end of the plant, where the material type is relatively homogeneous, and easy to collect and sort and contains few other impurities. While, obviously, post-consumer waste is less easy to recycle because it is highly dispersed and usually mixed with impurities, and there are certain logistics costs to collect them.

6.2.7 Aerobic Composting

The deep resource treatment of mixed organic waste is largely dependent on naturally occurring microorganisms. Humans can enhance this process with certain conditions and facilities, where treatment processes requiring aerobic bacteria are commonly known as aerobic composting, often referred to as composting.

Aerobic composting is originally an ancient natural fertilizer manufacturing process. In agriculture it originally refers to the process of plant, animal remains and excrement which contains fertilizer components, mixing with soil and minerals, after going through fermentation, maturation and microbial decomposition in high temperature and humid conditions, to make organic fertilizer. Long-term application of organic compost can not only obtain high yields, but also improve soil quality and ground strength significantly. Since the aerobic composting process is also applicable to the treatment of mixed organic waste generated from human activities, it has been rapidly developed industrially and professionally—the benefits of this waste treatment have even exceeded its original purpose for making fertilizer.

There are two kinds of modern aerobic composting: normal composting and high-temperature composting. The former one requires lower fermentation temperature while the latter one needs higher fermentation temperature at first and then compressing later on. Aerobic composting process requires a lot of natural conditions. The location needs to be on the high terrain, lee ward and close to water with convenient transportation. Since composting is an aerobic process, it produces relatively little odor and the process is not too complicated (compared to anaerobic digestion); however, most aerobic composting of waste needs to first reduce its water content, which may require additional energy to heat and dehydrate in areas with insufficient sunlight, and occupies a certain amount of land; and in a highly industrialized and urbanized area, aerobic composting may be limited in scale, and the organic fertilizer, if to be sold as commodity, may meet market access and regulatory challenges.

Manufacturing companies seldom generate waste suitable for aerobic composting. Such organic waste usually comes from human residence. The waste sorting is also important for aerobic composting as it could prevent unnecessary residue.

6.2.8 Anaerobic Digestion

In contrast to aerobic composting, which relies on aerobic bacteria, the process of deep resource treatment of mixed organic waste by anaerobic bacteria is generally referred to as anaerobic digestion. A more specialized definition is the digestion technique in which organic compound is broken down into CH_4, CO_2, H_2O and H_2S by facultative bacteria and anaerobic bacteria under anaerobic conditions.

Anaerobic digestion is one of the most important biomass utilization technologies today. Through the four stages of hydrolysis, acidification, hydrogen/acetic acid production and methanation, solid organic compound is converted into dissolvable organic compound, and then the energy contained in the waste is converted into biogas for combustion or power generation to achieve resource and energy recovery. The amount of residue after anaerobic digestion is small and the nature is stable; meanwhile, the reaction equipment is closed and the emission of bad odor can be controlled. Anaerobic digestion greatly improves the energy balance of the organic waste treatment process, and has greater economic and environmental advantages.

Compared with aerobic composting, anaerobic digestion costs 1.2~1.5 times more in investment, and is more demanding for equipment's operational stability and safety. However, it takes smaller place and barely needs any energy input from outside (to achieve energy self-sufficiency). In addition, it can generate power into the grid if connected, which can directly reduce greenhouse gas (CO_2, CH_4) and odor emission.

According to the different sources and types of organic waste, many anaerobic digestion technologies with different operation processes have been developed around the world, such as wet continuous multi-stage fermentation system and dry single-stage fermentation system, etc. The applications of these technologies have their own advantages and disadvantages, which will not be detailed here. At the same time, new and efficient processes combined with aerobic composting, such as sequential batch anaerobic composting process, dry anaerobic digestion + aerobic composting, semi-dry anaerobic digestion + aerobic composting, two-phase anaerobic digestion in leachate bed, etc., have been more and more popularly applied with the development of related scientific research and upgrading of facilities and equipment.

Manufacturing companies, unlike aerobic composting, rarely generate waste directly suitable for anaerobic digestion (partially food waste), but may generate a large amount of secondary sludge due to the plant's biochemical waste water treatment facilities, which needs to be further reduced or rendered harmless by anaerobic digestion. This part will be described in more detail later in Chap. 7 on secondary waste.

6.2.9 Biofuel

Biofuel (or biomass fuel), generally refers to solid, liquid or gaseous fuel composed of or exacted from biomass, replacing gasoline and diesel made from petroleum. It is an important direction for renewable energy development and utilization. The biomass mentioned here is any and all organic matters living on photosynthesis using the atmosphere, water and earth (all living organic matters that can grow, including plants, animals and microorganism, different from traditional fuel like petroleum, coal and nuclear energy, etc.). And the biomass concept in waste diversion also includes the organic waste produced by human activities.

Some of the organic matters in nature becomes waste during the production process of human being. A typical example is the bagasse made from sugar production. Some other organic matters turn into waste after human beings' utilization, typically the restaurant waste grease. The former waste is pre-consumer waste and the latter post-consumer waste.

They are all biomass, whether it's pre-consumer or post-consumer waste organism, and are possible to be made into biofuel just like a natural organic matter—biodiesel, bioethanol and biobutanol etc. Using wasted biomass to produce biofuel, compared with using natural biomass, has the following merits, except for being safe and pollution-free:

① No need to change the status quo in agroforestry, no competition with food production for water and land resources.
② Various raw materials can be used, such as crop straw, forestry processing residues, livestock manure, organic waste water residue from food processing industry, urban garbage, etc.
③ Cost effective, only needs to establish or improve the collection and transportation system from decentralized raw material.
④ The benefits of comprehensive management of oil and grease waste are significant, especially the processing of recollected waste cooking oil or gutter oil into biodiesel with supervision can greatly reduce the risk of unclean oil usage in the catering industry.

Therefore, although there are still many controversies and restrictions on the production of biofuels from natural biomass, the production of biofuels from waste biomass is a waste diversion method already being encouraged and developed in various countries and regions around the world.

6.2.10 Repairing

Generally speaking, repairing includes also maintenance. The specific operations may have replacing parts, repairing parts, restoring or upgrading according to functions, and so on. No matter what kind of operation, product A after repairing is still product A, it does not involve any quality guarantee and intellectual property issues.

Different types of consumer products have different specific items of repairing. For example, for mobile phones, software updates can also be regarded as repairing; for cars, paint touch-up can also be included in the scope of repairing.

The repairing of industrial products is more common, which mainly involves the repairing of equipment in the factory—the technical activities carried out to restore the function of the equipment after the deterioration or failure of the equipment, including various planned maintenance, unplanned fault repairing and accident repairing.

All these repairing activities have only one purpose, that is, to convert the product and equipment into normal things at the end of their service life or when they are about to end and become waste. Different from reuse, repairing is not a simple process. It requires professional technology and tools, and has a fixed workflow and standard. Therefore, repairing has a certain cost. The cost depends on the complexity of repairing. In short, it depends on the repairing time (man-hour) and the value of parts to be replaced. Obviously, the shorter the repairing time and the simpler the parts to be replaced, the higher the efficiency of repairing business and the higher the value of repairing activities.

When it comes to repairing efficiency and repairing value, it naturally involves two different repairing methods: local repairing and factory return repairing.

Local repairing takes place where the product or equipment is used. In principle, whether the products to be repaired are sent to the designated sales stores for repairing or the professional engineer/technician bring tools and accessories for on-site repairing, the after-sales logistics of products or equipment is not involved (here specifically refers to reverse logistics, and the relevant contents will be discussed separately in Chap. 10).

Easy to understand, factory return repairing refers to the return of products or equipment to the manufacturer (here reverse logistics is involved), and using the original manufacturing resources to carry out repairing—because generally only the original manufacturer can provide the most professional repairing service—which is also the most efficient way.

No matter what kind of repairing, the whole product or equipment can be avoided to become waste, even if it is only due to a small part or even software failure. Of course, the repairing itself will also produce secondary waste, such as replaced parts, auxiliary materials used in maintenance operations, and so on. Compared with the complete waste of the whole product or equipment without repairing, even if the secondary waste generated has to be sent to incineration or even landfill, it is much less than the former (of course, there are other corresponding diversion methods for these secondary wastes, see Chap. 7, Sect. 7).

6.2.11 Refurbishment

The definition of refurbishment is very tricky, which can be approximately considered to be between repairing and remanufacturing. Although product A has been refurbished, it is still product A, but re-entering the market for sale after the refurbishment involves the quality guarantee and intellectual property of the "new products".

At first, refurbishment was limited to the worn-out products. After special processing, the appearance or performance of the worn-out products could be restored to the greatest extent. With the progress of relevant technology, the used products with financial scrap or performance degradation were transformed into new products, which were included in the scope of refurbishment.

Due to some existing violations in the market, refurbishment has a negative "reputation" for a long time. Criminals collect used products (most of which are relatively high-tech consumer electronic products) through various channels, clean them with special chemicals, replace the case, batteries, chargers and counterfeit or forged packaging, passing off as new products and entering the market for sale.

In fact, if the original manufacturer of the product can effectively provide recycling channels for the used products and carry out the business of refurbished products in an open, transparent and compliant manner, the social and economic benefits will be very significant. Because:

① The used products for refurbishment usually will not be reused simply because of consumers' subjective factors (fond of the new and tired of the old). The "official" refurbishment of manufacturers can just eliminate the restriction of personal subjective factors.
② Although the refurbished products also need specific processes, these processes generally already exist in the original manufacturing plants, which do not require additional investments of equipment and management by enterprises, and are easy to operate economically.
③ Although the products that can be refurbished are used, they generally have no major failure or damage, so the refurbishment process will not produce more secondary waste, and the environmental benefit is good.

Enterprises with certain social responsibility usually go through strict internal process control for refurbished products, including deep cleaning, renewing case and package, and routine testing according to the same strict quality standards as the new products, so that the refurbished product in the hands of end users can really "like new". In addition, in order to encourage consumer to buy and use, refurbished products generally have special discounts on prices, and sometimes provide additional quality guarantee.

In a word, the commercialization, popularization and standardization of refurbished products not only need the relevant policies, regulations and standards issued by the national market supervision department, but also need to change the concept of individual consumers through publicity and education, so that the public can gradually accept the formal refurbished products and avoid some unnecessary waste.

6.2.12 Remanufacturing

Remanufacturing is a new mode of waste diversion which has developed rapidly in the early twenty years of the 21st century. It can also be considered that it is the highest level of waste diversion under the support of science and technology in the new century. It may even greatly surpass the repairing and refurbishment in industrial scale. Different from repairing and refurbishment, product A may return to product A, or be transferred into product B after remanufacturing the whole or parts. Therefore, when remanufactured products enter the market, they have to reconsider the quality guarantee as new products. At the same time, if they return to product A, they will involve intellectual property, and if they are transferred into product B, they will not involve any intellectual property of original product A.

In the initial concept, remanufacturing is an industry of high-tech repairing and transformation of damaged products. Firstly, it industrializes the dismantling of damaged products, and then carries out secondary engineering design on the basis of failure analysis and performance evaluation for dismantled parts. Due to the application of a series of more advanced manufacturing technologies, the quality of remanufactured products can reach or even exceed the original products. Later, after the theoretical research and operational practice of remanufacturing, the concept of remanufacturing has been gradually expanded and deepened. Today, it is far beyond the narrow scope of dismantling parts to produce new products—remanufacturing is almost omnipotent.

So why is remanufacturing the highest level of waste diversion? It is mainly considered from the following aspects:

① Theoretically speaking, if the normal loss is ignored, remanufacturing can go on indefinitely as long as there is enough energy input. The only premise is that remanufacturing should be considered at the design phase of the product. The greener design (more reasonable) is, the simpler it is to remanufacture the waste products at the end, and the less energy input is required. On the contrary, although remanufacturing can always be carried out, due to technical and economic factors, the more unreasonable such remanufacturing is, the more difficult it is to achieve.

② Strategically speaking, remanufacturing is a system engineering, which needs the coordination of industry, country and even global supplier chain. Through remanufacturing, the upstream and downstream of the industry, production and supervision, manufacturing and service will be opened up. Once the remanufacturing ecosystem is formed, it is bound to continue stably for a long time, its comprehensive benefits will be very obvious, and the enthusiasm of the participants is self-evident.

③ In a broad sense, after industrialization, human beings are actually slowly remanufacturing the Earth—a celestial body in the universe. Due to the current technological and economic constraints, this "remanufacturing" is still mainly concentrated in the area of human activities (biosphere) on the Earth's surface. However, with the ambition of human beings to transform the world, as long as human beings do not die out due to accidental astronomical events, all the resources on the Earth, including all the waste generated before, will be all "remanufactured" into a world more suitable for human habitation.

Of course, it does not mean that remanufacturing can replace all other diversion methods, but that once the remanufacturing system is formed, other diversion methods will automatically become effective complementary means and join in remanufacturing. At present, the remanufacturing system urgently needs to be standardized, including product standards and supply chain standards. Only by standardizing the detailed indicators of remanufacturing in their respective industries, can this "advanced" diversion method be promoted and developed step by step, and reflect its strong vitality.

6.2.13 Conclusion

With further development of human society, science and technology, there may be more advanced waste diversion methods. However, the environmental benefit and economic benefits of various diversion methods are different. The environmental benefit mainly depends on the diversion efficiency and the additional energy consumption in the diversion process, and the economic benefit mainly depends on the investment and operating costs of waste diversion. Of course, it also depends on the comprehensive benefits of environment and economy.

According to their own actual situation, enterprises can give priority to the implementation of waste diversion methods which are easy to achieve in a short period of time, and then gradually consider long-term planning and move forward to the goal of "zero waste" in stages.

Chapter 7
Waste Treatment and Disposal Technology

The strategies and methods of waste diversion have been found, which shows the way for manufacturing companies to practice their social responsibilities. However, at the operational level of waste diversion, waste-generating companies need to, by themselves or entrust other companies with corresponding qualifications, find the most suitable waste treatment and disposal technologies based on their diversion methods.

The waste generated in different industries is different in varieties and features. It's impossible to list them all here due to limited knowledge and length. This chapter will focus on several typical industrial wastes to study and share their treatment and disposal technologies.

7.1 Chemical Waste

There might be no waste other than chemical waste—discarded chemicals, which can draw so much attention from the society and the public—no matter in which country and region in the world. Theoretically, the types of chemical waste are just as many as the types of chemicals.

Chemical waste normally doesn't have elementary substance, as one would be out of his mind to cast away elementary substance, which can be directly used as chemical industry raw material. Chemical waste usually refers to compound containing certain impurities which can't easily be removed, or a mixture of different compounds. Those wasted compounds can be divided into, obviously, inorganic waste compounds and organic waste compounds.

7.1.1 Inorganic Waste Compounds

Inorganic waste compounds (referred to as inorganic waste hereafter) don't have complicated varieties and origins. They are mainly derived from the initial mineral collection and front-end physical or chemical processing from a full product life cycle perspective.

7.1.1.1 Tailing

The sorting operation of mineral separation will sort out those of which the target component content is too low and cannot be used in the production—called tailings. Tailings cannot be used for production means that it is not suitable for further sorting under the current technical conditions, but with the development of science and technology, the target components of tailings may also have other economic value for recycling. Therefore, tailings are not completely useless and it has potential for comprehensive utilization. And waste-free is to make full use of mineral resources and protect the ecological environment.

Different types and structures of ores require different beneficiation processes; and the tailings produced by different beneficiation processes often have certain differences in various physical and chemical properties, especially in particle morphology and grain composition. Tailings can be divided into the following types according to the beneficiation process: hand-selected tailings, heavy-selected tailings, magnetic-selected tailings, flotation tailings, chemically-selected tailings, electrically-selected tailings, etc.

The rapid development of human economy sees the exponential increase in the demand for natural resources, especially mineral resources in various industries, with a larger and larger scale of mining. Correspondingly, the number of tailings generated by large-scale mineral beneficiation is also increasing. If not treated and disposed of, the large amount of tailings will cause a great burden to the mining industry itself, as well as to the local environment and economy. As shown in Fig. 7.1.

Large amount of tailings will result in environmental and economic problems, including resource waste, land occupying and beneficiation effluent pollution.

First of all, as a "wasted" mineral resource, tailings still contain useful components such as re-choosable metallic and non-metallic minerals. When the main mining enrichment process has taken away the most valuable minerals from the original ore, it's a pity to just discard the tailings directly.

Secondly, the storage of tailings occupies a large amount of land, and is mainly open ground storage—so the ecological impact of soil erosion and vegetation destruction around the mine area cannot be ignored. If the mining area's environment cannot be restored to its original state, various potential ecological risks will gradually emerge.

Additionally, certain components of the tailings and residual beneficiation chemicals can also cause direct damage to the natural environment, especially for tailings

7.1 Chemical Waste

Fig. 7.1 Tailings' landscape

containing heavy metals. The oxidation of sulfides will produce acidic beneficiation effluent which may permeate heavy metals, which, if flow away, will harm the soil, surface water and ground water of the entire mining area.

To deal with the above-mentioned problems, current tailing treatment and disposal technologies focus on the following areas:

① Try comprehensive utilization of useful components in tailings resources, and develop some auxiliary mining or beneficiation technologies to obtain relatively low-value mineral sands or other construction materials—use mineral sands that do not contain chemical leachate to build roads directly, or to build fields around the sea; use some tailings to process and manufacture cement, bricks and tiles, concrete, glass, refractory materials, etc.

② Tailings that cannot be comprehensively utilized can be made into water-sand filler or cemented filler to backfill the original underground mining void areas. Or directly mulch the tailings dumps to create fields, plant crops or plant trees if soil and water conditions allow.

③ Constructing tailing ponds according to local conditions to collect and treat tailings water. The tailing pond can be set in the valley, slope, river bank or flat land by using the terrain, surrounded by dikes. In the pond, drainage wells and drainage ditches along the edge can be set up. If tailing water stays in the pond for at least one day and night, the water can be clarified, purified and overflow, while the original suspended particulate matter will precipitate in the pond bottom—the longer the effluent stays in the pond, the better the treatment effect. When the tailings particles are very fine and partly colloidal, coagulants and flocculants can be added to the tailings water to accelerate the precipitation process and improve the treatment effect.

④ Tailings pond overflow water can also be recycled. For re-chosen, magnetic separation and simple flotation of single metal ores with low water quality requirements, the recycling rate of overflow water can be up to 80%, or even no drainage at all. The overflow water that cannot be discharged into natural water bodies if it does not meet the standard, and further treatment is required—removal of heavy metals can be done by lime neutralization and roasted dolomite adsorption, removal of flotation agent can be done by lead and zinc ore and activated carbon adsorption (activated carbon adsorption is more effective but more expensive), removal of cyanide is mainly done by chemical oxidation, and recovery of sodium cyanide can also be considered for high concentration cyanide-containing waste water.

The treatment and disposal of tailings is still a great challenge nowadays. The demand for minerals in today's industrial development is increasing and the volume of tailings generated is staggering. Even with deep utilization and resource-based treatment and disposal, it is still difficult to achieve complete diversion of mineral waste—and this is exactly what human beings need to think about. From a life-cycle perspective, mining is the "cradle" stage of the product, and the importance of waste diversion is self-evident. At the same time, the difficulty of tailings treatment and disposal is prompting mankind to give more consideration to the reuse and recycling of industrial waste to reduce the pressure on the demand for virgin minerals.

7.1.1.2 Nuclear Waste

Nuclear waste is a highly sensitive topic. The disposal of nuclear waste, at the same time, is one of the greatest challenges in the development of human science and technology, especially when the demand for energy from human beings reaches a certain level.

Nuclear waste broadly refers to the radioactive waste generated during the production process of nuclear fuel and at the end of the use of nuclear reactors. It can also specifically refer to the spent fuel used in nuclear reactors, in which the usable nuclear materials such as plutonium-239 is recovered, but waste like uranium-238 is left unwanted and still radioactive. It is necessary to point out that the nuclear waste discussed here does not include various low-level radioactive wastes generated by irradiation or contamination in some locations that use radioactive materials, such as hospitals, factories, schools and research institutes (which can be treated and disposed of according to the corresponding waste requirements after being tested safe).

Nuclear waste can easily distinct itself from other wastes, by its radioactivity in the first place. The radioactivity of nuclear waste can't be eliminated by general physical, chemical or biological methods, but can only be reduced by the decay of the radionuclides themselves. Secondly, the distinction lies in its harmfulness. When the radiation emitted by nuclear waste passes through substances, it will cause ionization and excitation so that organisms will be damaged. Furthermore, nuclear waste releases heat when radionuclide decays. When the nuclide content is high, the heat released will cause the temperature of nuclear waste itself to rise, with solids melting and liquids boiling by themselves.

Those features of nuclear waste have determined a different diversion principle for it from other wastes. The elimination of nuclear waste seems impossible at least for now, its reduction is nowhere to begin with, with reuse and recycling almost out of existence. Depleted uranium is the only so-called reused part as the by-product of nuclear fuel, mainly containing less radioactive uranium-238, and minimal uranium-234/uranium-235. Unfortunately, it seems that the only "outlets" that the countries producing nuclear fuel have been able to find for depleted uranium are weaponry and warfare applications: depleted uranium ammunition for attack, or depleted uranium armor for defense, using its high density, hardness, self-sharpening, easy oxidation, and residual radioactivity—obviously, the radiological toxicity (mainly alpha rays) and chemical toxicity (heavy metal poisoning) of depleted uranium make it difficult to use depleted uranium as a weapon. The radiological toxicity (mainly alpha rays) and chemical toxicity (heavy metal poisoning) of depleted uranium is contrary to the nuclear ethics of mankind. So, such an "outlet" is not worth mentioning at all.

At present, the most popular nuclear waste disposal method is landfill in the ocean or in the land. After cooling and dry storage, the nuclear waste will be put into metal tanks and dropped under at least 4,000 m of selected sea waters, or be buried in the nuclear waste repository in underground lithosphere. The U.S., Russia, Canada and Australia normally landfill nuclear waste in the land due to vast territory and wilderness. In order to ensure the absolute safety of nuclear waste disposal, countries must accept international supervision when placing it. As shown in Fig. 7.2.

Fig. 7.2 Nuclear waste disposal repository

7.1.2 Organic Waste Compounds

The types and sources of organic waste compounds (hereafter referred to as organic waste) are a lot. It's mainly because humans have developed too many organic chemical substances, especially organic ones. Let's take a look at three examples, which are chemical fiber, plastics and rubber.

7.1.2.1 Chemical Fiber

Chemical fibers are fibers with textile properties made from natural polymer compounds or synthetic polymer compounds as raw materials, through the preparation of spinning solution, spinning and post-treatment processes. Therefore, chemical fibers can be divided into two kinds: synthetic fibers and man-made fibers, according to the different raw materials.

After hundreds of years of industrial development, synthetic fibers are categorized, according to the structure, as carbon chain synthetic fibers, such as polypropylene fibers (polypropylene), polyacrylonitrile fibers (acrylic), polyvinyl alcohol formaldehyde fibers (vinylon), and miscellaneous chain synthetic fibers, such as polyamide fibers (nylon), polyethylene terephthalate (polyester), etc. By function, synthetic fibers are also classified as heat-resistant fibers, such as polybenzimidazole fiber, heat- and-corrosion-resistant fibers, such as polytetrafluoroethylene, high-strength fibers, such as poly-phenylene terephthalamide, radiation-resistant fibers, such as polyimide fibers. In addition, there are flame retardant fibers, polymeric optical fibers, etc.

If we take waste synthetic fiber raw materials, including pre-consumer materials from the production process and post-consumer recycled materials with necessary treatment, to melt or dissolve them into new fibers, the product is called recycled synthetic fibers. As shown in Fig. 7.3.

Fig. 7.3 Regenerated synthetic fiber

7.1 Chemical Waste

Most of the discarded pure chemical fiber products or trimmings can be cracked into polymer monomers, re-polymerized into fibers that meet the standards of textile raw materials, to further be processed into carpets, ropes and fishing nets and other products. But for the discarded mixed textiles, they are not easy to be re-decomposed and polymerized due to too much impurities. But they can be recycled and used to produce floor tiles and road fillers by mixing with resin.

Of the regenerated synthetic fibers, the production and utilization of regenerated polyester is particularly noteworthy. Regenerated polyester uses recycled polyethylene terephthalate (PET for short) as a raw material to regenerate discarded plastic and soft drink bottles into usable textile fibers, also called PCR (Post-Consumer Recycled) fibers, indicating that before reprocessing, they had been used and discarded by consumers. The process of regenerating polyester starts with color sorting, sterilization, and shredding of recycled and discarded plastic bottles into small, fine pieces, which are then melted and stretched into filaments, softened in hot water, drawn, crimped, dried, and finally cut into short fibers, basically the same as the production process of ordinary polyester.

PCR fibers can be spun pure or blended with various proportions of polyester to make plain woven fabrics and a variety of novel fabrics such as luggage cloths, purse cloths, outerwear, swimwear, skiwear, knitted polo-neck shirts, etc. The fabrics are so close to pure polyester fabrics in terms of feel, appearance and inner quality that they are difficult to distinguish. This recycling gives polyethylene terephthalate more than one industrial life, it reduces waste generation and creats new product value at the same time.

7.1.2.2 Plastics

Plastics are polymer compounds made from monomers, polymerized by addition or condensation reactions, and can freely change their composition and shape. They are composed of synthetic resins and additives such as fillers, plasticizers, stabilizers, lubricants, and colorants. According to the complexity of monomers and the presence or absence of additives, plastics can be generally divided into two categories: general plastics and engineering plastics. And according to the different behaviors when subjected to heat, plastics can be broadly divided into thermoplastics and thermosets.

The five major varieties of general plastics, produced in large quantities, with good moldability, wide application and relatively inexpensive prices, are polyethylene (PE), polypropylene (PP), polyvinyl chloride (PVC), polystyrene (PS), and acrylonitrile–butadiene–styrene copolymer (ABS). These five categories of plastics account for the majority of plastic raw materials used. The remaining plastics can basically be classified as engineering plastics, such as: PPS, PPO, PA, PC, POM, etc., mainly used in the engineering industry, defense-related technology and other high-tech fields, such as automotive, aerospace, construction, telecommunications, etc.

Due to the complexity of the monomer and the functionality of the additives, thermoset plastics are relatively difficult to recycle after disposal, some even difficult

Fig. 7.4 Regenerated plastic grains

to incinerate, with secondary pollution hard to control. Thermoplastics, on the other hand, can generally be recycled effectively after disposal, and various recycling technologies and process equipment have been well developed. As shown in Fig. 7.4.

Followed is the summary of the regenerating features of all the five general plastics. It is easy to see that even though they can be recycled, there is still a certain difference in the quality of the regenerated products, which means it's difficult to make the same primary products as virgin plastics after recycling, and they have to be downgraded, until little usage after certain times of regeneration. Of course, being able to regenerate is always good, to avoid direct waste generation and to reduce the dependence on petrochemicals.

① PE: Its performance gets reduced after regeneration, and the color becomes yellow. Several times of extrusion will reduce the viscosity of high-density polyethylene, and increase the viscosity of low-density polyethylene.

② PP: The color barely changes after the first time of regeneration, but the melt index rises. Regenerated for more than twice, its color will darken with still rising melt index. The breaking strength and elongation will decrease after regeneration, but it won't affect the usage.

③ PVC: There is apparent color change after regeneration. First time extrusion after regeneration will bring about light brown color, and opaque dark brown after three times of extrusion. Its viscosity barely changes after twice of generation, but tends to decrease for more than twice generation. Whether PVC is hard or soft, stabilizer should be added when regenerating; 1%~3% ABS is often added when regenerating in order to make the products shiny.

④ PS: After regeneration, the color turns yellow, and the decline of the performance of the regenerated material is proportional to the time of regeneration. Its breaking strength does not change significantly when the amount of admixture is less than 60%, and the ultimate viscosity does not change significantly when the admixture is below 40%.

⑤ ABS: There's apparent color change after regeneration, but no obvious performance change if less than 20%~30% of regenerated ABS is mixed.

7.1 Chemical Waste

Thanks to the features of general plastics, various waste plastics from production and life, such as agricultural film, packing tape, food bags, sandals, electric wire, wire board, pipe, barrel, basin, etc., can be crushed, granulated into plastic raw materials. Or necessary additives can be added into the regenerated plastics with special processing technology to make engineering plastics for functional parts and decorative building materials.

7.1.2.3 Rubber

Rubber (raw rubber) is a highly elastic polymeric material with reversible deformation, which can produce large deformations at room temperature with a small external force and recover after the force removed. There are two kinds of rubber: natural rubber and synthetic rubber. Natural rubber is made from the gum extracted from rubber trees and rubber grass, while synthetic rubber is made from various monomers by polymerization reaction.

The disposal of waste rubber has gradually become one of the serious problems facing mankind today as rubber products get widely used in all areas of industry or life. In order to meet the ever-improving performance requirements, rubber gets developed in high strength, wear resistance, stability and aging resistance. At the same time, the discarded rubber cannot be naturally degraded for a long time. Not only the discarded rubber wastes valuable resources, but also causes black pollution which is more difficult to deal with than plastic pollution. There are millions of tons of waste rubber produced worldwide every year, and in order to reduce the volume of the pile, the world's major industrial countries, in addition to burning waste rubber products as fuel, have also been studying more effective waste rubber recycling technology since the early 21st century.

Usually recycled rubber refers to plastic and viscous rubber can be vulcanized again, transforming from discarded vulcanized rubber in an elastic state through crushing, regeneration (desulfurization) and refining. The nature of the regeneration process is the partial destruction and degradation of the vulcanized rubber network under the combined physical and chemical action of heat, oxygen, machinery and regenerating agents, making the broken position both cross-linked bonds and macromolecules between the cross-linked bonds, which is the key principle and step of rubber regeneration. As shown in Fig. 7.5.

In addition to the traditional rubber recycling methods, various other methods of rubber recycling processes have emerged. For example, the new method of freezing and crushing waste rubber to make rubber powder of different particle sizes and then directly using it as rubber filler is still under research and development.

Due to the limitation of the regeneration process, the various physical and chemical properties of recycled rubber cannot be identical with raw rubber. If within the quality requirements, recycled rubber can partially replace raw rubber, to save raw rubber and carbon black, and to improve certain properties of rubber products in a targeted manner.

Fig. 7.5 Recycled rubber blocks

7.2 Construction Waste

7.2.1 Management of Construction Waste

Due to the large area, long construction period and large number of participants in mega construction projects, a large number of solid wastes, including various construction wastes and domestic wastes, will be generated in the process of construction and workers' daily life. The volume of domestic waste is relatively small, which generally needs to be treated and disposed according to the relevant municipal environmental protection requirements in location; while the construction waste (generally refers to the spoil, waste concrete, waste masonry and other wastes generated in the construction activities of people engaged in demolition, building, decoration and houses repairing) have usually large volume and complex types, therefore there are special requirements for stacking, transportation and disposal.

Basically, construction waste dumps that comply with regulation should be set on construction site:

① Administrative staff should be arranged at the location of construction waste dumps to monitor construction wastes and make sure that the wastes are all at the right place, and transportation vehicles are cleaned before leaving.
② At construction waste dumps, there should be walls that meet the specifications (as the height is higher than 2 m) and the way to get in and out should be built with hardening treatment.
③ Set spray or other measures for dust suppression, and maintain regular function of dust-proof facilities.

④ Set vehicle cleaning area and transportation vehicle washing facilities at the exit.
⑤ Divide stacking area from the road; clean scattered materials timely; keep road clean and do road washing in time.
⑥ If there is no work at the dumps within 2 days, sprinkler measure is needed; if there are no work dumps within 1 week, then cover measure is needed.

In addition, construction waste includes mud generated in the process of foundation which needs special permission issued by the local municipal administration for transportation and disposal. Although the management methods of different countries and cities are not the same, but usually the permit like "construction waste disposal license" is required.

7.2.2 Sources of Construction Waste

It is very important to find the sources of construction waste for the reasonable and efficient treatment or disposal of construction waste. Let's take a look at the three most common and largest types of construction waste: spoil, cement concrete and packaging wood, and how they are generated.

7.2.2.1 Spoil

Any mega construction project, as long as it involves excavation (most likely), there is a challenge of earthwork balance. Because buildings basically have underground structure as foundation—the volume of underground structure is the minimum volume of "spoil" to be excavated. Of course, for the convenience of underground construction, the excavation is usually larger and more, and some "spoil" is backfilled around the underground structure after the completion of underground structure. In the end, the residual "spoil" that cannot be backfilled (to excavated foundation pit) needs to be removed and disposed. As shown in Fig. 7.6.

7.2.2.2 Cement Concrete

Cement, as the main structural support material of construction project, is widely used. In addition to special purpose cement, Portland cement is the most common type, and also the main cementitious material in concrete. In the process of mega construction projects, a large number of temporary structures need to be used in the construction site, such as temporary roads, temporary leveling land, temporary warehouse, etc. At different stages of construction, the above structures need to be demolished or rebuilt to generate abandoned cement concrete blocks. As shown in Fig. 7.7.

Fig. 7.6 Spoil

Fig. 7.7 Cement concrete

7.2.2.3 Packaging Wood

Mega construction projects, especially those that ultimately need a large number of mechanical equipment, will generate a large number of packaging materials in their transportation and storage stages, especially wooden packaging, such as ordinary wooden cases, frame wooden cases, plywood boxes, fiberboard boxes, wooden pallets, etc. Because of the irrecoverability of the material, the wood will be directly disposed as waste by the contractor of the project after one use. As shown in Fig. 7.8.

Fig. 7.8 Packaging wood

7.2.3 Common Disposal Methods of Recyclable Materials

7.2.3.1 Spoil

In a strict sense, spoil cannot be regarded as waste, because soil itself is also a kind of resource (provided that spoil does not contain other construction waste, it is pure "soil"). In the project planning, earthwork balance calculation should be carried out first—earthwork balance is also a kind of mass balance. As discussed in the previous chapter, the better the mass balance is, the less waste will be generated, so is earthwork balance. That is to say, the earthwork volume to be excavated and the earthwork volume to be backfilled should be calculated, and the in and out should be balanced as far as possible. The volume of "spoil" that will be generated in the end of the project, which means the amount of spoil to be transported and disposed of, should be well known.

For mega construction projects, several or even more than a dozen general contractors may be involved, so at the beginning of the project, the construction management department of the owner company should confirm the earthwork balance of the construction area with each general contractor; with the different nodes of each bid section of the project, some general contractors still need to transport earthwork, while some general contractors have started to carry out earthwork return. At this time, the construction management department of the owner company should coordinate and manage the earthwork operation of each general contractor according to the actual situation of the project progress. If necessary, the excavation of contractor A can give priority to the backfill of contractor B. Good earthwork balance management has following advantages:

① Reduce the cost of purchasing soil, including the cost of testing the purchased soil and the cost of the soil itself.

② Reduce the cost of outward transportation of soil, including the cost of handling residue permit and receiving place.
③ Reduce the cost of excavation and load/unload the soil.
④ Reduce the energy consumption of engineering vehicles and excavation equipment.
⑤ Reduce dust emission and road cleaning pressure.
⑥ Optimize the layout of the construction site and reduce the impact of soil piling on the construction operation.

For the finished earthwork, the soil should be sealed, sprayed and covered with covering net as soon as possible to control the degree and scope of soil exposure. If the soil is piled up for a long time, the growing season can be properly considered and plants can be planted. This can not only effectively control dust, but also prevent local soil erosion. As shown in Fig. 7.9.

Fig. 7.9 Bare soil cover and grass planting

7.2.3.2 Cement Concrete

(1) Recycled aggregate concrete

Recycled concrete is prepared by using recycled aggregate as part or all of the aggregate instead of natural aggregate. Most of the processing methods of recycled aggregate are the integration of various crushing equipment, transmission machinery, screening equipment and impurity removal equipment. Through crushing, screening, impurity removal and other processes, recycled aggregate meeting the quality requirements can be obtained. Compared with natural aggregate, recycled concrete produced by general production process contains about 30% hardened cement slurry.

(2) Recycled cementitious materials

Recycled aggregate is produced from waste concrete by separating aggregate, and the remaining hardened cement slurry can be used as foundation modification material, so as to realize 100% utilization of waste concrete. At present, there are few practical applications of using waste concrete hardened cement slurry to produce recycled cement. It is said that about 30 tons of recycled cement can be obtained for every 100 tons of waste concrete. The production cost of this kind of recycled cement is only half of that of ordinary cement, and it does not produce carbon dioxide in the production process, which is more conducive to environmental protection.

7.2.3.3 Packaging Wood

(1) Used as coating material

Wood waste is rich in lignin, which can be used to prepare coating materials for controlled-release fertilizers.

(2) Used to extract bio oil

Generally speaking, 1,500 L bio oil fuel can be produced from 2,000 kg wood. Bio oil has high thermal efficiency and is convenient for storage, transportation and modification. However, the technology has high requirements for equipment, and has not been widely used in the industry.

(3) Used for gasification

Wood waste can also be used for gasification. The gasification process is a special way of combustion. Through incomplete combustion (including three stages of combustion, pyrolysis and reduction), the energy in the fuel is transferred to the generated combustible gas. These gases include carbon monoxide, hydrogen, methane, and so on.

(4) Used to press wood briquettes

The direct combustion of wood waste will produce a lot of waste gas, and the combustion efficiency is not high, so it is not the best method for rational utilization. In order to overcome this shortcoming, wood waste can be processed physically to produce wood briquette, that is, densification. It can be stored in dry environment for a long time, and will not be spontaneously combusted, rot, and mildew. It is an excellent large and medium-sized boiler fuel.

7.2.4 Regulations and Examples of Construction Waste Recycling in Various Countries

According to relevant statistics, developed countries have invested a lot in the construction waste recycling since the 1970s, and a series of achievements have been widely promoted, so the utilization rate of construction waste is relatively high. As shown in Fig. 7.10.

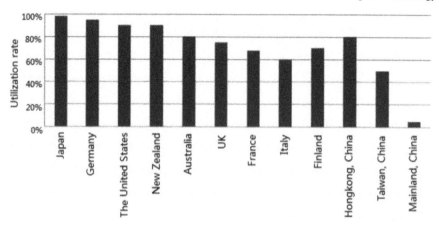

Fig. 7.10 Utilization rate of construction waste resources in some countries and regions

7.2.4.1 Japan

Japan has set up recycling plants to deal with waste concrete. Japan's recycled aggregate is divided into three grades, namely grade H, grade M and grade L. Grade H is made by heating and grinding method to completely remove the old mortar, so the recycled aggregate can be used at the same time with natural aggregate without any restrictions; grade M is mostly made by crushing method, containing old mortar, which is allowed to be used in the secondary position such as foundation cushion and construction road; grade L has more impurities, which is allowed to be used in the backfill level.

In the same time, Japan has a strong support for waste wood recycling by laws and regulations. At present, the forest coverage rate of Japan has reached 68%, but the recycling rate of waste wood is as high as 82%. Among them, the recycling rate of construction waste wood in 2004 was as high as 89%. In Japan, the laws and regulations on the recycling of waste wood include the Basic Environmental Law, Fundamental Plan for Establishing a Sound Material-Cycle Society, Waste Management and Public Cleansing Law, Law for the Promotion of Effective Utilization of Resources, the Containers and Packing Recycling Law, the Law on the Recycling of Construction, and the Green Purchasing Law, etc., which stipulate that the enterprises producing waste shall be responsible for recycling, and all construction waste must be recycled by the contractor.

7.2.4.2 Germany

There are large-scale construction waste reprocessing plants in every region of Germany, and there are more than 20 in Berlin alone. At present, recycled concrete is mainly used for highway pavement. In August 1998, the German Committee for

Reinforced Concrete put forward the Application Guidance of Recycled Aggregate in Concrete, which requires that the concrete prepared with recycled aggregate must fully meet the national standard of ordinary concrete. Germany already has examples of successful application of recycled materials to structures, such as ViblerWeg and Waldspirale buildings in Darmstadt, Germany.

At present, recycled waste wood is divided into five categories in Germany, according to the grade of wood and the type of impurities. A1 and A2 grade recycled waste wood can be used to produce wood-based panels. By using secondary waste wood processing technology, materials meeting different applications can be produced economically and effectively. The cost of purchasing these materials is low. Particleboard, medium density fiberboard and oriented particleboard manufacturers save energy when drying these materials with low moisture content. After treatment, the contaminated A3-A5 grade wood is a good material for energy generation.

7.2.4.3 The United States

Local governments in the United States play an important role in the recycling of construction waste. The government provides technical support for enterprises, promotes education programs and instruction manuals, and holds seminars. The government also guarantees the recycling of construction waste by allowing enterprises to pay a deposit. Setting up a special fund for construction waste recycling research provides economic support for enterprises. Superfund formulated by the U.S. government provides legal protection for the development of recycled concrete, which stipulates that "any enterprise producing industrial waste must dispose of it by itself and shall not dump it without authorization". In the mid-1980s, Kansas State Department of Transportation used recycled concrete as aggregate for new cement pavement. Through years of observation, it shows that it is technically feasible to use waste concrete for pavement surface.

There are many ways to recycle waste wood in the United States. In addition to building materials, some waste wood is also converted into liquid fuel by extraction. In the late 1960s, Appell and others in the U.S. put wood chips, sawdust, cellulose and municipal solid waste into sodium carbonate solution, and back pressed to 2.8×10^4 kPa with CO to make the raw materials react at 350 °C to obtain 40%~50% liquid products. This is the very famous "PERC" method.

7.2.4.4 China

(1) Waste concrete used as road cushion

The main functions of road cushion are water proof, drainage, anti-freezing and improving the working conditions of earth foundation. Because the cushion material requirements are not high, so the waste concrete can be used for road cushion. The concrete itself has good water resistance, so it can meet the requirements of water stability; the broken fragments of concrete have high porosity, so it can meet the requirements of thermal insulation of cushion.

(2) Waste concrete used in earth rock dam

Soil impervious core is the most widely used impervious structure in earth rock dam, and the amount of soil material used as impervious core is very wide. For waste concrete, most of these properties can be better than ordinary clay, so it partially replaces the traditional materials used in earth rock dam. However, the economic cost should be considered. The materials used for earth rock dams are usually local materials, and the use of non-local waste concrete may require higher transportation costs.

(3) Waste concrete made into concrete road for reuse

For mega construction projects, due to the complex construction process, the construction site often excavates and breaks the road, some contractors choose pre-made recycled concrete pavement blocks. The use of these concrete blocks not only reduces the use of concrete and steel, but also reduces the generation of construction waste when the temporary road is demolished. According to the theoretical calculation, the carbon emission of 1 m^3 of concrete is 240 kg. Therefore, the recycled concrete pavement block has great promotion value. As shown in Fig. 7.11.

Fig. 7.11 Precast concrete pavement block

(4) Wood based panels made from waste wood

The rapid development of wood-based panel in China has broken through the bottleneck problem of raw material restriction—the recycling of used wood has solved the raw material source of wood-based panel production. In the use of waste wood processing MDF (Medium Density Fiberboard), particleboard, some large enterprises have made significant progress, both equipment and technology are becoming increasingly mature.

(5) Production of wood plastic composites from waste wood

The recycled wood can be processed together with plastics to produce wood plastic composites. Beijing University of Chemical Technology has developed a new generation of wood plastic composite production technology. It uses waste wood and waste plastics, adding a special adhesive, to make structural profiles after high temperature and high-pressure treatment, and then directly extrudes them into products or reassembles them into products, such as pallets or packaging boxes. This new wood plastic composite material has good mechanical properties, and 98% of the raw materials are waste wood. It is cheap and easy to maintain. It can be sawed, planed and nailed, and it's 100% recyclable.

7.3 Electronic Waste

Electronic waste is also known as e-waste, normally referring to all waste electrical and electronic equipment (WEEE).

Electronic waste has many kinds and varieties. But in general, they can be divided into two categories: one is large used electrical products containing relatively simple materials and less harmful to the environment, such as refrigerators, washing machines, air conditioners and other household appliances, as well as medical and scientific research appliances, etc. The dismantling and treatment of these products are usually not very complicated. The other is the used precision electronic products containing relatively complex materials and more harmful to the environment, such as computers, monitors, cell phones, tablets, etc. These products contain complex chemical elements and a variety of tiny components with high integration, leaving it difficult to be dismantled and treated.

7.3.1 The Hazardous Substances in E-Waste

It is not easy to fully lay out all the hazardous substances in e-waste. In the early days of electrical and electronic industry development, the hazards were not exactly known to man due to limited technology. It is only after several occurrences of environmental pollution and human health incidents that people started to put forward the concept of restricted substances for the production of electrical and electronic industry. The most influential one is the RoHS standard of the European Union, that is, the Restriction of the Use of Certain Hazardous Substances in Electrical and Electronic Equipment. Despite the fact that this standard has been widely adopted and implemented in all major industrial countries around the world, there are still a considerable amount of hazardous substances in existing e-waste, due to their functionality and the production in the past. The most commonly seen ones are:

(1) Lead

Lead can damage human central nervous system, blood system, kidney and reproductive system, and it can negatively affect the brain development of children. The main parts of computers containing lead are: the glass screen of computer monitors (1.4–3.5 kg per monitor), the solder of circuit boards or other components.

(2) Cadmium

Cadmium compounds can accumulate in the human body, especially in the kidneys. Cadmium is contained in SMD resistors, infrared generators, semiconductors, etc. Cadmium is also a curing agent for plastics and is contained in old cathode ray tubes.

(3) Mercury

Mercury can cause damage to many organs, including the brain, kidneys, and ovaries. Mercury is commonly used in thermometers, sensors, hysteresis devices, converters (e.g., in circuit boards and measuring devices), medical devices, lamps, cell phones, and batteries; it is also used in flat-panel display screens, gradually replacing the original cathode ray tube displays.

(4) Barium

Even short-term exposure to barium can cause brain swelling, muscle weakness, and damage to the heart, liver, and spleen. Barium is commonly used on computer monitor cathode ray tube screens.

(5) Beryllium

Beryllium is considered to be a carcinogen for lung cancer. The ash and fog produced by beryllium wear can easily lead to "beryllium chronic disease". Workers who are exposed to beryllium for a long time, even in very small doses, can easily get skin diseases. Beryllium is widely used in computer motherboards and keyboard backings (an alloy of beryllium and copper is used to strengthen the elasticity of the connector while maintaining electrical conductivity).

(6) Hexavalent chromium

Hexavalent chromium can easily cross cell membranes and be absorbed, destroying and damaging DNA in cells, making it an extremely toxic substance in the environment. Hexavalent chromium is used for rust protection of steel sheets and for hardening and beautifying treatments.

(7) Inks

The main component of black inks is carbon black, which can strongly irritate the respiratory system when inhaled. The International Agency for Research on Cancer (IARC) has classified carbon black as a Group 2B carcinogen, which is probably carcinogenic to humans. Some reports indicate that colored inks (blue, yellow and red) may also contain carcinogenic heavy metals. External computer devices such as printers contain black or colored inks.

(8) Plastics containing PVC

PVC, like many other chlorinated compounds, can produce dioxins when discarded and burned incompletely. The average old computer has almost 6 kg of plastic parts each, and nearly a quarter of that is PVC, which is used to wrap wiring and computer cases because of its excellent fire resistance.

7.3.2 Treatment Technology of E-Waste

As long as the materials, whether metal or plastic, can be disassembled (see Chap. 9, Sect. 2 on disassembly) and tested to be free of hazardous substances, they can be recycled in the same way as ordinary waste. What really represents the technology of e-waste treatment is the recycling and utilization of two special parts: circuit boards and batteries.

7.3.2.1 Circuit Board

The waste circuit board contains nearly 20 kinds of non-ferrous metals and rare metals, besides heavy metals such as lead, mercury, hexavalent chromium, as well as polybrominated biphenyls (PBB), polybrominated diphenyl ethers (PBDE) and other toxic chemicals as components of flame retardants. The economic value of recycling waste circuit board is considerable, making it a treasure to be mined. In order to develop this potential renewable resource, the world has developed a series of relatively mature circuit board treatment technologies, such as physical, chemical and biological methods. As shown in Fig. 7.12.

(1) Physical methods

Physical methods are mechanical means, to retrieve various substances using their different physical properties. There are generally two steps—crushing and sorting.

1) Crushing

Crushing is to dissociate the metal in the circuit board from the organic matter as much as possible to improve the sorting efficiency. It is found that when the crushed particles are at 0.6 mm, the metal can be 100% dissociated in general, but the actual choice of crushing method and extent depends on the subsequent process.

Fig. 7.12 Waste circuit board

2) Sorting

Sorting uses different density, particle size, electrical conductivity, magnetic conductivity and surface properties and other physical properties of material to separate them. At present, the more widely used are wind shaker technology, flotation separation technology, cyclone separation technology, and vortex sorting technology, etc.

(2) Chemical method

Chemical method is the process of extract those substances using their chemical stability difference.

1) Thermal treatment

Thermal treatment is mainly used to separate organic matter and metal by means of high temperature. It includes incineration, vacuum pyrolysis and microwave, etc.

① Incineration: incineration is to put waste circuit boards and other e-waste which are crushed to a certain particle size into a primary incinerator to decompose the organic components, separating the gas from the solids. The residue after incineration is the bare metal or its oxide and glass fiber, which can be recovered by physical and chemical methods respectively after crushing. The gases containing organic components are then discharged into a secondary incinerator for combustion treatment. Since this method generates a large amount of off-gas and toxic substances, its process control is extremely demanding.

② Vacuum pyrolysis: pyrolysis is also called dry distillation in industry, which is the process of placing electronic waste such as circuit boards in a container under the condition of air isolation and heating, controlling the temperature and pressure so that the organic substances in it are decomposed and converted into oil and gas, which can be recovered after condensation and collection. Unlike traditional incineration, the vacuum pyrolysis process is carried out under oxygen-free conditions, so the production of dioxins and furans can be suppressed, and the amount of waste gas produced is relatively small, same for the pollution to the surrounding environment.

③ Microwave: microwave recycling method is to first crush circuit boards and other electronic waste, and then to heat them with microwaves, so that the organic matter is decomposed by heat. Heating to about 1,400°C makes the glass fibers and metals melt to form a vitrified substance. When this vitrified substance is cooled, gold, silver and other metals can be separated in the form of small beads, and the recycling of the remaining glass material can be recycled as construction materials. This method is significantly different from the traditional heating method and has obvious advantages of high efficiency, high speed and low energy consumption.

2) Hydrometallurgy

Hydrometallurgy technology is to remove metals from electronic waste such as circuit boards by dissolving them in acids like nitric acid, sulfuric acid and aqua regia, and to recover them from the liquid phase. It is a more widely used method to deal with electronic waste such as circuit boards. Compared with pyrometallurgy, hydrometallurgy has the advantages of less off-gas emission, easy treatment of residues after metal extraction, significant economic benefits, and simple processes. Of course, due to the use of strong acids, chemicals safety becomes very important.

(3) Biological method

Biological method uses microbial adsorption and microbial oxidation to solve the metal recovery problem. Microbial adsorption can be divided into two types: using the metabolites of microorganisms to fix metal ions and using microorganisms to fix metal ions directly. The former is the use of hydrogen sulfide produced by bacteria to fix metal ions. When the surface of the bacteria adsorbed ions reached saturation, it can form flocs and settle down. The latter is the use of ferric ion oxidability to oxidize other metals in the alloy so that they are dissolved in the solution while precious metals can be exposed to recovery. Biotechnology extraction of gold and other precious metals is relatively simple, with low cost and convenient operation, but the leaching time is long, and the yield is low, making it not widely applied so far.

7.3.2.2 Battery

Battery refers to a device that holds an electrolyte solution and a metal electrode to produce an electric current in a cup, tank or other container or part of the space of a composite container that converts chemical energy into electrical energy. There are many types of batteries, and the main ones related to electronic waste are dry batteries (such as manganese zinc batteries, nickel cadmium batteries) and lithium batteries (including lithium metal, lithium alloy, lithium ion, and lithium polymer batteries). As shown in Figs. 7.13 and 7.14.

(1) Dry battery

Dry batteries are mainly zinc-manganese batteries and alkaline zinc-manganese batteries. So, the recycling can obtain mercury, zinc, cadmium and other metals, and completely solve the pollution caused by the battery. There are three main recycling technologies: manual sorting, fire recovery, and wet recovery.

Manual sorting is to separate carbon batteries from alkaline ones, then cut them out and manually separate zinc skin, manganese dioxide (further demercurization needed), charcoal stick and plastic cover, etc. This is a way to fully recycle the batteries.

Pyroprocessing is to sort and crush the dry cells and send them to the high temperature furnace. The zinc and zinc chloride are oxidized into zinc oxide and discharged with smoke, and the powder is recovered by cyclone dust collector and then further synthesized into zinc oxide products. The manganese dioxide and hydromanganese stone left with the residue, and depending on the economic value, it can be determined whether to recover manganese powder again.

Fig. 7.13 Waste dry batteries

7.3 Electronic Waste

Fig. 7.14 Waste lithium battery

Wet recovery mainly uses chemical reactions: dry batteries are divided into carbon and alkaline batteries and then crushed. The crushed materials will be placed in a leaching tank, and 100~120 g/L dilute sulfuric acid is added to obtain zinc sulfate solution, and then zinc metal is obtained by electrolysis. After separating copper grease and carbon rods, the remaining manganese dioxide residue and hydromanganese stone are calcined to produce manganese dioxide.

Nickel-cadmium battery is actually an alkaline battery with positive plate of nickel hydroxide, negative plate of cadmium, and electrolyte of potassium hydroxide or sodium hydroxide solution. In order to recover the cadmium, nickel, iron materials and plastics from Ni-Cd batteries, the following treatment procedures are generally used:

① Mechanical disassembly and discharge of electrolyte: separate the holder and shell of the large cell, neutralize the discharged potassium hydroxide acid into potassium salt and discard it.
② Crushing, sieving and physical separation: sieving and magnetic separation according to the particle size and magnetization rate of different materials. Obtain fine-grained electrode materials and coarse-grained stainless steel, iron scrap and plastic.
③ Chemical metallurgy treatment: chemical metallurgy treatment of active electrode materials to obtain metallic cadmium, nickel or their compounds.

(2) Lithium battery

Although lithium batteries can be repeatedly charged and discharged to provide electrical energy for devices, however, they still have a limited service life and inevitably end up as waste that needs to be disposed of. Used lithium batteries contain a large number of precious and rare metals, of which cobalt accounts for 5%~20%, nickel 5%~12%, manganese for 7%~10%, and lithium for 2%~5%—which can be completely recycled and reused.

There are three main methods of recycling lithium batteries: physicochemical, chemical and biological methods. Compared with other methods, hydrometallurgy is considered to be a more ideal recovery method due to its low energy consumption, high recovery efficiency and high product purity.

1) Physicochemical method

This method uses the physicochemical reaction to treat lithium-ion batteries. The common physicochemical treatment methods are crushing flotation and mechanical grinding.

① Crushing flotation method uses the difference of physicochemical properties of material surface, that is, after first crushing and sorting the complete waste lithium battery, the obtained electrode material powder is heat-treated to remove the organic binder, and finally flotation separation is carried out according to the difference of hydrophilicity of lithium cobaltite and graphite surface in the electrode material powder, so as to recover the cobalt-lithium compound powder. The crushing and flotation method is a simple process, which enables effective separation of lithium cobaltite and carbon materials, and the recovery rate of lithium and cobalt is high. However, as all the various materials are crushed and mixed, it causes difficulties to the subsequent separation and recovery of copper foil, aluminum foil and metal shell fragments. And because the crushing tends to make the electrolyte $LiPF_6$ react with H_2O to produce HF and other volatile gases, it may cause environmental pollution. Thus, special attention needs to be paid to the crushing method.

② The mechanical grinding is to use the thermal energy generated by mechanical grinding to induce a reaction between the electrode material and the abrasive, thus converting the lithium compounds originally adhered to the collector fluid in the electrode material into salts. The recovery rate varies with different types of grinding aid materials, with higher recovery rates of 98% for Co and 99% for Li being achieved. Mechanical grinding is also effective to recover cobalt and lithium from lithium batteries. The process is relatively simple, but requires high instrumentation and prone to cobalt loss and difficulty in recovering aluminum foil.

2) Chemical method

Chemical method is the use of chemical reaction for lithium-ion batteries, with two kinds in general—pyrometallurgy and hydrometallurgy.

① Pyrometallurgy, also known as incineration or dry metallurgy, is to remove the organic binder in the electrode material by high temperature incineration, and at the same time to make the metal and its compounds undergo redox reaction to recover the low boiling point metal and its compounds in the form of condensation. The metal in the slag is recovered by sieving, pyrolysis, magnetic separation or chemical methods, etc. Pyrometallurgy is not strict on the components of raw materials and suitable for large-scale processing of more complex batteries. But combustion will certainly produce off-gas which pollutes the environment, and high temperature also requires more processing equipment, at the same time purifying and recovering equipment is needed, which all add up to the cost.

② Hydrometallurgy is to selectively dissolve the cathode material in used lithium-ion batteries with suitable chemical reagents and to separate the metal elements in the leachate. Hydrometallurgy is more suitable to recover lithium batteries with relatively single chemical composition, which can be used alone or in combination with pyrometallurgy, with low equipment requirements and low processing costs, and is a very mature processing method, suitable for small and medium-sized waste lithium batteries.

3) Biological method

Biometallurgy, which is still under research, uses the metabolic process of microbial bacteria to selectively leaching of metallic elements such as cobalt and lithium. The biological method has low energy consumption with low cost, and the microorganisms can be reused with minimal secondary pollution. However, the cultivation of microbial bacteria requires very strict conditions, long cultivation time, low leaching efficiency, thus the technology still has room for improvement.

7.4 Medical Waste

7.4.1 Types and Hazards of Medical Waste

Medical waste is the waste with direct or indirect infectious, toxic and other harmful effects generated by medical institutions in the course of medical, preventive, health care and other related activities, including following types.

(1) Infectious waste

Infectious waste refers to medical waste carrying pathogenic microorganisms with the risk of spreading infectious diseases, including items contaminated by patients' blood, body fluids and excreta, and waste generated by patients with infectious diseases.

(2) Pathological waste

Pathological waste refers to human waste and medical test animal cadavers generated in the course of medical treatment, including discarded human tissue generated during surgery, discarded human tissue after pathological biopsy, pathological wax blocks, etc.

(3) Damaging waste

Damaging waste is discarded medical sharps capable of piercing or cutting the human body, including medical needles, scalpels, glass test tubes, etc. As shown in Fig. 7.14.

(4) Pharmaceutical waste

Pharmaceutical waste refers to expired, obsolete, spoiled or contaminated waste drugs, including generic drugs, cytotoxic drugs and genotoxic drugs.

(5) Chemical waste

Chemical waste refers to waste chemical items that are toxic, corrosive, flammable and explosive, such as waste chemical reagents, chemical disinfectants, mercury sphygmomanometers, mercury thermometers, etc.

These wastes contain a large number of bacterial viruses, and have characteristics of spatial pollution, acute virus transmission and latent infection. If they are not well managed, discarded at will, and allowed to mix with domestic waste and spread to people's living environment, they will pollute the atmosphere, water sources, land, animals and plants, causing the spread of diseases and seriously endangering people's physical and mental health.

Fig. 7.15 Medical waste

7.4.2 Methods of Treatment and Disposal of Medical Waste

Depending on the treatment principle, medical waste treatment and disposal generally includes sterilization and disinfection, high-temperature incineration, plasma, pyrolysis, etc.

(1) Sterilization and disinfection

There are many sterilization and disinfection treatment ways for different medical wastes, which are mainly through high temperature, high pressure, chemical reagents, certain frequency or wavelength of microwave technology, etc., to destroy the living environment of microorganisms and viruses, and to reduce the degree of health and environmental hazards of medical waste. But there are many limitations to the sterilization and disinfection effect, and the type of various medical wastes is very different. So sometimes the best sterilization and disinfection effect may not be achieved. Since sterilization and disinfection do not change the volume and weight of the waste, it is generally used as a pretreatment and, in some cases, prior to final landfill.

(2) High-temperature incineration

According to the study, 92% of the total weight of medical waste is combustible components, and the non-combustible components are only 8%, which can be completely burned into ashes given sufficient temperature and oxygen. Incineration treatment is a deep oxidation chemical process. The medical waste in the incineration equipment, under the action of high-temperature flame, will go through drying, ignition, incineration and transform into residue and gas. Pathogenic microorganisms and harmful substances in the incineration process is also effectively destroyed thanks to the high temperature. The volume and the weight are also reduced effectively along the way. The incineration method is applicable to all kinds of infectious medical waste and is the mainstream technology in the field of medical waste treatment.

(3) Plasma treatment

The plasma treatment is an innovative technology for treating medical waste. It sterilizes and disinfects medical waste by killing all microorganisms in medical waste with the high temperature generated by the plasma arc furnace, destroying toxic drugs and toxic chemicals left in the cells, and melting metal sharps and inorganic chemicals so that they are completely destroyed.

(4) Pyrolysis treatment

The pyrolysis treatment is the process of using the thermal instability of organic matter to heat the organic components of medical waste at high temperature under anaerobic or anoxic conditions, using heat energy to break the chemical bonds of compounds, so that the large molecular weight of organic matter is transformed into combustible gas, liquid fuel and coke. Compared with incineration, this treatment technology requires lower temperature, no open flame combustion process, with heavy metals mostly kept in the residue. It can recover a large amount of heat energy, solve various problems of medical waste incineration treatment.

(5) Electric arc furnace treatment

Electric arc furnace is a batch reaction furnace heated by electric arc, its combustion temperature is about 1,650~3,300 °C, residence time is about 8~10 min. The electrode bar in the furnace uses alternating current to produce a strong magnetic stirring effect so that the waste and molten steel can be fully mixed. The combustible waste can be cracked and oxidized to CO_2 and H_2O, and infectious bacteria can be completely destroyed in a very short period of time. The non-flammable syringes, glass bottles and other non-metallic wastes will form residues floating on the surface of the molten steel, while the needles, instruments and other metal wastes will be melted together into the steel.

(6) Irradiation treatment

Irradiation treatment uses electron beams to kill microorganisms and bacteria. Electrons excited by a source of ionizing radiation (e.g. Co-60) interact with electrons in the molecular structure of the treated object, and the accumulated energy can break the chemical bonds of organic compounds, thus destroying the microorganisms by cleavage. However, irradiation techniques cannot be used to treat radioactive materials and require increased protection of the operator.

(7) Liquid alloy treatment

Liquid alloy treatment involves heating special low-melting-point alloys such as Sn, Bi, etc. to about 400 °C to become liquid, and then putting medical waste into the liquid alloy. It allows water evaporation while killing bacteria and viruses. The volatile gases are heated to 800 °C, where volatile organic compounds are completely burned and discharged.

(8) Sanitary landfill

With necessary pre-treatments being carried out, the residual waste can be hygienically landfilled if it can meet corresponding legal and technical requirements. The waste is landfilled by layer in a court with bottom impermeably treated and then compacted and covered with soil on the top, so that the waste (organic material) is anaerobically fermented under controlled conditions, to achieve harmless treatment.

7.5 Kitchen Waste

7.5.1 Sources and Types of Kitchen Waste

Kitchen waste mainly refers to waste generated during food pre-processing, food preparation and food service in catering industry, which contains much oil, starch and animal or plant fibers. It has different classifications according to its forms.

7.5 Kitchen Waste

(1) Kitchen waste water

The main components are leftover food and water. Their composition is organic matter such as starch, food fiber, and animal fat, with the characteristics of high nutrient content, high water content, high oil and salt content, perishable, fermentable, and odorous. As shown in Fig. 7.16.

Fig. 7.16 Kitchen waste water

(2) Kitchen off-gas

The main components are the fumes and high temperature vapors produced during cooking, which include settleable particulate matters, fine particulate matters and hydrocarbon substances. Their composition is oxidized organic matters, with some acetaldehyde, formaldehyde and acetone which cause high temperatures and odors. As shown in Fig. 7.17.

(3) Kitchen solid waste (commonly known as food waste)

The main components are food waste and food residues, rich in organic matters and nutrients, high water content, perishable, and prone to odor and sewage. Their composition is proteins, fats, and carbohydrates, causing effects such as spoilage and acidification that produce harmful substances and indirectly affect ground water and the atmosphere. As shown in Fig. 7.18.

Although food waste does not cause sudden pollution to the environment, it will have a lasting and widespread negative impact on the environment if not properly

Fig. 7.17 Kitchen off-gas

Fig. 7.18 Kitchen solid waste

treated due to its nutrient enrichment. It can also cause the growth and spread of pathogens and indirectly cause harm to the people. Treatment and disposal methods vary according to the characteristics of different forms of food and beverage waste, especially kitchen waste water and kitchen off-gas.

7.5.2 Oil and Water Separation

(1) Physical method

① Oil–water separator: a special oil–water separation device is used to carry out oil–water separation of oily waste water. The waste water enters the separator from the water inlet and the solid residue is removed by the screen. The oil in the water goes from the bottom to the top after emulsion breaking and adsorption, and some of the oil floats to the water surface and is then collected by the oil filter tank, while the clear water is discharged from the bottom outlet.

② Coarse granulation: coarse granulation filter media is lipophilic and hydrophobic at the same time. When the oily waste water passes through, tiny oil beads will be attached to its surface to form an oil film, and after reaching a certain thickness, under the action of buoyancy and water flow shear, it will be separated from the surface of the filter media and form large particles of oil beads to float to the water surface.

(2) Chemical method

The use of detergent causes the oil in the waste water to be emulsified, making it difficult for the general oil and water treatment equipment to effectively separate oil from water. The chemical method is to use emulsion-breaking agents to break the emulsified oil, so that the oil and water can be rapidly stratified.

(3) Electroflocculation

The reaction principle of electroflocculation is to use aluminum, iron and other metals as the anode, and under the action of direct current, the anode is dissolved, producing Al^{3+} and Fe^{3+} ions, and then through a series of hydrolysis, polymerization and oxidation process, developing into various hydroxyl complexes, polynuclear hydroxyl complexes and hydroxides, so that the oil and water in the waste water are separated. At the same time, the charged pollutant particles swim in the electric field will be partially neutralized so as to destabilize, coagulate and precipitate.

7.5.3 Waste Water Treatment

(1) Coagulation method

Kitchen waste water, using coagulants, will go through coagulation, sedimentation, sand filtration and activated carbon adsorption to meet the discharge standard. It can be further disinfected to be used as domestic miscellaneous water.

(2) Biological method

The pollutants of restaurant waste water, mainly containing COD and BOD of oil, are biodegraded using activated sludge treatment, biological contact oxidation and membrane bioreaction.

7.5.4 Off-Gas Treatment

(1) Condensation method

It is commonly used to purify and absorb organic off-gas by making use of the physical property that substances have saturation vapor pressure at different temperatures. By lowering the system temperature or increasing the system pressure, the pollutants in the vapor state could condense and separate from the off-gas. When the oil smoke at a higher temperature passes through a certain closed channel, the oil smoke in the channel will collide with each other while rising up; the temperature gradually decreases till a certain point that the oil smoke began to condense into oil droplets; oil droplets becomes bigger, pulling downward by gravity and eventually drop into the collection pool down below. The upper layer of floating oil can be skimmed out after a while.

(2) Cyclone separation method

It is to use the centrifugal force generated by the rotating airflow to separate the particles in the oil smoke. The main advantage of the cyclone separator is the simplicity of the equipment, but the disadvantage is the low removal rate for small particles. Due to the high viscosity of soot particles, cleaning and maintenance work is tedious. It often works as primary stage equipment in multi-stage treatment. Most of the domestic off-gas hoods are this type.

(3) Activated carbon adsorption method

With this method, the oil smoke is adsorbed in the purifier through a large area of activated carbon in order to remove harmful gases from it. The advantage of this method is that it has a small footprint and high purification efficiency, and can effectively remove oily smoke, odors, and various harmful substances that cause cancer and deformation. However, the activated carbon is easily saturated and it is difficult to regenerate the activated carbon, resulting in high operating costs. So, it is normally used as the last stage in multi-stage oil smoke purification.

7.5 Kitchen Waste

(4) Static electricity removal method

It is to use the corona discharge generated by the DC high voltage electric field, to purify the oil smoke flowing through the purifier and then gets it discharged. Through the smoke pipe, the oil smoke is ionized by the DC high voltage electric field inside the purifier, decomposed to form tiny charged particles. Due to the air extraction, these small charged particles are adsorbed when they pass through the flat plate dust collector inside the purifier, and the adsorbed oil, smoke, water and dust particles are finally deposited into the oil storage chamber at the bottom of the purifier. At the same time, the ozone generated by the corona discharge of DC high voltage in the purifier also has the effect of odor removal and sterilization on the oil and smoke flowing through the purifier.

(5) Liquid washing method

The soot is guided through the exhaust pipe and passes through a layer of filler first. The washing liquid is showered down evenly from the top of the device through the water distribution plate, forming a large liquid film in the pores of the filler. The residual soot not retained through the filler layer will be mixed and absorbed with the washing liquid from above, while continuously replenishing the liquid film at the filler layer. The washing liquid finally returns to the reservoir and is recycled by the pump for repeated use. When the device is not in use, the purifying liquid containing oil and smoke is separated from oil and water in the water tank. The oil on the liquid surface is discharged, the oil and smoke is purified.

7.5.5 *Solid Waste Treatment and Resource Recovery*

(1) Anaerobic fermentation

Using the metabolism of different microbial anaerobic bacteria, the organic matter in kitchen waste is fermented in a closed space (container) under certain temperature conditions through a mature and stable anaerobic fermentation technology to produce biogas. The digestate produced after fermentation can be used to produce organic fertilizer and the digestate can be used to produce liquid fertilizer.

(2) Aerobic composting

The biochemical process of organic matter degradation relies on the action of specialized and parthenogenic aerobic bacteria to degrade organic matters. The organic matters to be composted and filler material are mixed by a certain proportion, with the right moisture, aeration conditions, microorganisms will multiply and degrade the organic matter, thus generating high temperature and killing the pathogenic bacteria and weed seeds, for the organic matter to achieve stability. In the process of aerobic composting, the soluble small molecule organic substances in organic waste are absorbed and utilized by microorganisms through their cell walls and cell membranes. The insoluble macromolecules are first attached outside the microorganism, and then decomposed into soluble small molecules by the extracellular enzymes secreted by the microorganism, and then input into the microorganism's cells for use. Through the life activity of microorganisms (synthesis and decomposition processes), part of the absorbed organic matter is oxidized into simple inorganic substances and provides the energy needed for the activity, while another part of the organic matter is converted into new cellular substances for the microorganisms' own reproduction.

(3) Feeding treatment

Feeding treatment is to ferment food waste by using microbial organisms, using the growth, reproduction and metabolism of microorganisms to accumulate useful organisms, enzymes and intermediates, and make protein feed after drying. By killing and sterilizing the food waste, it can retain the nutrients to the maximum extent and fully develop the feeding value of food waste under the premise of meeting the feed hygiene standard, and the future is promising.

7.6 Laboratory Waste

Laboratories, due to their diversity of functions and material uncertainty, also have diversity and variability in the types of waste they generate—laboratories in different industries will have completely different waste at different times. The only constant is that, depending on the state of the waste, laboratories are still primarily concerned with off-gas, waste water and solid waste.

7.6.1 Laboratory Off-Gas

For laboratory off-gas, partial treatment and areal treatment need to be considered. As shown in Fig. 7.19.

Partial off-gas treatment, mainly for gases emitted from laboratory operating tables, or facilities such as biological safety cabinets, fume hoods where chemical biological operations, or experiments that need to be operated under protective conditions takes place. Its main pollution factors are: dust particles, combustion fumes and smoke, odor gases, toxic and harmful gases, etc. Given the size of the laboratory and the instability of the experiments, the main technologies applicable to the treatment of partial off-gases in laboratories are absorption, adsorption and catalytic conversion.

(1) Absorption

Absorption is a mass transfer process in which a solution or solvent is used to absorb harmful substances from laboratory off-gases and separate them from clean gas (air). Absorption is the primary method of reducing or eliminating the flow of hazardous laboratory gases to the atmosphere.

7.6 Laboratory Waste

Fig. 7.19 Laboratory off-gas

(2) Adsorption

Adsorption is a purification operation process that uses unbalanced or unsaturated molecular forces on the surface of porous solids to absorb one or more harmful components of laboratory off-gases onto the surface of the solids and remove them by separating them from the gas stream.

(3) Catalytic conversion

Catalytic conversion is a method in which laboratory off-gases are converted into harmless or easily treatable and recoverable substances by catalytic reactions in a catalyst carrier.

Areal off-gas treatment, mainly for gases emitted in large spaces throughout the laboratory (or laboratory building) in order to maintain certain experimental conditions during laboratory operations. The pollution factors within this off-gas are more complex, but the concentration of pollutants is relatively low, and adsorption methods and high-altitude discharge are usually adopted.

7.6.2 Laboratory Waste Water

Waste water generated by laboratories may contain high concentrations of chemicals or biohazardous components depending on the laboratory's different processes—if the design capacity of the laboratory's local waste water treatment facilities is exceeded, appropriate waste water treatment and disposal management processes should be developed in accordance with the characteristics of such waste water.

Even low concentration waste water from laboratories, including liquids generated from laboratory processes, liquids from laboratory equipment (e.g., liquids from preparation of pure water implementation, cooling water equipment, and other related laboratory equipment), and liquids from ancillary laboratory processes (e.g., liquids from cleaning and cooling processes)—due to differences between such liquids and ordinary domestic waste water, they also need to be managed according to established treatment and disposal processes. As shown in Fig. 7.20.

Fundamentally, laboratory waste water treatment still involves the use of the following processes or combinations of processes for treatment and disposal, depending on the nature of their pollutants (insoluble state pollutants, infectious biological pollutants, organic pollutants in dissolved state, inorganic pollutants in dissolved state, heavy metal pollutants).

(1) Gravity separation treatment

It is one of the physical treatment methods of waste water, using the principle of gravity to separate the suspended matter in waste water from the water, removing the suspended matter and purifying the waste water. It can be divided into sedimentation method and uplifting method. The specific gravity of the suspended matter is greater

Fig. 7.20 Laboratory waste water

than that of the waste water to settle, and less than that of the waste water to float. The main factors affecting the rate of settling or floating are: particle density, particle size, liquid temperature, liquid density and absolute viscosity. Pre-treatment of laboratory waste water is mostly done by gravity separation.

(2) Anaerobic biological treatment

Also known as "anaerobic digestion", anaerobic biological treatment is a method that uses anaerobic microorganisms to degrade organic pollutants in waste water in order to purify it. The use of anaerobic biological treatment is limited by the small volume and unstable quality of laboratory waste water.

(3) Aerobic biological treatment

A treatment method that uses aerobic microorganisms (mainly aerobic bacteria) to break down organic pollutants in waste water and render it harmless. As with anaerobic biological treatment, aerobic biological treatment of laboratory waste water is rarely used due to the small volume and unstable quality of water.

(4) Chemical treatment

A waste water treatment method in which the physical or chemical properties of pollutants in waste water are altered by chemical reactions to change them from a dissolved, colloidal or suspended state to a precipitated or floating state, and then removed from the water. The use of chemical methods for laboratory waste water treatment is very common and easy to implement due to its small water volume.

(5) Disinfection treatment

A treatment process that uses physical or chemical methods to destroy pathogens that remain in the waste water. Even if it is not a medical laboratory, some general laboratory waste water still contains a large number of bacteria and viruses that cannot be completely exterminated by normal waste water treatment processes. *Escherichia coli*, for example, can only be removed by 80%~90% using ordinary biofilters in a typical waste water treatment system, and by 90%~95% using activated sludge methods. In order to prevent the spread of disease, most laboratory waste water needs to be disinfected. Common disinfection treatment methods include: chlorination disinfection, ozone disinfection, sodium hypochlorite disinfection, chlorine dioxide disinfection, etc.

7.6.3 Laboratory Solid Waste

Solid waste in laboratories refers to solid or highly concentrated liquid and semi-solid waste generated in the course of experiments that have an impact on the environment, mainly including general laboratory waste such as packaging materials, test samples, etc., but also some semi-finished products from the R&D process.

Laboratory solid waste may contain a variety of hazardous pollutants that are combustible, explosive, corrosive, reactive, highly toxic, radioactive, infectious and pathogenic, many of which are very difficult to degrade or dispose of; in addition, the types and quantities of laboratory solid waste are highly uncertain and unclear, and difficult to reuse. Therefore, laboratories that generate solid waste will generally treat and dispose of all of it as hazardous waste in accordance with relevant regulations—usually including incineration and pyrolysis. As shown in Fig. 7.21.

Fig. 7.21 Laboratory solid waste

(1) Incineration method

Incineration is an integrated process of high-temperature decomposition and deep oxidation of solid waste. For laboratory wastes, incineration has the advantage of breaking down large quantities of hazardous substances, especially synthetic intermediates of organic matter of unknown hazard, into harmless substances.

(2) Pyrolysis method

Pyrolysis is the decomposition of organic matter into gas, liquid and solid products by heating it at high temperatures (500~1,000 °C) under anaerobic or anoxic conditions. Pyrolysis is also very suitable for organic wastes that are mixed together in the laboratory, yet are not suitable for incineration.

7.7 Secondary Waste

7.7.1 Sources and Characteristics of Secondary Waste

Secondary waste is inevitable in the process of normal treatment and disposal of all kinds of waste, which is different from the original waste in composition proportion, physical properties and chemical properties. They mainly include:

(1) Sorting waste

It mainly includes impurities after mechanical or manual sorting of wastes, as well as residues from aerobic composting and anaerobic digestion.

(2) Incineration waste

It mainly includes the residues of waste (garbage) after incineration, such as bottom ash, slag, fly ash, etc.

(3) Mineralized waste

It mainly includes minerals that cannot be avoided in the process of solidification, vitrification or stabilization of various wastes.

(4) Diverted waste

It mainly includes the non-hazardous wastes from the physical and chemical treatment of hazardous wastes, the activated sludge from the biochemical treatment of various organic wastes, and the landfill leachate.

Generally speaking, in the sorting process, as long as the waste is properly classified with not much mutual contamination, there will not be too many sorting wastes. It is also normal and acceptable that the sorting waste in the industry doesn't exceed 1% of the total mass. For incineration waste, as long as the thermal treatment (incineration) process is reasonable, the waste types and sources are stable, there will not be many incineration wastes or what cannot be oxidized or decomposed (usually within 10%), and they have already been burned harmless. The bottom ash and slag can either be used in construction, or be landfilled or sea dumping in accordance with the regulations. And although the mass ratio of various minerals in the mineralized waste is not certain, the total content is very limited, and there is no problem of hazardous substance migration after stabilization, with little impact on the ecology and environment.

What is really worth mentioning is the diverted waste. After the hazardous waste is transformed into ordinary waste, it must be treated and disposed of according to the characteristics of the target waste. The activated sludge produced by biochemical process also needs to be further dehydrated or incinerated; the landfill leachate should be considered in the design of landfill site and collected for disposal according to the regulations.

At present, the biggest problem is the activated sludge produced by municipal waste water treatment system, given its considerable volume. The following section

7.7.2 Municipal Sludge

Municipal sludge is a derivative of municipal waste water treatment, which usually contains pathogenic microorganisms, parasitic eggs, harmful heavy metals and a large number of non-biodegradable substances. It will cause secondary pollution to the environment if not treated thoroughly. As shown in Fig. 7.22. Therefore, there is a saying in the industry that "treat waste water but not sludge, and transfer pollution". With the improvement of urbanization and the rapid development of waste water treatment facilities, the capacity of municipal waste water treatment is constantly improving, and the waste water discharge standards are also further improved, followed by the increase of sludge production year by year. Taking China as an example, by the end of June 2018, more than 5,000 municipal waste water treatment plants had been built in cities nationwide, with a waste water treatment capacity of 190 million cubic meters per day, and an annual output of more than 50 million tons of sludge (excluding 40 million tons of industrial sludge) with 80% water content. According to statistics, the total annual output of municipal sludge in China will reach 60 million to 90 million tons by 2020. According to the "Action Plan for Prevention and Control of Water Pollution" in China, the harmless treatment and

Fig. 7.22 Municipal sludge

will take it as an example to study municipal sludge treatment and disposal technology thoroughly, and explore the challenges and opportunities of secondary waste.

7.7 Secondary Waste

disposal rate of municipal sludge at prefecture level and above should reach more than 90% by the end of 2020.

The composition of sludge is complex, which contains not only organic matters, but also harmful substances such as microorganisms and heavy metals from domestic and industrial waste water. As the first by-product of waste water treatment, improper treatment will cause serious secondary pollution to the environment. Still take China as an example, 70% of the sludge produced by waste water treatment plants has not been properly treated, and the problem of random stacking of sludge and re-pollution has been highlighted. Sludge is considered as a kind of recyclable resource because it contains a lot of organic matter and nutrients. Therefore, how to realize the harmlessness, stabilization, reduction and resource utilization of sludge has become the focus of social attention and the research hotspot in the industry.

At present, after thickening, dehydration and drying, the sludge treatment methods mainly include landfill, natural drying, incineration, aerobic composting, anaerobic digestion, building materials, and so on. In many countries and regions, landfill accounts for a large proportion.

The characteristics of municipal sludge vary greatly in different countries with different economic development levels. The VSS/SS of developed countries is generally 60%~70%, while that of developing countries is lower, generally 30%~50%. The content of heavy metals will directly affect the feasibility of sludge recycling, while the organic matter and calorific value will affect the economic benefits of sludge recycling. According to the output and nature of sludge, cities in developed countries usually take resource utilization as the main goal of sludge treatment and disposal, while cities in developing and underdeveloped countries usually take harmlessness and stabilization as the short-term priority goal of sludge treatment and disposal.

7.7.2.1 Sludge Reduction

From the point of view of mass balance, the production of municipal sludge is to transfer carbon from dispersed liquid phase (COD and BOD in waste water) to relatively concentrated solid-liquid mixed phase (activated sludge), and then stabilize carbon to solid phase (fertilizer, building materials or landfill) or gas phase (oxidation to carbon dioxide) by various methods. Because the potential pollution to the environment in the three phases is actually the transitional phase—solid-liquid mixed phase (carbon neutral is not considered for the time being), a natural and preferred choice when considering reduction is to find a way to transfer carbon directly from the liquid phase to the gas phase, thus skipping the troublesome intermediate steps of aerobic composting, anaerobic digestion or incineration.

At present, in the process of municipal waste water treatment, sludge reduction is mainly based on the uncoupling growth method. This method increases the energy level difference between catabolism and anabolism of microorganisms in sludge by adding uncoupler, so as to reduce the energy used for anabolism, inhibit anabolism, reduce the growth rate of sludge microorganisms, and achieve the purpose of reducing the amount of excess sludge. Because this sludge reduction method usually does not need to make a major adjustment or improvement to the existing waste water treatment process, it only needs to add a dosing device, and the investment is very low. Therefore, this method has far-reaching environmental and economic significance.

Generally, the uncouplers in the research include nitrophenol [such as 2,4-dinitrophenol (DNP), p-nitrophenol (p-NP), m-nitrophenol (m-NP), etc.], chlorophenol [such as p-chlorophenol (p-CP), m-chlorophenol (m-CP), pentachlorophenol (PCP), etc.], 3,3',4',5-tetrachlorosalicylidene aniline (TCS), aminophenol, etc. These uncouplers are generally liposolubility weak acid, which pollutes water more or less.

Some uncouplers, such as tetra hydroxymethyl phosphate sulfate (THPS), a water-soluble quaternary phosphate salt, were discovered in the 1980s. It has a special quaternary structure with only one long and short side chain of carbon atom, which determines that it has the advantages of wide spectrum, high efficiency and rapidity of quaternary ammonium salt. At the same time, it can be quickly oxidized into tris (hydroxymethyl) phosphine oxide (THPO) with no bactericidal activity and almost no toxicity. However, THPO is easy to be further biodegraded into orthophosphate. It is because of these characteristics that THPS is widely used in cooling water system, oilfield water system, fire sprinkler system, paper making and other fields. In addition, THPS is also used to control the bacterial biomass in aqueous system to reduce the excess sludge production in the process of municipal waste water treatment.

The main process of using THPS is that in the traditional municipal waste water treatment system, a part of the sludge discharged from the bottom of the sedimentation tank is introduced into the mixing tank through the sludge pump, where it is mixed with the THPS introduced in the storage tank, and then the mixed liquid flows back to the aeration tank for continuous aeration together with the waste water and the original sludge; and another part of the sludge discharged from the bottom of the sedimentation tank is normally used as excess sludge discharge, and it keeps cycling like this. As shown in Fig. 7.23.

By improving the traditional activated sludge process, this method can reduce the amount of excess sludge produced in the municipal waste water treatment process by about 20%~60%, and significantly improve the sludge settling performance by about 5%~20%. The process has almost no effect on the removal efficiency of other pollutants in waste water (including COD, BOD_5, SS, TN, TP, NH_4^+-N, etc.), and has the advantages of simple equipment, less investment, simple operation and management, low operation cost, etc., which can be widely used in the treatment of various municipal and industrial waste water.

7.7.2.2 Sludge Thickening

Sludge thickening methods includes gravity thickening, mechanical thickening and air flotation thickening. In China, 71.5% of sludge is thickened by gravity, 21.4% by mechanical and 7.1% by air flotation.

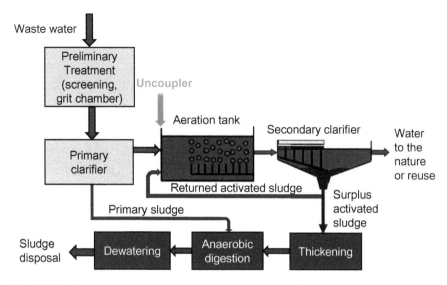

Fig. 7.23 Sludge reduction process using uncoupler in municipal waste water treatment

(1) Gravity thickening

At present, gravity thickening is still an important method for sludge thickening in municipal waste water treatment plants in many developing countries. For excess sludge with high organic matter content, gravity thickening has poor effect, but gravity thickening is the most economical method for primary sludge treatment. Gravity thickening process is simple in technology, structure and operation management, but it has some disadvantages, such as large area, poor sanitary conditions, long residence time, sludge in thickening tank is easy to float due to anaerobic digestion, which affects the thickening effect. On the other hand, gravity thickening will lead to the secondary release of phosphorus. In recent years, due to the improvement of the total phosphorus discharge standard of municipal waste water in many countries and regions, the traditional gravity thickening process has been greatly challenged.

(2) Mechanical thickening

Mechanical thickening uses centrifugal, belt type, drum type and screw type thickeners. Mechanical thickening has the characteristics of high thickening efficiency, short cycle, highly continuous and quantitative operation, and can avoid the secondary release of phosphorus from sludge. It has become the main direction of sludge treatment equipment in municipal waste water treatment plants nowadays—however, the power consumption of this technology is high. Before using the belt thickener, drum thickener and screw thickener, it is usually necessary to add chemicals for sludge conditioning.

(3) Air flotation thickening

Air flotation thickening relies on a large number of micro bubbles attached to the sludge particles around, reducing the proportion of particles and forced floating.

According to the different ways of producing bubbles, air flotation process can be divided into pressure dissolved air flotation, biological dissolved air flotation and vortex concave air flotation. Air flotation thickening has the advantages of fast thickening speed (treatment time is only 1/3 of gravity thickening), less land occupation, convenient sludge scraping and simple operation; however, air flotation thickening has the advantages of high capital construction and operation cost, complex management, high operation cost (operation cost is 2–3 times of gravity thickening), certain odor in operation, and sensitive to sludge settling performance (Sludge Volume Index, SVI). It is suitable for activated sludge treatment system with small excess sludge production, especially for excess sludge in biological phosphorus removal system.

7.7.2.3 Sludge Stabilization

The goal of sludge stabilization is to reduce the content of biodegradable organic matter in sludge, kill pathogens, and reduce water content to reduce sludge volume. The organic matter in sludge is gradually transformed into $CH_4/CO_2/H_2O$ and other inorganic compounds through artificially biological, chemical or other "sludge stabilization technology", so as to achieve the ultimate containment of microbial reaction or effective control. That is to say, the sludge after stabilization treatment can no longer cause odor in the follow-up treatment process, improve the sanitary conditions in the follow-up treatment process, or be more suitable for agriculture, horticulture or forestry production. Therefore, the process of sludge stabilization can realize harmlessness, reduction and resource utilization at the same time. Among them, harmless treatment is the basis, reduction treatment is the core, and resource usage is the ultimate goal.

From the perspective of the whole chain of sludge treatment and disposal, if the sludge is not stabilized properly, it will lead to the release of various pollutants in the follow-up treatment, and increase the constraints of the follow-up treatment. At present, sludge stabilization methods include anaerobic digestion, aerobic digestion, sludge composting, wet oxidation, supercritical oxidation, etc.

(1) Anaerobic digestion

Anaerobic digestion is a process in which organic matters in sludge are mineralized into CH_4, CO_2, H_2O, H_2S and NH_3-N by microorganisms under anaerobic conditions. Anaerobic digestion is the most economical sludge treatment method for large-scale waste water treatment plants because it can realize the degradation and transformation of pollutants in sludge, recover energy and nutrients from sludge, and achieve the goals of sludge stabilization, reduction and energy generation. Sludge anaerobic digestion process is very complex, and it is generally considered that it needs to go through three stages: hydrolysis acidification stage, acetic acid stage and methanation stage. Each stage is interrelated and influenced by each other, and each stage has its own characteristic microbial community. At present, the methods to improve sludge digestion performance and anaerobic digestion efficiency include collaborative anaerobic digestion technology with organic waste, combined anaerobic digestion technology with moderate temperature and high temperature, and anaerobic digestion technology with high solid content.

(2) Aerobic digestion

Aerobic digestion of sludge is an endogenous metabolic process of microbial organisms in sludge. By aeration, the microbial organisms of activated sludge oxidize and decompose into carbon dioxide, water and ammonia. Aerobic digestion of sludge can inactivate pathogenic bacteria in sludge, and eliminate the odor of final product. COD and BOD_5 in supernatant are relatively low (BOD_5 can reach below 10 mg/L).

Of course, there are some problems in sludge aerobic digestion, such as long digestion time, large amount of facilities, high operation cost and low treatment efficiency. However, due to the advantages of convenient management, flexible operation, small investment and stable output, aerobic digestion is an effective and practical sludge stabilization technology for waste water treatment plants with small load ($\leqslant$ 20,000 m^3/d).

There are two kinds of aerobic digestion: ordinary aerobic digestion and thermophilic aerobic digestion. Ordinary aerobic digestion is similar to activated sludge process, which mainly depends on delayed aeration to reduce the amount of sludge. Thermophilic aerobic digestion uses the heat released by microorganisms when they oxidize organic matter to heat the sludge and raise the sludge temperature to 40~70 °C. Compared with ordinary aerobic digestion, thermophilic aerobic digestion reacts faster, has shorter residence time, and can kill almost all pathogens without further disinfection.

(3) Sludge composting

Sludge composting is a process that makes the organic matter in sludge degrade and stabilize continuously through the action of microorganism under certain conditions, and produces suitable product for land use. Sludge composting technology can achieve the effect of "harmlessness", "reduction" and "resource utilization" in practice, which has the characteristics of no need of additional energy and no secondary pollution. Generally, composting can be divided into aerobic composting and anaerobic composting. At present, aerobic composting is basically adopted in sludge composting. The process consists of four stages: heating stage, high temperature stage, cooling stage and maturation stage.

In practice, there are many ways of sludge composting, according to the state of sludge, it can be divided into static and dynamic; according to the degree of mechanization in the composting process, it can be divided into open-air composting and rapid composting; according to the complex process of composting technology, it can be divided into strip stack, forced ventilation static stack and bioreactor system. The stacking surface of strip stack can be trapezoid, triangle or irregular quadrilateral, which can ensure the aerobic state in the pile body by turning the pile regularly; the static stack with forced ventilation is based on the strip stack, which supplies oxygen to the pile body through forced ventilation instead of turning the sludge—the composting time is short, the temperature and ventilation conditions can be well controlled, and the operation cost is low; the bioreactor system is actually a closed fermentation bin or tower, which covers a small area and can collect and clean up the odor, but the investment and operation costs are high.

(4) Wet oxidation

Wet oxidation (WO) of sludge includes hydrolysis, pyrolysis and oxidation steps. It is a process in which the sludge is placed in a closed reactor, air or oxygen is introduced as oxidant under high temperature and high pressure, and the organic matter in the sludge is oxidized and decomposed according to the principle of submerged fuel, and the organic matter is transformed into inorganic matter. Wet oxidation can oxidize 80~90% of organic matter for excess sludge, so it is also called partial incineration or wet incineration.

Wet oxidation is a new sludge treatment method in the world, which can make almost all organic matter in sludge be oxidized and decomposed. It not only has a high degree of decomposition, but also can be continuously adjusted according to the needs of treatment objectives. Due to the change of sludge structure and composition in the process of wet oxidation, the main components of treated sludge become mineral inorganic substances, so the specific resistance of sludge is small, and the dewatering performance is greatly improved (usually it can be directly filtered and dehydrated, and the water content of filter cake is low). Its disadvantages are require equipment with high temperature and pressure resistance, large one-time investment cost, high operating cost and easy corrosion.

(5) Supercritical oxidation

Supercritical oxidation refers to the process of treating high water content carbon sludge in supercritical reactor by using the characteristics of fast reaction speed, complete reaction and high heat exchange efficiency of water in supercritical state. In supercritical oxidation process, sludge and water are mixed in a certain proportion to make carbon containing slurry, which is heated and pressurized to the temperature and pressure above the critical point (usually 374.3 °C and 22.1 MPa), so that the water in carbon containing slurry is converted into supercritical water, and then the organic pollutants in sludge are oxidized and removed by supercritical oxidation reaction.

In the sludge supercritical oxidation process, carbon is converted into carbon dioxide, hydrogen is converted into water, nitrogen is converted into nitrogen gas, sulfur is converted into sulfate, which is stable in ash—compared with the traditional sludge treatment and disposal, there is no secondary pollution. The organic matter conversion rate and volume reduction rate of the sludge treated by supercritical oxidation are more than 99% and 90%, respectively. The effluent is clean and can be discharged to natural water if it meets the standard. In addition, the heat generated by the oxidation of pollutants can also be recovered.

7.7.2.4 Sludge Gasification

Sludge gasification is a process of partial oxidation of dry sludge at high temperature (700~1,000 °C) to convert its organic matter into synthetic combustible gas (mainly composed of H_2, CO and CH_4). Sludge gasification includes four stages: drying, pyrolysis or devolatilization, combustion, carbon gasification reduction. According to gasification conditions, sludge gasification can be divided into air gasification, steam gasification and supercritical gasification. Gasification can reduce the volume of sludge, and fix the heavy metals in the sludge in the residue, so the leaching toxicity is low and the treatment cost is relatively low.

As an efficient, clean and energy self-sufficient sludge treatment technology, sludge gasification is attracting more and more attention from academia and industry. Compared with the traditional sludge gasification process, supercritical water gasification, plasma gasification and catalytic gasification of sludge also attract great interest of researchers due to their higher energy utilization rate.

At present, the research on the properties of sludge gasification tar is not deep enough, and the utilization of sludge gasification residue needs to be further explored. In addition, the development of sludge gasification technology focuses on the design of efficient, cheap and simple gasifier, the establishment of sludge gasification eval-uation criteria, and the determination of the best gasification conditions within the operation range.

7.7.2.5 Sludge Pyrolysis

Sludge pyrolysis is a process in which organic matter is converted into bio-oil, char, synthetic gas and reaction water by thermochemistry in anoxic ambience. The process is usually carried out in a dual reaction system: in the first reactor, more than 60% of the dewatered sludge (with solid content of 90% ~95%) volatilizes at 450°C; in the second reactor, the gas-phase components and the scorched products are combined to produce various reactions to obtain bio-oil. Sludge pyrolysis is a very complex chemical reaction process, including macromolecular fragmentation, small molecule polymerization and isomerization.

Generally, sludge pyrolysis can be divided into three stages: the first stage is the precipitation of water in sludge, the second stage is the precipitation of volatile matter in sludge, and the third stage is the stage of coke burnout. The yield of products is different with the pyrolysis temperature. Compared with sludge incineration, the main advantages of sludge pyrolysis are as follows:

① Although the volume reduction rate of sludge is lower than that of incineration, it can still reach more than 50% (depending on the nature of sludge), and the amount of fly ash produced by sludge pyrolysis is less.
② The pyrolysis of sludge is carried out under anoxic or anaerobic ambience, which does not produce dioxins and other toxic substances, and plays a good role in fixing the heavy metals contained in the sludge.

③ Sludge pyrolysis products can effectively recover resources—the residue can be made into adsorption material or solid fuel, the liquid can be used as fuel oil, and the gas can be stored as combustible gas.
④ Sludge pyrolysis equipment occupies a small area, with low investment and stronger adaptability.

7.7.2.6 SludgeRecycling

(1) Building materials

Because the sludge contains 20%~30% inorganic matter, especially the sludge from coagulation process, it contains a lot of aluminum, iron and other components, after incineration, the ash can replace part of cement raw materials; if a certain amount of lime is added, the quality of ecological cement can meet the corresponding standards after high temperature incineration. Sludge cement technology is mature, simple management, easy operation, in line with the strategy of circular economy and sustainable development.

Sludge brick can be made by mixing sludge with other raw materials (such as clay, shale, coal gangue and fly ash) after certain treatment and screening, pressure molding and roasting. This method can not only kill the harmful bacteria in the blank, but also make full use of the calorific value of sludge and reduce the energy consumption of brick firing. By process optimization, the sludge bricks have not only main indexes that reach the corresponding standard of ordinary fired brick, but also many voids, light brick, and a certain effect of sound and heat insulation. There are two common methods of sludge brick making, namely sludge incineration ash brick making and dry sludge direct brick making. At present, dry sludge direct brick making is the main method in the market.

Sludge is used as the main raw material, clay and slag are used as auxiliary raw materials—after roasting and pelletizing (commonly used rotary kiln incineration), sludge ceramsite with certain hardness is formed. However, there are certain requirements for making ceramsite from sludge, that is, the chemical composition and basic indexes of sludge should be kept stable, such as SiO_2 content of 52.0%~60.0%, Al_2O_3 content of 16.0%~17.5%, Fe_2O_3 content of 6.9%~9.0%, CaO content of 0.9%~1.8%, MgO content of 1.2%~1.9%.

(2) Fiberboard

Because the sludge contains a certain amount of bacterial protein, the sludge can be made into biochemical fiberboard by using the property that the crude protein (organic matter) and globulin (enzyme) contained in the activated sludge can be dissolved in water and dilute acid, alkali and neutral saline solution. Firstly, the sludge was heated, dried and pressurized under alkaline conditions to denature the protein, and then the activated sludge resin (also known as protein glue) was made. Then, the bleached and degreased waste fibers were pressed into boards. The quality of this kind of fiberboard is better than that of some hard fiberboard, and the felling of wood is reduced at the same time.

7.7 Secondary Waste

(3) Binder

Municipal sludge contains a lot of organic matter, which has a certain bonding performance and calorific value, and can be used to prepare briquette binder. Replacing white sludge with municipal sludge can improve the internal pore structure of briquette at high temperature, improve the gasification reactivity of briquette, reduce the residual carbon in ash after combustion, and improve the carbon conversion rate; meanwhile, sludge is treated in high temperature gasifier, and the potential secondary pollution is eliminated.

(4) Adsorbent

Activated carbon is a kind of efficient adsorbent. In theory, any carbonaceous matter can be used as the raw material for the preparation of activated carbon. The municipal sludge is rich in organic carbon, which can be made into activated carbon like adsorbent in chemical way at a certain temperature. In turn, it can be used for various waste water treatment.

(5) Feed

Because the municipal sludge contains protein, vitamin and trace elements, using the purified municipal sludge as protein feed or mixing the purified sludge with other feeds can increase the production of fish and poultry. However, if the municipal sludge is directly made into sludge feed without pretreatment, some toxic and harmful substances may accumulate in the animal body and bring potential harm, and the risk needs to be further studied and evaluated.

7.7.2.7 Final Disposal

As with all other wastes, no matter what technology is used, there are always parts of sludge cannot be completely diverted and need to be disposed of. The final disposal methods of sludge include high temperature incineration, sanitary landfill and soil utilization.

(1) High temperature incineration

High temperature incineration is a common method for the final disposal of municipal sludge. It refers to the technology that the organic matter in the sludge is completely converted into CO_2 and H_2O after combustion reaction with sufficient oxygen under high temperature conditions, so as to realize the sludge volume reduction, mass reduction and harmlessness. In order to achieve a good treatment effect, the "3 T" principle should be met, that is, to ensure the appropriate incineration Temperature, the sufficient Turbulence of combustibles and oxygen, and the residence Time required for the completion of the reaction.

Generally, increasing the incineration temperature is beneficial to the decomposition and destruction of organic toxicants in waste, and can inhibit the generation of black smoke. However, under high temperature conditions, the sludge temperature rises fast, and the precipitation of moisture and volatile matter is also fast, which will make the sludge easy to break in the initial stage of incineration and increase the loss of fly ash; at the same time, too high incineration temperature will not only increase the fuel consumption, but also increase the amount of nitrogen oxide and the volatility of heavy metals, causing secondary pollution. The suitable temperature is determined by experiment under a certain residence time.

Air is another important factor affecting municipal sludge incineration. When sludge is incinerated, oxygen must be used to support combustion, and oxygen is provided by air. If the air flow is insufficient, the combustion will not be sufficient. If the air flow is too much, heating the air will consume additional energy. Generally, 50%~100% excess air flow is appropriate.

There are generally two different ways of sludge feeding for municipal sludge incineration. When intermittent sludge feeding is adopted, the residence time of sludge in the furnace is determined by the feeding cycle and input amount, and the longer the residence time is, the better the incineration treatment effect is; when continuous sludge feeding is adopted, the incineration amount is determined by the input amount and the residence time in the furnace, and the longer the residence time is, the worse the incineration treatment effect is.

Incineration can quickly and effectively sterilize and reduce the sludge. Generally, the heat energy can be self-sufficient, and even the residual energy can be obtained from the incineration exhaust gas for grid connected power generation, and the combustion products can also be effectively disposed. Of course, sludge incineration also has some problems. The water content of primary sludge is higher (more than 60%) and the net calorific value is lower, which leads to large investment in pretreatment facilities, high energy consumption and maintenance costs. Sludge incineration is also prone to produce fine particles and toxic and harmful gases. In order to avoid secondary pollution, the discharged flue gas must be treated. These problems are also worth of attention and solution.

(2) Sanitary landfill

Sanitary landfill refers to the transportation of municipal sludge to a designated area (mountain, canyon, flat land, abandoned mine pit, etc.) to be spread and compacted into a thin layer, and then covered with inert soil to a certain thickness; the closed landfill is covered with the final covering layer composed of cohesive soil, on which green plants can be planted.

Sanitary landfill can be divided into mixed landfill and separate landfill. Mixed landfill refers to the full mixing, spreading and compaction of municipal sludge and domestic waste, and landfill disposal together; separate landfill refers to the simple sterilization of municipal sludge, and landfill disposal in a special landfill site, with necessary ecological restoration.

The operation of sanitary landfill is simple, the sludge does not need to be highly dehydrated (natural drying), non-toxic and harmless, and the comprehensive cost is low. But at the same time, there are many problems in sanitary landfill, such as long treatment period (sludge stabilization time is 2~7 years), serious land occupation, landfill leachate may lead to soil and ground water pollution. Because of these shortcomings, the landfill method is limited, so some countries and regions explicitly stipulate that only the sludge without any comprehensive utilization possibilities can be disposed by sanitary landfill.

(3) Soil utilization

Municipal sludge is rich in organic matter, nitrogen, phosphorus, potassium and other beneficial components, with strong viscosity and strong water absorption, which can significantly improve the physical and chemical properties of soil, help to form soil aggregates, enhance water holding capacity, reduce soil erosion, significantly improve soil fertility and biological activity, and realize a virtuous cycle of agricultural ecological environment. Therefore, soil utilization is also one of the important potential ways of municipal sludge disposal, which can be applied to farmland, vegetable land, orchard, municipal greening, and soil restoration and reconstruction in local areas.

Chapter 8
Zero Waste Theory and Practice

We discussed the treatment and disposal technologies of several typical industrial waste in previous chapter. However, there are many industries which generate different kinds of waste. One industry may possibly generate multiple kinds of waste while different industries may produce one same kind of waste. It is actually necessary to study waste management and to find zero waste theory and practice in different industries.

8.1 Chemical Industry

Chemical industry takes an important position in the national economy and is the foundation and pillar industry of a country. The speed and scale of chemical industry's development has a direct impact on all sectors of the social economy. According to incomplete statistics, the annual value of the world's chemical products has exceeded 1,500 billion USD.

There are various categories in chemical industry with complex process and diverse products, therefore the waste produced in processing, storage and utilization might be in wide variety, large volume and high toxicity. To realize zero waste in chemical industry, green chemistry must be introduced at the very beginning.

8.1.1 Green Chemistry

Although the industry has different and various definitions, green chemistry can generally be considered from chemical substances and chemical processes in terms of their ecological impact.

Green chemistry, substance wise, promotes the use of natural or bio-based raw materials for subsequent processing as far as possible. Those materials can be obtained directly from nature, thus avoiding tailings from the mining and waste from the consumption of auxiliary raw materials during mineral purification. Additionally, the residue from natural or bio-based raw materials, regardless of the material efficiency, are also natural or biological, which either do not need to be treated or can be easily degraded. In short, there is no waste too difficult to be treated during this process, which itself is zero waste.

There are numerous examples of natural raw materials, as many chemicals in nature can be utilized directly, and most of the times they are developed locally. Bio-based raw materials have also seen significant development in recent years. Let's take ethanol production as an example. Although the direct use of food to manufacture ethanol is still controversial in the international academic community, the use of agricultural and forestry by-products to manufacture ethanol, such as sugar cane molasses waste water fermentation, or the fermentation of straw from some food plants, is an uncontested zero waste practice.

The chemical processes of green chemistry require lower energy consumption under the same conditions, or higher material efficiency under different conditions. Lower energy consumption will reduce carbon dioxide emissions, though the solid waste may not be reduced but it's already environment-friendly. Higher material efficiency will directly contribute to waste reduction, although 100% material efficiency is not possible… However, the few percentages that cannot be reached can be complemented by reuse or recycling.

So how to improve material efficiency by changing the conditions?

To choose better equipment is the first thing to do. Better mass balance can avoid wasting the raw materials in the reaction process for no reason. As mentioned earlier in Chap. 4, it is the most unfortunate thing if raw materials are wasted and then emitted, as it is both an economic loss and environmental loss. So, the integrative equipment as well as the closed operation will help with material efficiency.

Next is to choose a better process pathway, for instance, by adding catalysts to influence the reaction equilibrium, or by reducing the number of steps—each reaction step has its upper limit of conversion, therefore, more steps mean lower final conversion. Proper catalyst use increases the overall conversion of a multistage reaction with fewer steps by reducing the activation energy of the reaction, influencing the endpoint of the reaction with a change in thermal equilibrium to achieve a higher single-stage conversion, or changing the pathway of the target product with a different reaction mechanism.

The last but not least important condition change is the optimization of production management. Green chemistry requires a green plant, and a green plant comes from a high level of production management. Having a complete quality system, with corresponding Standard Operating Procedures (SOP), is a necessary prerequisite to ensure non-technical losses. Plant practice has shown us that training within the system can significantly improve the efficiency of a unit operation.

8.1.2 Treatment Process Selection

However, even if green chemistry is achieved, the generation of chemical waste cannot be completely eliminated. It is important for a chemical plant to adopt a technically-appropriate and cost-efficient waste treatment process (including supporting facilities and external services).

Chemical plants are usually located in specific industrial parks, for the sake of governmental control and economic benefits (the overall waste treatment and disposal options for the parks are discussed in detail in Sect. 8.7 of this Chapter). Chemical plants are expected to take full advantage of the resources and services available in the park to achieve zero waste.

① If it is a chemical park of the same industrial type, then the park will generally be designed and built with waste treatment and disposal facilities in accordance with the scale of the industry.
② In the case of integrated upstream and downstream parks, one enterprise can usually recycle and reuse the other enterprise's waste in the park.
③ Even if there are no supporting services for waste treatment and disposal or recycling in the park, facilities such as administrative approval, quota coordination and unified logistics are usually provided, so that the various wastes in the park can be properly connected to external resources for treatment and disposal.

With the full consideration and use of various internal and external resources, the choice of treatment process becomes relatively clear and definite. Although there are many different process options for waste treatment and many specialized treatment companies, the choices are largely in the following directions.

(1) Mobile phase to stationary phase

Fine particles of waste dispersed in the gas phase (mostly carried by air) or liquid phase (mostly carried by water) are generally less easy to be treated directly.

① In the case of the gas phase, particle capturing can refer to industrial dust removal processes where waste particles will be collected from the air before further treatment.
② In the case of the liquid phase, waste particles (including very high dispersion colloids) need to be separated from the waste containing "waste water" by coagulation, flocculation, sedimentation, filtration, dewatering or even drying before further treatment.
③ For waste in the gas or liquid phase that is not in large amount, physical means are occasionally adopted. The change in temperature and/or pressure can directly transform the waste to solid phase which is easier for subsequent transfer or treatment.

(2) From organic to inorganic

In the discussion in Chap. 7, it is apparent that inorganic waste is relatively simple and thus easier to reuse as resource than organic waste, which has great diversity and thereby is complex to be treated and difficult to evaluate in terms of environmental hazards. Consequently, an important principle in the treatment of chemical waste is to transform organic waste into inorganic one. The main methods are as following.

① Carbon in organic matter in the gas phase can be directly oxidized through incineration so that it can be emitted as carbon dioxide.
② Carbon chains of organic matter in the liquid phase can be broken by strong oxidizing agents (hydrogen peroxide, etc.), thus large-molecule organic matter is decomposed into small-molecule organic matter for further decomposition into inorganic matter, while some small-molecule organic matter being transformed into inorganic carbon dioxide or carbonates (depending on other cations in the liquid phase and the pH of the solution).
③ Organic waste in the solid phase can be directly incinerated if it has no recycling value, while those with recycling value can be transformed into inorganic matter with the help of high-temperature furnaces in the metallurgical industry, and the various metals contained therein can be recovered.

(3) From hazardous to harmless

Any chemical company would like to reduce hazardous waste, in other words, to make the waste harmless, for the sake of easier management and more efficient cost of disposal. This is because the storage, transfer, treatment and disposal of hazardous waste require special qualifications, processes and permits, and the related cost could be more than ten times those of non-hazardous waste. Hazardous waste is usually rendered harmless in the following ways.

① Chemical methods. Common chemicals and simple reaction paths are used to convert hazardous waste into other waste or even into chemical feed stocks that can be used for other purposes. This method is cost-efficient and is a preferred method.
② Biological methods. Some hazardous wastes can be partially degraded by specific organisms (mainly microorganisms)—though neither eliminated nor reduced, the hazardous components of the waste are transformed into other components by biological action. Although the biological reaction time is longer and the transformation is less complete, it is nevertheless an option.
③ Physical methods. Physical methods are basically thermal decomposition, namely the decomposition of hazardous components in hazardous wastes at high temperatures (with the application of catalysts, when necessary, to lower the temperature required for decomposition). Unlike high-temperature incineration, the strategy here is not to completely oxidize the hazardous waste, but rather to break down the hazardous components to harmless ones; however, similar to high-temperature incineration, physical method is a last resort due to the high demand for equipment and energy.

8.2 Machinery Industry

What we generally call the machinery industry refers to the machinery industry in a narrow sense, namely the machine manufacturing industry, which mainly includes the manufacturing of agricultural machinery, mining equipment, metallurgical equipment, power equipment, chemical equipment and machine tools. Machinery industry is known as the "heart of industry", which is the means of production of other economic sectors and the foundation for the development of all economic sectors. The development level of the machinery industry is an important indicator of the industrialization degree of a country.

8.2.1 Industry Characteristics

The machinery industry is a "big" and "difficult" waste generator.

First of all, raw materials and products in machinery industry are always large and heavy. The waste generated in this industry, no matter during which process, is large in volume and weight, which requires rather substantial human and material resources as well as energy to treat and dispose of it.

Secondly, there are more molding processes in the machinery industry. When the shape and size of raw materials do not meet the final requirements (due to primary manufacturing and logistic reasons, the shape of raw materials is generally regular and the size often large), cutting, grinding and drilling are bound to produce a variety of wastes that are small, scattered and mixed (containing auxiliary materials and auxiliaries), compared with the raw materials. And they are often difficult to treat.

Thirdly, the machinery industry is mainly discrete based, process supplemented and assembly focused. This characteristic has decided the following features that will have a great impact on waste generation and treatment in machinery industry.

① The development of production plans and the management of production tasks are relatively heavy. In general, discrete machinery manufacturing enterprises are mainly engaged in single-piece and small batch production; the process of the product is frequently changed; and production is mainly organized according to orders, resulting in the difficulty to make forecast. Therefore, the time and amount of waste generated is very uncertain.

② The level of automation is relatively low. Machinery manufacturing enterprises are largely dependent on the skill level of workers for product quality and productivity due to mainly discrete processing. Automation is mainly at the unit level, like CNC machines and flexible manufacturing systems, etc. As a result, differences in the skill level of operations lead to uncertainty in the waste generation rate (material efficiency) as well.

③ The arrangement of production equipment is generally determined by process rather than by product. Since the process may be different for each product, complex scheduling of the processed materials is required and intermediate goods need to be transferred across workshops or regions. As a result, a variety of waste is also generated from the packaging, protection and marking required during the transfer process.

8.2.2 Corresponding Measures

Targeted measures shall be taken to accommodate the above-mentioned characteristics in order to achieve zero waste in machinery industry, normally from three perspectives.

(1) Collecting the pieces and dealing with them altogether

As waste generation is quite random in terms of time and volume, waste generating unit doesn't need to spend much energy in dealing with waste produced at the moment. The waste can actually be sorted and stored until enough is accumulated and can be transported to waste treatment companies for further treatment.

(2) Balancing supply and demand

As discussed in mass balance in Chap. 4, operations and processes decides material efficiency, which is key to waste generating in machinery manufacturing. If the supply and demand can be effectively communicated and balanced between the upstream and downstream manufacturers, for example, to match the size of the machinery required by the downstream manufacturer directly with the raw material needed for the upstream supplier, it will not only save the whole supply chain cost, but also reduce the unnecessary loss in the discrete processing process.

(3) Building scaled and collaborative industrial parks

Transfers within and across plants due to complex manufacturing process, are the source of packaging, protection and marking waste. As a result, scaling up and collaborating across industries is particularly important for waste reduction. Waste generation per unit of Gross Domestic Product (GDP) can be reduced by building scaled or collaborative industrial parks. This will be further discussed in Sect. 8.7 of this chapter.

In fact, as a traditional industry with a long history, there has been active exploration of waste diversion for a long time.

Machinery and equipment, especially the large ones, are usually quite expensive and are depreciated as fixed assets in an enterprise's financial statements. At the end of the depreciation, regardless of the service life, the equipment can be scrapped financially. However, it is likely that the equipment itself is not completely damaged. To scrap it simply due to the wear and tear of the parts, or customer demand upgrade, is quite a pity. Therefore, the repairing of "obsolete" machinery and equipment (including hardware and software upgrades) becomes the preferred option.

The recycling system for machinery and equipment was also established early and is relatively well developed in the major industrial countries. After complete scrapping of large machinery and equipment, the vast majority of the metal material can be well recovered and re-smelted into new metal raw materials. This will not be detailed here.

In addition, remanufacturing, which has enjoyed fast development in recent years, in fact, also started in the machinery industry. When end-of-life machinery and equipment could not be repaired or upgraded, and not to the extent of being made into iron, the idea of remanufacturing naturally emerged. As mentioned earlier in Chap. 6, remanufacturing was initially an industry that implemented high-technology repairing and modification of discarded products. High-technology repairing and modification is different from repairing and upgrade using the original process. Key components in large machinery and equipment can be restored to their original function by different methods, thanks to the emerging process technology. Typical examples are the surfaces of precision bearings, which were initially cut and polished by precision machines to achieve the required flatness, but can now be repaired repeatedly with ion-plating overlays to achieve the same effect.

Of course, the use of discarded machinery and equipment, through the disassembly and combination of its original parts, with other necessary parts and components to create a new mechanical product, has now been seen a lot in the developed industrial countries. In fact, this idea may have first appeared in the former Soviet Union. It's said that after World War II, people removed the turrets and armor from many scrapped tanks, and added necessary auxiliary mechanical structures to turn the tanks into sturdy and reliable tractors. Those tractors from then diligently served the agricultural farming of Siberia for quite some years!

8.3 Automotive Industry

Automobile manufacturing plays a pillar role in the economy of developed industrial countries: it accounts for a large proportion of output value and sales revenue; the development of automobile manufacturing inevitably promotes the development of many related industrial sectors; and it is a highly technology-intensive industry, concentrating new materials, equipment, processes and technologies in many scientific fields.

A broad sense of automobile industry includes not only manufacturing, but also sales, maintenance and finance of automobiles, etc. But our discussion of zero waste here will only focus on automobile manufacturing. Therefore, we will discuss how to reduce waste and the various ways to recycle waste by looking at the process of automobile manufacturing—mainly the four major workshops of the automobile production line.

8.3.1 Source of Generation

There are four well-known workshops in an automobile manufacturing plant, whether it's traditional or new energy car manufacturing: stamping workshop, where various metal plate and parts of automobiles are produced as required; welding workshop, where the sheet metal parts are welded together to form the body-in-white as required; painting workshop, where the body-in-white is treated with surface electrophoresis and top coating to prevent rust and corrosion; final assembly workshop, where the assembly of all parts and components of the whole car is completed and offline test finished so that the vehicle is ready for sale. Obviously, these four workshops will produce various kinds of waste; and based on the scale of production lines of today's automobile manufacturers in order to reduce unit costs, the total amount of waste produced by each of the four workshops is also extremely huge.

(1) Stamping workshop

In the stamping workshop, there are various large machining equipment such as cranes, openers, spreaders, rollers, benders, shears, hydraulic machines, punch presses, etc., in which the operation of shears and punch presses is the main source of waste in the workshop.

The steel sheets (mainly coiled steel or aluminum alloy sheets of different sizes) purchased from steel manufacturers for automobiles are generally fixed in size due to the limitations of the forging equipment in steel plants. So, they have to be cut and trimmed according to the size of the specific car model when they arrive at the automobile manufacturing plant (some small and medium-sized automobile manufacturing plants also outsource this process), and the sheet metal trimmed off becomes a large part of the workshop's waste.

At the same time, the steel sheets required for different models will have windows, holes and slots in the necessary parts for the installation of various components—which in turn requires stamping processes. The metal blocks produced by the press are also not re-usable in the automobile manufacturing process and become metal waste together with trimmed off materials.

Of course, as in other machinery plants, the various dies and molds in the press shop that are regularly scrapped for model changes and cannot be reused are themselves part of the metal wastes. In addition, there are various waste lubricant oils and cutting oils (fluids) in the workshop—according to the corresponding laws and regulations, they are generally considered as hazardous wastes.

(2) Welding workshop

The main equipment in the welding workshop includes a traveling crane, sewing machine, cutting machine, arc welder, CO_2 shield welder, pipe bender, skin tensioner, resistance welder, plasma cutter, and adjustable fitting platform. In addition to saws and cutters, which continue to generate a small percentage of metal waste similar to that of a stamping workshop, a large number of welding and assembly operations (mainly arc and spot welders, excluding laser welding) generate welding slag spatter—particles of metal oxide; also, the use of anti-spatter fluids and sealants in welding workshops will leave containers with residual liquid, which become a large part of the solid hazardous waste.

The production line generates a certain amount of metal fume, mainly composed of iron oxide, manganese oxide, silicon dioxide, silicates, etc. This part of the fume and dust is collected by electrostatic dust removal or filter dust removal equipment, and the fine metal oxide particles (smaller than welding slag) are also part of the waste from the welding workshop.

(3) Painting workshop

The painting workshop normally has transplanting cranes, pure water preparation system, electrophoresis system, high temperature drying room, stabilized gas storage tank, paint spraying room, low temperature drying room, sanding room, lifting platform, hydraulic lifting rail, ground conveyor chain, translating car, paint mixing system, automatic spraying machine, air conditioning system, CO_2 firefighting system, sewage treatment system, venting system, etc. Unlike stamping and welding, which are mechanical and physical processes, the painting workshop introduces a large number of chemical and electrochemical processes, so that the types of waste are also very different from those of the stamping and welding workshops.

Metal parts of automobiles must be cleaned effectively before painting. A typical cleaning process will leave residual surfactants in the waste water after degreasing as COD and get discharged from the workshop. Residual zinc, manganese, iron, nickel and phosphate after the phosphating process will also flow into the waste water. Similarly, pure water cleaning after painting will bring residual electrophoretic paint into the waste water… The painting workshop produces a large amount of waste water with high COD and even metal ions, and the treatment of such waste water converts these pollutants into physical and biochemical sludge—a major source of solid waste in the painting workshop.

Of course, before the waste water in painting workshop leaves, one more process is needed to remove the larger paint sludge from the water, in order to reduce the pressure on the water treatment facilities. If wet Venturi water adsorption is used, the paint residue scraped from the water curtain and filtered from the recirculating water becomes solid hazardous waste after filtering through a filter press; if dry lime powder adsorption is used, the paint residue adsorbed by quicklime (powder), forming a mixture of calcium oxide and (paint body) resin although containing traces of metal components (from paint color additives), is generally recognized as ordinary waste.

Additionally, due to the use of various solvents, electrophoresis drying, gluing PVC spraying, medium coating spraying line, medium coating drying, top coating spraying line, top coating drying, plastic parts spraying line, plastic parts drying, etc. will all generate VOCs. In order to ensure the health of workers without polluting the atmosphere, various exhaust devices in the painting workshop are usually equipped with VOCs treatment facilities. Depending on the volume of off-gas from the painting shop, the common VOCs treatment process, such as zeolite rotor and RTO (Regenerative Thermal Oxidizer), can achieve a VOCs treatment efficiency of over 90%

or even 99%. But after a certain number of years of use, the scrapped zeolite can become hazardous waste.

Besides waste produced in above mentioned processes, there are actually a large number of waste paint and glue drums in the painting workshop. Most of these drums cannot be recycled, and they become hazardous waste. The amount of waste paint and glue drums is proportional to the daily production of new cars, the more the new cars, the more the waste drums.

(4) Final assembly workshop

The main equipment involved in the final assembly workshop is basically related to the assembly of various parts, such as cranes, manual rolling machines, profile cutting machines, electric saws, electric planes, CO_2 protection welding machines, plate conveyor chains, turntables, electric feeders, manual forklifts, pipeline seal testing machines, vehicle inspection lines, synchronous lifters, etc.

The final assembly workshop, theoretically, will not generate a lot of waste. But as the supply chain in the automobile industry is highly developed and differentiated, a large number of packaged parts from other factories and protected parts from other workshops will be delivered here. A variety of packaging materials will be in the final assembly workshop (or the warehouse), those not able to be reused by the supplier will be treated as packaging waste.

In addition, there are still some processes in the final assembly workshop (such as glass lamination) that require the application of glue. So, the glue drums will be the hazardous waste in final assembly workshop.

8.3.2 Zero Waste Opportunities

As from the previous description, even without considering the sale, repair and finance of cars, or the automotive chain, just the four main workshops of an automobile manufacturing plant generate a large amount of waste every day—industry data shows that for every car produced, there will be approximately 1 ton of waste water, 200 kg of solid waste, 20 kg of hazardous waste and 0.5 kg VOCs emissions. Of course, the more waste generated, the greater the opportunities for elimination, reduction, reuse and recycling, and thus the greater the drive for zero waste and the benefits.

(1) Stamping workshop

Metal scraps from cutting, shearing and stamping are materially equivalent to the sheet metal for automobiles, if not contaminated by machine oils or chip oils (fluids) in the workshop. They can be sent directly back to the steel manufacturer's plant for re-smelting into new products of the same material. In the blast furnace of a steel mill, the temperature of the melt zone is about 1,350~2,000 °C (the theoretical value of the flame temperature of the combustion zone can be more than 2,000 °C), which is already much higher than the incineration control temperature for general hazardous waste (more than 1,100 °C), and also higher than the incineration control temperature for PCBs hazardous waste (not less than 1,200 °C). It means the small amount of oils and fluids carried by the metal trimmings can be completely oxidized and rendered harmless in the iron-making blast furnace.

Of course, as with all other wastes, total reliance on smelting and recycling is not the preferred option. How to reduce the difference between the size of the sheet and the design of the car body, and how to use the trimmings from cutting, shearing and stamping for the manufacture of small metal parts, are the priorities to be considered by the stamping workshop, together with car design department and the raw material procurement department.

As for the various molds that have to be scrapped periodically and cannot be reused, it is also necessary to avoid and delay the generation of such metal waste from the perspective of optimizing the structural design of the car body, sharing the manufacturing platform of the model and extending the market life of the car. For lubricant oils and cutting oils (fluids), which are indispensable for the operation of various machinery and equipment, good quality and long-life brands can be used to reduce their usage as much as possible, as long as costs permit; some bio-based lubricant oils and chip oils (fluids) can also be considered—they are usually biodegradable, non-(low) toxic and renewable.

(2) Welding workshop

In the welding workshop, both the relatively large particles of metal oxides in the weld slag spatter and the relatively small particles of metal oxides collected from the fume by electrostatic de-dusting or filter de-dusting can be sent to the blast furnace of the steel manufacturer's plant to be reduced to metal.

Waste drums containing residual spatter and residual sealant can generally only be disposed of as hazardous waste to a qualified processor. To make it zero waste, on the one hand, larger barrel packaging is needed wherever possible. For example, there are both 25 kg/drum and 200 kg/drum packaging of welding anti-spatter agent in the market, and for the same amount of anti-spatter agent consumption, the total weight of the waste drums is less by choosing the latter packaging. Or, automobile manufacturers can cooperate with raw material suppliers to return the waste drums to the raw material suppliers for refilling. Furthermore, there are also many professional cleaners of drums in the market, to thoroughly clean whatever number of drums or whatever kinds of drums automatically in the assembly line—the vast majority of which can be directly reused, and those that are broken can be recycled as plastic or metal. They are no longer hazardous waste.

(3) Painting workshop

Sludge generated from waste water treatment systems in paint workshop, whether for reduction, thickening, stabilization, or resource recovery, is essentially similar to municipal sludge treatment and disposal technologies, see Chap. 7, Sect. 7, and will not be detailed here.

As for the reduction of paint residue, it also needs to be addressed by upgrading the painting process, for example, by maximizing the paint adhesion rate of the various painting processes so that the paint is on the surface of the material rather than wasted in the water—process improvement projects that reduce paint waste can have a significant return on investment.

The total amount of waste such as zeolite generated due to the VOCs treatment process is not large and will be further reduced or even eliminated with the continuous innovation of the VOCs treatment process. But for the large amount of waste paint drums and waste glue drums in the painting workshop, its zero waste outlet is basically the same as that of waste liquid drums and waste glue drums in the welding workshop, namely, overall reduction, direct reuse, and reuse or recycling after cleaned harmless.

(4) Final assembly workshop

Since the waste generated by the final assembly workshop is mainly a variety of packaging materials, how to reduce packaging waste will be key to achieve zero waste for final assembly workshop, or to be more precise, the entire automobile manufacturing industry. In fact, the reduction of packaging waste is a big topic, not only in the automobile industry, but also in the consumer electronics and retail industries which will be discussed later.

The treatment and disposal technology of packaging waste varies based on the type of packaging materials. Packaging plastics mainly go to recycling granulation, packaging paper mainly to recycling paper, packaging metal to recycling smelting, and packaging glass (mainly glass containers) to recycling glass… What's relatively more difficult is the composite packaging materials. Its function usually requires it to be made of two or more different materials, and the inability to separate the materials makes it unable to be recycled, and only suitable for incineration.

In fact, all industries involved in packaging must consider the following three points in order to achieve packaging zero waste: homogeneity, versatility and durability.

① Homogeneity: the packaging waste can be well recycled only when it is made of single material. Regardless of what composite materials are used, or if the packaging material becomes contaminated during the packaging function and is difficult to clean, the high cost of separating or cleaning out a single material will drive companies away from recycling packaging waste.
② Versatility: no matter how many types of packaging needed, if they are all of the same material, such as all polypropylene film or all corrugated paper, no matter what shape they are in, they can be collected and recycled to plastic or paper factories. The comprehensive disposal cost of packaging waste will be greatly reduced in this way.
③ Durability: the more durable industrial products and consumer goods, the longer the life cycle, the smaller the total amount of waste generated within a certain period of time. By the same token, if the packaging material is robust and durable, then the need for secondary packaging and over-packaging will be greatly reduced. And robust and durable packaging materials can even be reused directly after unpacking in the same way. Although the basic cost of robust and durable packaging materials is higher than simple disposable packaging

materials, in the long run, for enterprise using a large amount of such packaging, the comprehensive cost may be lower, taking into account the increasing cost of waste treatment and disposal.

8.4 Consumer Electronic Industry

The consumer electronic industry is the most emerging, the most high-end, and the most complex of all industries. It's mainly because the products involved in this industry, or consumer electronics—although late in their emergence—are a comprehensive expression of the highest human intelligence.

Consumer electronics are electronic products for everyday consumer use. However, it has different definitions in different countries and regions which are at different levels of development. It also means different scopes at different development stages even in the same country and region.

Initially, consumer electronics were audio and video products for personal and household use: television sets, video players (VCD, SVCD, DVD), VCRs, camcorders, radios, record players, combination stereos, jukeboxes, laser jukeboxes (CDs), etc.; in some developed countries, telephones, personal computers, small printers, electronic health care devices, car electronics, etc. are also classified as consumer electronics. With the development of technology and the emergence of new products and applications, digital cameras, mobile phones, handheld computers (PDA) and other products have also become emerging consumer electronics. After entering the twenty-first century, the leap of electronics and information technology, through miniaturization and intelligence, has made more electronic products from industrial and commercial products into personal consumer goods. At the same time, the functions of traditional electronic products are highly integrated and portable, and many products tend to be owned by everyone (such as smart phones), even suitable for wear and implant (in human body).

8.4.1 Industry Characteristics

The myriad of consumer electronics products and the constant quest for new products by consumers has pushed the industry to considerable prominence. At the same time, the waste from the consumer electronics industry is far more extensive and complex than the e-waste described in Chap. 7. It has the following reasons.

(1) Wide range of spare parts

While ordinary electronic and electrical products have a large number of components, consumer electronics products are not only diverse but also highly integrated for purposes such as miniaturization and portability. The smaller and more complex the electronic components are, the more difficult it is to separate and sort the waste generated at the end of the electronic components life (in fact a mixture of various metals, non-metals and semiconductor materials). The electronic components will turn into a huge quantity of e-waste that occupy great volume (see Chap. 7, Sect. 3).

(2) Complex supply chain

The division of labor in today's world is so fine that even in the same industry, the components of the final product are provided separately and by individual suppliers stepwise; numerous components of consumer electronics are assembled by a huge supply chain (which itself covers many industries) level by level, and finally tested and packaged at the brand's own plant or its subcontracting plant. Then, through specific logistics systems, they reach consumers through warehousing and retail—a huge and intertwined supply chain that generates different amounts, sizes and materials of waste in each transfer, assembly and packaging procedure (including protective packaging in the middle of production and commercial packaging in the final sale). The sorting and treatment of this waste at each plant is itself a major challenge.

(3) Globalization of materials

The manufacture of consumer electronics requires many kinds of special raw materials, some of which are rare and precious metals with very limited global origins and production capacity. The mining and processing of raw materials and logistics is globalized, and the waste generated in these processes are equally globalized and exoticized, and therefore manufacturers must comply with the controls and restrictions of the corresponding international laws and conventions, which further increases the overall difficulty of waste treatment and disposal.

(4) Labor-intensity

Although the manufacturing of electronic components, especially microelectronic components, is highly automated, their final assembly and testing, as well as part of the packaging process, is very dependent on human manual labor. So, the consumer electronics industry in general is still a labor-intensive industry. Many consumer electronics production plants or original equipment manufacturer (OEM) plants could have tens or even hundreds of thousands front-line workers. Such a huge base of workers makes the plant's domestic waste, including kitchen waste in huge quantities. And many plants will have staff dormitory in order to organize production and management of workers better. The amount of comprehensive waste generation, therefore, is comparable to that of a small city. The difficulty to treat and dispose of waste in this kind of large plants is also comparable to that of municipal waste.

8.4.2 Sources and Streams

If we omit the commercial aspects of raw mining, materials manufacturing, and product logistics and sales at the top end of the consumer electronics industry supply chain, and examine only the parts production and final assembly and packaging, we can roughly summarize the waste types, sources, and general streams of the consumer electronics industry, as shown in Table. 8.1.

8.4.3 Stream Analysis

After observing the sources and types of common wastes in the consumer electronics industry and carefully examining the general streams of these wastes, we can summarize the basic status of waste in the consumer electronics industry in comparison with the various waste diversion methods in Chap. 6, which can be broadly classified as follows.

8.4.3.1 Internal Reuse

Many small and fine parts used in consumer electronic products need to be stored or transferred among different warehouses, production lines and workshops using a large number of pallets and turnover boxes, which in general are of plastic. Instead of using cheap, disposable, or easily damaged plastic pallets and boxes, it is better to use relatively robust and durable pallets and turnover boxes made of plastic or even metal, so that they can be used repeatedly for a relatively long time. It's inevitable that they will wear and tear, or have to be scrapped due to product modification, but it's still better than generating a large amount of plastic waste every day.

8.4.3.2 External Reuse

The upstream and downstream suppliers in the consumer electronics industry also use a lot of transfer equipment, large ones include boxes and pallets, while small ones are like turnover boxes and trays in plants. This transfer equipment is usually disposable, and the supplier will not take them back after giving them to the customer (the cost is included in the total price of the goods), and the downstream plant will dispose of this transfer equipment as waste after taking out the parts. If relatively robust and durable equipment can be used, and if the necessary cleaning processes are added so that the transfer equipment can be used repeatedly between upstream and downstream plants, not only will this waste be reduced, but some of the costs should also be reduced.

8.4.3.3 Material Recovery

The larger plants in the consumer electronics industry generally have a material recovery department, one of whose main tasks is to collect recyclable materials and

Table 8.1 Consumer electronics industry production and assembly waste at a glance

Waste	Types	Sources	General streams
Raw material	Metal edges	Metal cutting	Metal recycling
	Metal scraps	Metal grinding	Metal recycling
	Plastic scraps	Plastic forming head	Plastic recycling
	Defective raw materials	Unqualified raw materials	Raw material supplier processing
	Defective parts	Unqualified parts	Repairing or dismantling
	...	...	...
Production accessories	Plastic pallet/turnover box	In plant or inter plant material transfer	Plastic recycling
	Plastic bottle/barrel	Storage of liquid raw materials	Plastic recycling
	Packing foam	Packaging protection	Foam recycling
	Paper bag/carton	Packaging of raw materials and finished products	Paper recycling
	Wooden pallet	Forklift transfer	Incineration
	Scrap mold	Stamping and casting	Metal recycling
	Office furniture	Office upgrading	Dismantling and recycling
	Document paper	Office paper	Paper recycling
	Construction waste	New construction and reconstruction of plant	Landfill
	Ordinary sludge	Pool and pipeline sediment	Landfill or brick making
	...	...	...
Hazardous waste	Waste oil and waste fluid	Lubrication, cutting, cleaning, etc	Refining or incineration
	Waste activated carbon	Filtration adsorption	Regeneration or incineration
	Waste oil tank	Fuel oil	Cleaning and reuse
	Waste filter element	Filtration of waste water and off-gas	Regeneration or incineration
	Waste lamp	Factory lighting	Crushing landfill
	Waste battery	All kinds of electrical equipment and instruments	Dismantling and recycling
	Waste paint can	Painting	Metal recycling
	Waste solder can	Welding	Metal recycling

Table 8.1 (continued)

Waste	Types	Sources	General streams
Hazardous waste	Biochemical sludge	Water treatment facilities	Harmless landfill or incineration
	...	...	...
Domestic waste	Domestic garbage	Personal belongings	Incineration
	Household paper	Restroom	Incineration
	Glass bottles	Drinks	Glass recycling
	Plastic bottles	Drinks	Plastic recycling
	Cans	Drinks	Metal recycling
	Working clothes	Damage and season change	Incineration
	Melon rinds and fruit scraps	Personal snacks	Aerobic composting
	Vegetable leaves and fish bones	Canteen meal preparation	Aerobic composting or feeding pigs
	Waste grease	Canteen oil	Esterified soap or biodiesel
	Swill and slops	Leftover	Anaerobic digestion or feeding pigs
	...	...	...

send them to a qualified professional company for recycling. Recyclable, or valuable and worthy of recycling materials include metals (especially rare earth elements, precious metals and non-ferrous metals), plastics, paper, glass, etc.; in conjunction with this, the vicinity of these plants, or even inside the factory, there are usually material recovery companies to provide a "one-stop" service from sorting (in or out of the factory), packing, logistics to recycling and sales.

Certain mega-scale consumer electronics assembly plants have plastic recycling workshops or branches within their plants, which directly extrude, draw and granulate waste plastics from their plants to make recycled plastic materials. Some can even make recycled plastic products for sales.

8.4.3.4 Aerobic and Anaerobic

Kitchen waste like melon rinds, fruit scraps, vegetable leaves, fish bones, waste grease, swill and slops, is usually a problem for households or small restaurants, and can't be processed on a large scale due to the limited amount. But large assembly plant can take advantage of its scale to centralize the treatment.

Kitchen waste with the relatively low-water content, like melon rinds, fruit scraps, vegetable leaves and fish bones, etc., can be used for aerobic composting through the collaboration with nearby companies. These organic fertilizers, after a certain period of reaction and being identified qualified by in the relevant departments, can be applied to agricultural fertilization. For kitchen waste with relatively high-water content, like waste grease, swill and slops, the plant can work with kitchen waste treatment enterprises, to transport the waste for anaerobic digestion, generating biogas for power generation.

8.4.3.5 Biodiesel

In the aforementioned kitchen waste, if the amount of grease is relatively large and the oil-water separation is relatively well done, these waste oils can be processed into biodiesel through specific technique and mixed with ordinary diesel in different proportions, which can supplement the raw material sources of diesel locomotives and heavy machinery, and also reduce pollution emissions, as well as the risk for them to return to the table.

8.4.3.6 Livestock Feed

In areas where municipal support is relatively weak, all food waste can of course be fed to livestock—in most countries and regions mainly to pigs. However, all food waste must be steam-cooked before being fed to livestock, and the various meat residues must be sterilized and broken down into protein before being used as feed—for animal rights reasons, it would be highly inappropriate to let pigs eat pork directly without breaking it down.

8.4.3.7 Incineration for Power Generation

As with ordinary municipal waste, domestic waste from large plants can be sent to incineration for power generation after sorting and reducing as much as possible; to reduce logistics costs, small compactor stations can be set up inside the plant or living area to reduce the waste storage and transport volume.

8.4.3.8 Solidify and Landfill

The main types of waste generated by consumer electronics manufacturing plants that must be landfilled as a last resort are as follows:

(1) Construction waste

Same as municipal construction waste, construction waste from the plant may be landfilled at designated sites after obtaining the necessary landfill disposal permits, which also includes sea-fill (marine reclamation land).

(2) Ordinary sludge

Ordinary sludge without chemicals is mainly composed of silt. As it does not pose any pollution risk to the environment, it can be landfilled if local laws and regulations are met.

(3) Waste lamps

This type of waste cannot be recovered as metal, nor can it be simply landfilled due to the presence of a thin metal plating. Normally it is crushed (glass component) and cured with cement concrete and landfilled at a government-designated site.

(4) Biochemical sludge

Unlike sludge from municipal waste water treatment plants, biochemical sludge containing certain chemicals and microbial cells cannot be landfilled directly. It shall be dewatered and then stabilized at a government-designated site for landfill, if possible.

8.4.4 Zero Waste Practices

8.4.4.1 Consumer Electronics Industry's Advantages to Practice Zero Waste

As complex as the waste generated by the consumer electronics industry could be, the industry is still leading the way of zero waste practices in all industries. It has several inherent advantages despite all difficulties and challenges.

(1) Brand owner awareness

The consumer electronics nowadays tends to concentrate into a few major brands. And as consumer goods, those major brands attach great importance to building and maintaining their own brand image. At a time when zero waste is an advanced option for environmental management, brands are advocating zero waste to ensure compliance and to declare sustainability, killing two birds with one stone.

(2) Leading by values

As a typical representative of the high-tech industry in the world today, the consumer electronics industry as a whole is far ahead of other traditional industries in terms of values, and is even seeking to disrupt the traditional values. Whereas zero waste seems to be difficult to achieve in traditional industries, the consumer electronics industry is determined to succeed sooner rather than later.

(3) Top of the supply chain

Consumer electronics is a market with great potential as it's for consumers worldwide. It is also at the top of the supply chain and has a strong influence. So, the consumer electronics industry can pass on zero waste as a sustainability requirement to every level down the supply chain, right down to the primary raw material suppliers. In this way, just a few global brand companies can have a direct impact on thousands of manufacturing companies of all kinds and sizes.

(4) Profit margin guarantee

The vast majority of consumer electronics manufacturing companies have gained some brand premium in the rapid development of modern industrialization and information technology, and the overall high profit margins are an important guarantee that the consumer electronics industry can allocate sufficient budget to drive the entire supply chain toward zero waste.

8.4.4.2 Practical Experience of Consumer Electronics Industry

In fact, several of the world's leading consumer electronics brands, as well as the OEMs in the consumer electronics industry, have implemented their zero waste programs in a systematic manner and have gained some practical experience, which can be summarized as follows.

(1) Defining a strategic approach to zero waste in the enterprise

Although zero waste is not a compliance requirement and is a sustainable concept, enterprises need to be as careful to develop their own strategic approach to zero waste as they are to implement compliance requirements. They can either follow national waste management laws and regulations, or simply base on their own characteristics, to identify achievable goals, empowering an executing team to develop a plan that is feasible with a corresponding timetable.

(2) Prepare a certain project budget

A budget is required to support the project kick-off, roll-out, necessary hardware and software, as well as consultancy and certification, etc., even though potential revenue return is proven by some practices.

(3) Awareness-raising, training and mobilization in all areas

Similar to all sustainability projects, zero waste is not something that can be achieved spontaneously. Enterprises need to plan awareness-raising efforts, training activities and to supplement them with other possible means of mobilization. These are both for internal and external—after all, the implementation of zero waste projects requires the support of external suppliers from upstream and downstream and municipal services.

(4) Seeking technology support for waste diversion

Even the best ideas of an enterprise cannot be separated from processes and technologies, and the diversion of all waste directly or indirectly requires certain process methods and technical means. By seeking internal process modification or technological innovation, as well as external advanced treatment and disposal paths, eliminable waste returns to zero, and non-eliminable waste is diverted as much as possible after reduction.

(5) Introduction of project consulting and certification, as appropriate

The technology and experience of any one enterprise are in general not well-rounded. If budget allows, it is reasonable to bring in third-party consultants as needed, refer to their cross experience in different industries and different customer projects. Standard certification, at the same time, can be considered as a strategic approach to achieve an enterprise's zero waste goal, referring to mature zero waste international standards. See Chap. 13 for standard certification.

(6) Pilot in one location before rolling the experience out to all

It is indeed quite difficult to implement zero waste simultaneously in both the global division and the entire supply chain. A more feasible approach is to select one or a few plants as a pilot, rolling out the pilot experience globally or to whole supply chain after phased and regional achievement made. This is less risky, budget-controlled, and easy to report on the results of the phases and regions, thus gaining further support from all parties.

(7) Combined with the brand's marketing operations

Even the best projects cannot be separated from the necessary marketing operations. Since the consumer electronics industry leads the world in brand awareness and values, it is only natural to do some marketing campaigns based on objective facts. The marketing department or public relations department of an enterprise can publish the concept of zero waste, strategic objectives, milestones and regional results through various media channels, thus directly or indirectly enhancing the value of the brand and the social image of the enterprise, and also contributing to the visibility of the enterprise.

To sum up, consumer electronics industry is quite likely to continue to lead and drive zero waste theory and practice throughout industrial society for a relatively long period of time.

8.5 Retail Industry

An analysis of waste in the retail industry cannot be separated from the discussion of waste in the logistics sector that goes with it. In fact, the retail industry and the logistics industry themselves are inextricably linked. There are not many empirical approaches to achieving zero waste in the retail industry and the logistics industry behind it compared to other industries. It is also the most challenging.

8.5.1 Industry Characteristics

The retail industry refers to the sale of goods produced by industrial and agricultural producers directly to residents for domestic consumption or to social groups for public consumption. There are many different retail formats, each format means a different waste source. In order to find the opportunities for zero waste in the retail industry, it is necessary to analyze the characteristics of each business (format).

Based on the location, scale, target customers, merchandise structure, store facilities, operation methods and service functions, traditional retail formats can be broadly classified into eight types according to the history of their creation, including department stores, convenience stores, supermarkets, hypermarkets, warehouse membership stores, specialized stores, exclusive shops and shopping centers.

8.5.1.1 Traditional Retail Formats

(1) Department stores

It is a retail business in which different sale areas are set up in a large building for different categories of merchandise, through goods ordering, management and operations, to meet customers' needs for a diverse selection of products. Shanghai No.1 Department Store and Wing On Department Store in Shanghai, Yaohan and Takashimaya in Japan, Macy's in the United States and Galeries Lafayette in France are all representatives. This is the most familiar and mature type of retail operation. As there's a complete range of products, the packaging wastes are of various kinds, making it difficult to be sorted; the busy customer traffic brings about diverse and complex personal waste; and the focus on the shopping environment and product display leads to waste generated by upgrading of shelves and auxiliary facilities. But the good thing is that almost all large department stores care a lot about their brand and reputation, thus usually do not shun the social responsibilities such as zero waste.

(2) Convenience stores

It is a retail format that aims at the convenience of consumers. It mainly provides convenience goods and services for a small community, with prices generally higher than that of supermarkets. FamilyMart and 7-Eleven are commonly seen in Asia-Pacific region. The positioning of this business dictates that it does not generate much waste, either from back house storage or in-store consumption. Even customers will take the waste generated in the convenience store to the municipal bins or household bins outside the store.

(3) Supermarkets

It is a retail format that adopts the a la carte sales method to sell basic food, fresh food, side food and household goods, which are the daily necessities of customers. Hualian and Lianhua, as well as NGS, are typical supermarkets in China. These supermarkets have partially replaced the traditional "wet market" (complete replacement of wet markets in some countries and regions), and they generate a lot of kitchen waste (pre-meal kitchen waste) in their back-house work areas due to fresh food sales. Moreover, in order to achieve standardization and barcoding, various kinds of transportation package and secondary package are also a major source of paper waste.

(4) Hypermarkets

It is also a retail format that takes a la carte sales approach but sells practical goods for mass-market at one-stop. Carrefour and Auchan in France are typical representatives of hypermarkets. Compared with supermarkets, they have a much larger business area, and more importantly, they have a full range of goods. Hypermarkets are the combination of department stores and supermarkets, with even larger scale. It also means the waste of hypermarkets are the combination of waste from both department stores and supermarkets.

(5) Warehouse membership store

Both Walmart and Metro are membership-based warehouse stores, but still their approach is different in their memberships: the ones represented by Walmart are aimed directly at individual and household consumers, while Metro and its kind are similar to a three-tier wholesaler and are aimed at social groups, small and medium-sized merchants. Either way, the large warehouse style business sells the manufacturer's products directly to end consumers, together with factory or logistics packaging, therefore the average packaging waste per unit of goods generated is less (the absolute volume of waste is still huge due to the large amount of goods). And because the membership system could lock the customers, they often shop with their own durable bags to put those simple packaged or unpackaged goods, which indirectly reduces package waste.

(6) Specialized stores

This kind of retail business mainly deals with one major category of goods, and is equipped with professional sales staff and appropriate after-sales service to meet the needs of consumers for a wide selection of goods. Typical examples include Decathlon for sports, Gome for electronics, and B&Q for building materials and household products. These stores have a wide range of brands to choose from in a particular product category, so whatever waste is generated (depending on the product), the type of waste is relatively homogeneous.

(7) Exclusive shops

It is a retail format that specializes in or is licensed with a specific manufacturer's brand to adapt to consumer demand for brand selection. Such exclusive stores often appear in the form of a chain store, operating the same brand of goods, but with many categories, such as the world-famous luxury brand Hermès, which covers a range of horse harnesses, leather goods, perfumes, clothing, silk scarves, dining porcelain, watches, jewelry, etc. Similarly, children's favorite brand Disney has exclusive stores selling clothing, stationery, toys, books, audio and video products, etc. These stores are generally small in size and do not have much traffic (except for flagship stores in some areas), so the total amount of waste generated daily is not very large (especially in luxury stores), but the types of waste are relatively diverse.

(8) Shopping centers

It is a commercial combination of various types of businesses and service facilities that are developed, owned, managed and operated by a company in a planned manner. It differs from a department store in that the property, management and operation are independent of each other. Typical shopping centers are Shanghai Global Harbor and Grand Gateway 66, as well as Outlets, which originated in the United States. The waste generated in shopping centers is also of large amount and great variety, together with the domestic waste brought about by huge customer traffic. All the waste will be disposed by property through charging a flat fee to the operator and management.

8.5.1.2 Retail Format Without Physical Stores

On top of these traditional eight types of retail with physical stores, we have been exposed to four other types of retail without physical stores.

(1) Door-to-door marketing

Corporate sales people go directly door-to-door and sell door-to-door in this business format. The internationally renowned beauty and cosmetic brand Avon is an example of this sales approach.

(2) Telephone and television sales

This is a relatively new form of retail without physical stores. It is characterized by the use of telephone and television as communication tools to deliver information about products to customers, who order directly by telephone and the seller delivers to their homes. In Shanghai there is the well-known Oriental CJ (OCJ).

(3) Vending machine

Since the World War II, vending machines have been used extensively for a wide range of goods, such as cigarettes, confectionery, newspapers, beverages, cosmetics, etc. Similar to brick-and-mortar stores, some vending machines are operated directly by brand owners and automatically sell a variety of goods under the same brand, while others are operated by properties or logistics companies, for example, and automatically sell a variety of goods under different brands.

(4) Purchase service

Retailers directly serve specific users in large organizations such as schools, hospitals, and government agencies through logistics channels are of this kind. Often the retailer gives a price discount to these specific contracted "members".

The above four types of retailing approaches, because of no existence of physical stores, will only generate waste in the back-house storage and logistics. Their business model, to some extent, has already achieved zero waste. As for the waste generated by logistics, it is inevitable as that of the traditional business.

The development of the Internet and telecommunications has led to a new retail model in the twenty-first century—the online stores. Because it operates online via the Internet, it is also known as "online" retail (the previously mentioned retail formats were also known as "offline" retail because they did not require an Internet connection to operate). The convenience of shopping at online stores far exceeds that of any other retail format, whether it is browsing the product pages through the Internet on a PC in the early days, or accessing a store's application on a smartphone with mobile Internet communications.

Businesses that specialize in online retailing are called e-merchants and their online retail platforms are also known as e-commerce platforms. Some of the world's well-known e-merchants are Amazon and Alibaba. Although online stores themselves do not generate any direct waste, they ultimately rely, if not entirely, on traditional warehousing and logistics, especially logistics, for the retail operations. This is because theoretically perfect online shopping can deliver goods directly from the manufacturer's production line to the final consumer, thus eliminating the need for warehouses; however, any kind of logistics still requires packaging of goods, and the required packaging generates waste that is not only unavoidable, but sometimes even more so than in traditional retail formats.

In recent years, there is another retail format that cannot be left out, called "new retailing". Individuals and enterprises use the Internet as the basis, through the use of big data, artificial intelligence and other advanced technologies and the application of psychological knowledge, to upgrade and transform the production, circulation and sales process of goods. It reshapes the business structure and ecosystem, and deeply integrates online services, offline experiences and modern logistics.

What about waste in the "new retailing" business? In the future, e-commerce platforms will disappear, and the new retail will be created by combining online, offline and logistics—online is the cloud platform, offline is the sales store or manufacturer. The new logistics will eliminate the inventory and reduce the amount of stockpiling. As you can see, the inventory is basically eliminated, and the storage waste will no longer exist; while the offline sales stores are "resurrected" and will still produce all kinds of waste in the traditional retail business. Therefore, the integration of manufacturing and retailing by the "new retailing" is very beneficial to boost the convenience of consumption; however, the contribution to waste reduction is very limited.

8.5.2 Zero Waste Practices

8.5.2.1 Restrictions of Retail Industry to Practice Zero Waste

The retail industry is not very motivated by zero waste, even the most basic waste reduction, in the vast majority of companies today. The reasons for this can perhaps be summarized as follows.

(1) Limited influence

The retail sector, as the end of manufacturing, has little influence on upstream manufacturing, especially branded companies in bulk goods, and also has no binding influence on downstream individual consumers (the customer is God), making the implementation of any plan or program on zero waste more difficult.

(2) Not sufficient budget

Profit margins in the retail industry are generally low, and it is difficult for retailers to allocate a certain budget to implement projects that have little or no return on investment for the retail industry. Even retailers on the Fortune Global 500 list are unlikely to undertake zero waste initiatives in all their stores at the same time.

(3) High dependency

The various retail formats are essentially located in areas with high population concentrations, either in or around cities, which leads to their dependence on municipal services—the level of local municipal waste collection and recycling directly affects the level of treatment and disposal of local retail waste.

8.5.2.2 Examples of Zero Waste Practices

Nonetheless, several prominent companies with global scale, in their traditional retail stores, as well as in their logistics supply chains, have also made some active explorations. We list a few companies here as representatives to see how they are thinking and practicing.

(1) Apple retail stores

The first thing that must be mentioned is the retail store of Apple. As shown in Fig. 8.1. In Apple's 2019 Environmental Responsibility Report, it's said that Apple is committed to the ambitious goal of zero waste to landfill in their multiple corporate facilities, hundreds of retail stores, and several data centers around the world, in addition to continuing to advance their zero waste to landfill program at their supply chain facilities—and the Apple retail stores are an important part of this ambition—we can take a closer look at several aspects of the environmental responsibility report.

8.5 Retail Industry

Fig. 8.1 Apple retail store

① Better use of materials through repair: if the equipment can be repaired rather than just replaced, the materials in it can have better utilization. As we all know, no matter how reliable a product is, it will inevitably malfunction or break due to external reasons. Apple has over 5,000 Apple Stores and Apple Authorized Service Providers around the world that are committed to providing safe and quality repair services. It is especially worth mentioning that Apple has also introduced a battery replacement service for all Apple products and ensures that the replaced batteries are recycled in a responsible manner, while further increasing the life of its products and extending their lifecycle through battery replacement.

② Refurbishing for a new life: durable products can often be used for a certain amount of time by the first user and then circulated to a second or even third user—Apple's Apple Trade In program allows users in different countries and regions to trade in their devices online or in Apple stores at a discounted price. If these devices can be repaired or refurbished as necessary and professionally, they can continue to be used by their next owner, rather than being manufactured brand new to meet the needs of a different user, which effectively reduces material consumption and carbon emissions.

③ Cutting down on plastic: Apple has used as much as 48% less plastic in packaging for products sold in the U.S. in the past three years. Starting with the iPhone 7 and iPad Pro, Apple switched from plastic trays in its packaging to trays made entirely of molded fibers. This change enabled the use of fiber-based materials for product packaging in the manufacture of the iPhone XS, iPhone XR, iMac Pro, MacBook Air, iPad mini and iPad Pro. As of March 2019, all of Apple's retail stores have switched to 100% fiber-based shopping bags. These new bags even feature paper woven handles and contain 80% recycled fiber.

④ Use of recycled paper: Apple wants to use as much recycled paper as possible in its packaging. In fiscal year 2018, Apple used an average of as much as 58% recycled paper. If virgin paper does need to be used, Apple also requires suppliers to source wood fiber from responsibly managed forests or wood controlled by the Forest Stewardship Council (FSC). All of Apple's packaging suppliers have been sourcing paper responsibly for two consecutive years, and Apple conducts regular reviews to ensure that suppliers are doing so.

As a result, Apple is leveraging their retail stores to offer a variety of repair services for their products and as a window for refurbishment services, thus to avoid, reduce and delay sold products from becoming e-waste; at the same time, Apple increases packaging waste diversion by cutting the use of plastic packaging and using a lot of recycled paper.

(2) Starbucks

Starbucks, a well-known coffee chain store, is another great example, shown as in Fig. 8.2. Being the world's largest coffee chain, Starbucks has nearly 21,300 locations worldwide across North America, South America, Europe, the Middle East, and the Pacific. Let's take a look at how they've built and run what is probably the largest green retail business in the world.

① A greener storefront: Starbucks has opened more than 1,200 LEED®-certified stores in 20 countries, accounting for 20% of the world's LEED®-certified retail projects. The LEED®-certified retail store provisions address waste management during the construction and demolition of stores, in effect making zero waste a requirement from the building itself in the first place.

② Development of a more environment-friendly cup: Starbucks has made significant progress in developing greener cups and recognizes that there is still a long way to go. Starbucks was the first company to offer discounts to customers who bring their own reusable cups, pioneered the incorporation of 10% post-consumer fiber (PCF) into their hot beverage cups, and has been leading the industry in advocating for increased recycling infrastructure. Starbucks' goal for 2022 is to accelerate the process of achieving greener cups, with plans that include doubling the amount of recyclables in hot beverage cups and exploring alternative materials for cold beverage cups; will continue its commitment to recycling and work to double the number of stores and communities that use

8.5 Retail Industry

Fig. 8.2 Starbucks coffee shop

cups for recycling; will promote and encourage "in-store drinking" and reusable cups. All of these actions are aimed at reducing the amount of waste used for food and beverage packaging.

③ Breaking the barriers to resource recycling: store recycling is an important part of Starbucks' comprehensive recycling program, and in 2014, Starbucks added consumer-facing recycling to more than 760 stores, representing 47% of company-directed stores across the U.S. and Canada. The vast majority of Starbucks' turnover is now generated through their stores, but at the same time, they are constantly working to incorporate environmentally friendly design into Starbucks' own manufacturing and processing systems, including roasters, coffee machines and juicers. Especially noteworthy is that the Starbucks York, Pennsylvania Roaster Equipment and Dispatch Center was certified by Underwriters Laboratories for 100% waste diversion to landfill (UL ECVP 2799 Zero Waste to Landfill, see Chap. 13, Sect. 2) in 2014.

(3) IKEA

Another courageous company is IKEA, the world's largest furniture retailer. As shown in Fig. 8.3. IKEA has stores in several countries around the world and sells flat-packed furniture, accessories, bathroom and kitchen items, so on and so forth. IKEA's sustainability philosophy includes value first and waste to treasure, with a resulting focus on recycling.

IKEA has put in a lot of efforts finding ways to make more products with fewer resources. They rethink everything, including the materials used, and how their products' service life can be extended through a circular model of repairing, reuse and recycling. Throughout IKEA's value chain, they are committed to using resources as

Fig. 8.3 IKEA outlet

efficiently as possible, ensuring that their products created are of great value rather than being wasted, and aiming to achieve the goal of using renewable or recycled materials in all products by 2030. Specific practices include:

① Doing the right thing from the very beginning: at the design stage, IKEA starts planning for the recycling of its products to win. To make more with less, IKEA uses renewable and recycled materials from sustainable resources, making all products easy to care for, repair, reuse, repurpose and recycle.

② Giving the product a second chance: IKEA wants customers to take care of their products for as long as possible—and even if customers don't, IKEA itself strives to do so. In Belgium, for example, to get furniture recycled, customers are offered five options: selling old IKEA furniture in malls; transforming furniture by repainting or reassembling it; providing replacement parts for repairing; returning old furniture through a shipping service; and donating it to social organizations. Globally, IKEA also offers replacement parts to all customers. For example, in most IKEA stores there is a mattress recycling program, whereby customers can return their old mattresses when they buy a new one, etc.

③ Working towards zero operational waste: IKEA has decided to reduce the waste generated by all its operations, working with suppliers and partners to improve the entire supply chain to produce and distribute IKEA products in the most efficient way possible. This includes minimizing waste in the supply chain and converting waste from manufacturing into new products.

8.6 Grand Event

Grand events are difficult to attribute to any one specific industry because they may be entertainment shows or sporting events; they may occur in one fixed location or be held in different locations, or even spread across the globe; some may end in one day, while others may extend over days or even months… In some ways, a grand event is somewhat similar to a project (hence why it is sometimes called a large event project)—though this project may be cross-industry, cross-geographical and cross-time.

A single grand event or a series of grand events has a limited spatial and temporal scope, but it is also enough to generate a huge amount of waste, which is often not paid enough attention and rarely well planned for waste reduction. In fact, although grand events are not part of a particular industry, we can use the analysis of the operational characteristics of the event organization to identify opportunities for implementing zero waste at grand events.

8.6.1 Characteristics of Grand Events and Their Waste Management

To be precise, a grand event is a specific activity task within a certain time and space, and the task identification, content, scope, available resources and means to complete it are decided by the relevant organizations or enterprises according to the specific requirements of the development of the industry involved in the activity at a specific stage and in a specific field. Considering that the organization of grand events has a huge social impact, involves many sectors, spans a long period of time and has a large professional span, we will discuss about zero waste management from the following characteristics.

(1)   Complex jurisdictional relationships

Grand events could have many themes, involving various industries and fields and even under the same theme, it could contain various activities, also involving various industries and fields. Besides, given the great impact that grand events may have on the normal social, economic and cultural order of the place where they are held, local public security, industrial and commercial authorities should approve it first. And in the case of international and national scale grand events, national or federal government approve the project as well.

Among all the administrative approval processes, the involvement of the department responsible for managing municipal waste treatment and disposal should not be overlooked. This is because, unlike normal events, the municipal authorities arrange waste treatment and disposal according to the normal population and commercial and industrial activities in the area. Grand events, on the other hand, generate a large amount of waste in a relatively concentrated space and time, often exceeding the normal municipal treatment and disposal capacity. So, the purpose is to get relevant municipal department better prepared for the event in advance. If the expected amount of waste generated is still within the upper limit of the treatment and disposal capacity, there's no need to go through too much trouble to find more resources; but if it exceeds the limit, the event organizer should be required to prepare a plan and budget to get extra resources; if the waste amount far exceeds the capacity and is difficult to disposed of even after the event, with experts panel assessment, the managing department may object to the event, so as to avoid the irreversible impact on the local ecological environment caused by the waste produced by the grand event.

(2) Complex organizational relationships

All kinds of grand events, objectively, affect the overall socio-economic image of the hosting place to some extent, and subjectively, they need the governmental influence to enhance their attractiveness. Therefore, the organization of grand events are complex, with the involvement of the organizer and co-organizer of the event, as well as the contractors and sponsors. International and national grand events are generally hosted by national authorities or organizations, and local grand events are generally hosted by local government or government authorities. Relevant government departments or industry organizations are generally co-organizers of those grand events; companies and organizations usually take care of event planning and organization as contractors, and companies, organizations exhibitors and advertisers are generally listed as sponsors to provide funds, in-kind or labor sponsorship.

Each of these "parties" has the potential to "create" waste for the event, but also has the potential to "reduce" waste in their own area of responsibilities, thus contributing to waste reduction. The key is that the event organizers makes zero waste one of the goals of the event—just like the environmental management goals of enterprises. It is especially helpful that government departments and industry organizations put forward this goal and use the administrative power to guide the implementation. The co-organizers of the event should assess the waste generated by the event in advance, anticipating the type and quantity of waste—similar to the environmental assessment of construction projects—and cooperate with the relevant municipal departments to prepare the necessary human and material resources to deal with the waste. The organizers of the event must find and cut off the source of waste from all aspects of the event plan, and implement the scheduled waste reduction plan during the event, and eventually collect and transfer the unavoidable waste to a designated location for disposal, or recycle the resource waste as planned—like a company's environmental management department—to achieve further sustainability based on the event's waste treatment and disposal compliance. The event sponsor can prioritize the provision of funds, goods or services to reduce or even eliminate waste at the event as much as possible. This can have some of the desired commercial effect and also be part of the social responsibility for the sustainability of the event itself.

(3) Complex relationship coordination

Grand events involve many sectors, industries, enterprises and individuals in terms of project jurisdiction, organization, investment and revenue distribution, and therefore very complex relationships to be coordinated during event organization and implementation. In summary, there are two main types of the coordination: external coordination and internal coordination. External coordination includes administrative coordination with relevant government departments, industry coordination with relevant industry organizations, economic coordination with sponsors, suppliers and advertisers, social coordination with the host community, marketing coordination with the target market, etc. Internal coordination includes the coordination of rights and obligations between project organizers, co-organizers, contractors and sponsors, the coordination of management levels within the project organizing body (organizing committee), the coordination of functional and professional division of labor between specialized committees, the coordination of economic contracts with project subcontractors, the coordination of public relations with event participants (special guests, journalists), the coordination of commodity exchange with event participants (consumers), etc. The coordination of the exchange of goods with the participants (consumers), etc.

If these complex relationships are not handled properly, it may lead to a chaotic situation in which the waste generated by the events becomes the responsibility of none—the organizers, co-organizers, contractors and sponsors. Zero waste is even not to be mentioned. To avoid such a situation, the management of waste must be coordinated well in advance, preferably with a dedicated person in charge of coordinating various relationships.

Specifically, internal and external coordination should all be done appropriately. Externally, the organizer and the co-organizer should take the main responsibility for coordination. The organizer should document the goal of zero waste and communicate it to all parties and individuals involved in advance. And the co-organizer should use the assessment of the potential waste situation to clarify the responsibilities of the external units and personnel required to cooperate with the activity (a coordination working group could be established and regular coordination meetings held). Internally, the organizers should directly allocate the waste reduction or zero waste work to each team involved in the event, and even to each person (an inspection task force can be set up to carry out regular inspections); while the sponsors should first manage the waste generated by their own sponsorship, they should not increase the burden of the organizers by providing sponsorship.

8.6.2 Organizational Operations and Zero Waste

Unlike a relatively fixed corporate organizational structure, the organizational structure of a grand event is temporary in nature, and the temporary structure will automatically be dismissed once the project is completed. Therefore, it is important to have a clear and efficient organizational structure during the event in order to accomplish the goals set for the grand event in a relatively short period of time, such as zero waste.

Temporary organizational bodies are usually established in order to implement the event with importance and authority, on top of previously mentioned organizers, co-organizers, contractors, sponsors, etc. that objectively existed originally (which only come together for a specific event), such as organizing committees and specialized committees at various levels. How should the organizing and specialized committees function to achieve zero waste in an event?

(1) Organizing committee

Once a grand event has been established, the coordination of the organization and implementation of the plan is entrusted to a temporary organizing committee. The organizing committee of a grand event will consist mainly of representatives appointed by the organizers and the contractors, also with a small number of co-organizer and sponsor representatives participating. Its responsibilities related to zero waste may include the following considerations:

To incorporate zero waste into management objectives during the overall development of the organization and management of the event;

To propose specific plans for waste reduction in the events organization and implementation;

To ensure zero waste earmarked funds and budgets when developing and implementing fund raising and budget plan;

To promote the concept of zero waste for the event during the development and implementation of the event marketing plan;

To ensure zero waste measures are included in the themed activities and sub-themed activities development and implementation;

To educate vendors and exhibitors about zero waste requirement when planning and executing investment and exhibition;

To consider waste management during the development of events related business travels and tourism;

To consider the disposal of construction waste during event venue design, venue hiring (including construction) and fitting out;

To plan a dedicated position for waste management when developing and implementing the staffing (including volunteer) plans;

To consider the disposal of service (including kitchen) waste during the development and implementation of reception plans;

To consider logistic waste during the development and implementation of the transportation plan for people and materials;

To consider the disposal of medical waste in the development and implementation of safety and health plans.

(2) Specialized committees

Specialized committees are specialized functional bodies under the organizing committee of a grand event, responsible for developing and implementing the plans for a specific business operation. The number of specialized committees depends on the nature, size, time span and complexity of the organization of the grand event, but their main types of work and responsibilities can be summarized in the following typical examples, which should also incorporate zero waste into their main responsibilities.

① Marketing and communication committee: this committee, during the development and implementation of marketing and promotion plans, should take into consideration the reduction of all kinds of paper documents (pictures, posters, flyers, etc.) for the events, making the event schedule, programs, invitation and appreciation letters electronic, and promoting concept of zero waste when issuing news and announcements for the event.

② Engineering committee: when formulating and implementing venue design and construction plans, this committee should select and book event venues or arenas with adequate infrastructure to reduce waste generated by the erection of temporary structures, give priority to waste removal vehicles when organizing traffic and parking management, consider plans for the cleanup of instantaneous excess waste when formulating various emergency plans, and maintain timely and effective communication with government waste management departments.

③ Finance committee: when this committee is drafting and implementing the budget, it should set aside the necessary cost for waste treatment and disposal compliance management (such as the possibility of adding additional budgets for zero waste practices), monitor and control the expenditure of waste management-related costs, and confirm the reasonable apportionment of waste treatment and disposal costs for each participating unit.

④ Catering committee: when this committee develops and implements catering plans, it should ensure that no or little disposable tableware is used and that the estimated number of diners is accurate in order to reduce the amount of kitchen waste; consider the timing of kitchen waste removal and, if necessary, the placement of temporary kitchen waste reduction or compacting facilities and equipment for grand event sites of longer duration.

⑤ Reception committee: when the reception committee is formulating and implementing hospitality service plans, it should try to select designated restaurants and family reception sites to reduce temporary kitchen waste from al fresco dining, train volunteers on zero waste projects when recruiting them, reduce the use of disposable materials if there are ceremonies, and include the waste reduction results of participating units in the award program if there is an award ceremony.

⑥ Ticketing committee: when developing and implementing a ticket sales plan that uses e-tickets wherever possible and, promotes the zero waste concept and the zero waste initiatives of the event through the use of e-ticketing platforms (or paper tickets) in conjunction with ticket sales.

⑦ Stage and exhibition committee: when developing and executing stage shows and exhibitions, this committee, together with the engineering committee, choose to build and set up stages, stands, etc., with the least possible waste, making the exhibition content as electronic as possible.

⑧ Themes and decor committee: when developing and implementing thematic design solutions for grand events, this committee should simplify the decor of the main arena and subareas as much as possible in order to reduce all kinds of decoration waste, while considering the reuse and recycling of decoration materials.
⑨ Transportation committee: when developing and organizing transport plans, this committee should prioritize the pathways for waste removal vehicles, with particular attention to the removal of food waste (since overnight storage has a significant environmental impact).

8.6.3 Zero Waste Requirements at Different Stages

The operation of a grand event can also be divided into four stages: initiation, planning, implementation and closing. If we do a solid job of waste management in these four stages, we can have a chance to achieve zero waste.

In the initiation phase of the project, the sustainability objectives of the project can be taken into account, whether it's the direct requirement of the client or indirect needs based on market analysis. Zero waste can be the most intuitive goal. After the whole project idea has been presented, certain research and studies are carried out, which also allow for a feasibility analysis of the implementation of zero waste. At this stage, the waste situation of similar projects is analyzed, the necessary data is collected, and the possible financial investment is projected and then justified in relation to the characteristics of the project.

After the feasibility study, a project plan is developed, which must then include a description of zero waste; the subsequent application (government or corporate) for a project will include the project budget, which must have zero waste funds earmarked. Once approved, the specific planning of the project is undertaken. The planning of a grand event project needs to clearly introduce the zero waste goals and programs, especially how many human resources and how much money are needed to achieve what result.

The implementation of the event is to turn the plan into reality step by step, including the idea of zero waste. There are two very important things to note here. First, the implementation of zero waste must be carried out with determination, with guidelines established and measures in place. And the implementation of the plan cannot be changed due to any human factors. The second is that the actual results of zero waste can be appropriately flexible, and that it is acceptable for guidelines and measures to fall short of the expected results due to changes in objective circumstances, even though all measures are taken 100% (reasons to be analyzed separately, of course).

The closing phase of a project is very important. For zero waste, there should be a summary of data and experience. The summary of data can show how far the zero waste project has been completed, so that it can be compared horizontally and vertically for improvement in the future; the summary of experience can review the initiation, planning and implementation to identify opportunities for future improvement.

8.6.4 Zero Waste Case Studies

8.6.4.1 2010 Shanghai World Exposition

The 2010 Shanghai World Exposition (Expo 2010 Shanghai) is second to none in terms of the length of time and number of participants in grand events. This is shown in Fig. 8.4. Many practices of zero waste are also worthy of reference for all other grand events.

In fact, during the Expo 2010 Shanghai, "how to deal with the many visitors' domestic waste" and "how to maximize the recycling of waste" have drawn much attention. It is expected that there will be about 70 million visitors to the Expo, with an average of 400,000 people entering the site every day. Assuming that each visitor brings a bottle of water, 70 million plastic bottles will be used, and the waste during the Expo is far more than just 70 million mineral water bottles! In fact, the generation of domestic waste amounts to 160 tons/day, and the generation of kitchen waste is about 30 tons/day. Among them, general domestic wastes are mainly plastics, metals, paper containers for drinks and food, and all kinds of advertising and promotional brochures, accounting for about 40% to 50% of the total, with a high proportion of recyclable components.

Fig. 8.4 Expo 2010 Shanghai

The organizing committee of Expo 2010 Shanghai has carefully studied the domestic waste source control technology, the domestic waste treatment and disposal and resource recycling facilities through a team of experts, finally achieving the goal of waste reduction, waste resource utilization, waste harmless-rendering in the park, as well as the goal of recycling. Let's take a look at some of the praiseworthy practices.

(1) Waste collection system

The domestic waste in the Expo Park is collected according to three categories: recyclable, combustible and hazardous waste, and the collection methods are divided into pneumatic conveying system, mobile compressing station and small compressing station. The pneumatic conveying system is responsible for the collection and transfer of waste, and its service area is mainly "one axis and four pavilions", covering a total area of about 0.5 square kilometers, with a total length of 4,230 m of vacuum convey pipes and a daily capacity of 60 tons of domestic waste. Mobile compressing stations and small compressing stations are mainly used for temporary venues, like the Expo Village, urban practice areas and construction coordination area.

The compressing station is equipped with a sorting and recycling function, and the recoverable materials collected are simply sorted and compressed for preliminary processing at the station before being sorted and sent out to the corresponding professional recycling companies or other treatment and disposal plants.

(2) Waste disposal pathways and integrated resource utilization technologies

To reflect the concept of turning waste into treasure, Expo 2010 Shanghai transformed both organic and inorganic waste into building materials, such as road base materials, sidewalk bricks as well as blocks and wave-proof stones, thus realized waste minimization, waste harmlessness and waste valorization. Through the combination of forward-looking and mature technologies, the utilization rate of recycled solid waste materials has reached 100%.

Recyclables, such as plastic bottles, cans, etc., are transported from small compressing stations by special transport vehicles to transfer stations for sorting, and then the recyclable parts are shipped out to recycling companies, and the residue is transported to incineration plants; most domestic waste, such as plastics, paper, clothes and other such hard-to-degrade chemical fibers, are developed into wood-plastic materials and paper-plastic materials, which become ideal substitutes for wood; other waste is transported from pneumatic conveying systems or small compressing stations to transfer stations by special transport vehicles and then transported to incineration plants; hazardous waste is separately collected and transported by special vehicles from dumpsters to designated storage points in Huangpu District, Luwan District and Pudong New District, and enters the unified disposal system of Shanghai.

The large amount of "kitchen waste" generated in the park has become an important resource. Some of the kitchen waste is treated by the biochemical treatment machine in the park and then used as fertilizer in the park; other kitchen waste is collected and transported by special enclosed food and beverage waste collection vehicles, and then transported to the Shanghai Kitchen Waste Treatment Station, where most of the grease is separated out and transported to the edible grease waste disposal plant through qualified collection companies to be made into organic fertilizer and feed protein powder, or used as raw materials for soap and paint. The residuals are transported to other designated places for aerobic composting.

(3) Integrated technology and demonstration of finished products from waste recycling

In addition to some environmentally friendly high-tech building concepts, more importantly, these concepts are put into practice by various means, resulting in the emergence of a variety of high-tech waste recycling, environmentally friendly materials and green products. These technologies and products are not only vividly demonstrated through models in venues such as "Shanghai—Eco Home", but are also perfectly reflected in most of the venues, and the following are some examples of the successful cases.

Case demonstration 1: Fermentation of organic waste at the United States Pavilion

The biggest highlight of the U.S. Pavilion is the rooftop sky garden. Modeled after the rooftop terrace garden built by Obama at the White House, the pavilion has an urban vegetable garden on top with green roof technology that has an additional thermal cooling effect and slows the drainage discharge of rainwater. Rooftop sky gardens are a portrait of the future of urban living—urban living produces a lot of waste, and by putting organic waste on the roof, the heating system bakes the roof hot in winter, and this heat promotes the decomposition of the waste and produces good soil. Residents could use this soil to grow vegetables and fruits, creating an urban farm.

Case demonstration 2: "Low carbon wall" in the Expo Park

Many of the building materials used in most of the Expo pavilions themselves are reused waste and can be continuously reused after the show.

The gate tower of the Beijing Case Pavilion was made from the construction waste of the athletes' village of the 29th Olympic Games in Beijing mixed with the "chicken blood red" tailings from Mentougou, Beijing; while the construction waste such as waste decoration materials and concrete, mixed with "tiger skin yellow stone" tailings, are processed into "people's wall", "projection ball" and pool base in the exhibition hall. The "National Olympic Village" was transformed from the Beijing Olympic Athletes' Village, and continues the green concept of "extensive use of energy-saving construction materials and increased energy utilization".

The theme of the Japan Industry Pavilion is "Good Living from Japan", and the concept of "reuse" was used throughout the construction project: not only was the old Jiangnan Shipyard renovated, but also the new structure was built using construction scaffolding that could be reused after dismantling; the interior decoration uses recycled paper tubes, and even the uniforms of the staffs use fabrics made from recycled old clothes.

Vanke Enterprise Hall uses straw pressed board as the main building material, and the exhibition hall structure is designed by seven independent "urban stacks", which are connected by a blue light-transmitting ETFE film on top.

Demonstration 3: The "Green Way" in the Expo Park—Baosteel's new steel slag paved "green" Expo Avenue

In the entire Expo Park, more than 60% of the permeable, breathable pavement paved with steel slag permeable concrete floor tiles. This environmentally friendly floor tile has high flexural strength, good wear resistance and other overall stability and pressure advantages, long-term use without "falling grain"; it can maintain good permeability, breathable function, and is conducive to inhibit the "urban heat island effect". By replacing cement with this product, it can not only save natural resources but also reduce carbon emissions, and the price of the product is lower than that of concrete of the same grade, so this concrete floor tile is widely used in major ground projects such as the central square, A13 square and the Expo Garden.

The Expo 2010 Shanghai not only integrates advanced international domestic waste management concepts, models, technologies and facilities, but also carries out domestic waste sorting, collection, recycling to a high standard, directly applying the concept and method of resource conservation in the Expo Park, and achieving the maximum resource utilization of domestic waste. This not only fully reflects the perfect image of the Expo Park and promotes the improvement of Shanghai's overall environment, but also provides an important reference basis for the management, sorting and recycling and resource utilization of domestic waste in Shanghai and nationwide.

8.6.4.2 2020 Tokyo Olympic Games

The Olympic Games is also a grand event that attracts worldwide attention, with various environmental protection and zero waste concepts being practiced and applied by the host countries. And the 2020 Tokyo Olympic Games are the one that stands out, creating a new miracle of zero waste.

On the one-year countdown to the 2020 Tokyo Olympic Games, the Tokyo Organizing Committee revealed the medal designs. The front of the gold, silver and bronze medals all feature Nike, the goddess of victory from Greek mythology, with the Panathinaiko Stadium in Athens, where the first Olympic Games were held, in the background, while the back of the medals feature the Tokyo 2020 logo—this is an otherwise modest design but a total of 2,500 gold, silver and bronze medals were all made from precious metals extracted from discarded mobile phones (e-waste) recycling nationwide! The gold medal (over 6 g of pure silver plating) weighs 556 g, the silver medal (pure silver) weighs 550 g, and the bronze medal (95% copper + 5% zinc) weighs 450 g. Not only that, even the ribbons used to hang the medals are made of recycled polyester. This is shown in Fig. 8.5.

The Japanese government actually started a collection campaign for used mobile phone appliances in April 2017. By the time the collection stopped in March 2019,

Fig. 8.5 Medals for the 2020 Tokyo Olympic Games

the city of Tokyo had collected about 79,000 tons of used cell phones and other small electronic devices, including more than 6 million used cell phones, for the production of Olympic medals. A total of 32 kg of gold, 3,500 kg of silver, and 2,200 kg of copper and zinc were extracted from the items collected during the campaign.

Such a large-scale government-led recycling initiative has indeed made the medals at this year's Olympic Games full of the relentless pursuit and aspiration of zero waste—in keeping with the Olympic spirit of "Higher, Faster, Stronger"—and has made all the medals shine even brighter.

8.7 Property and City

When waste leaves its immediate source—factories, activities and people in various industries—there is sometimes a process of "assembly" before it is finally disposed of. Depending on the source of the waste, this "assembly" may cover one or several buildings that are connected, similar in layout, and similar in function—often called a unit property (commonly called a small property); or it may be a campus or a residential area—usually called a comprehensive property (commonly referred to as a large property). At the extreme end of the spectrum, a comprehensive property is the property of a city.

At the level of waste management, there are two possibilities. The majority of "unit properties" do not have waste treatment and disposal capabilities, so the so-called "assembly" process is the initial collection and simple sorting of waste. The majority of "integrated properties" have some waste treatment and disposal facilities of their own, and the so-called "assembly" includes the treatment and disposal of part of the waste (sometimes all of it) in addition to the sorting and collection.

In the extreme case of cities, it is difficult to imagine a city without a comprehensive waste treatment and disposal capacity and relying on the help of other sister cities (except for individual types of waste, such as nuclear waste). Obviously, this would have many limitations and inconveniences. In an even more extreme case of a country, if it does not have the capacity to treat one or more types of waste, the consequences would be dire—relying on other countries with the capacity to treat and dispose of waste would inevitably be constrained by their own environmental protection policies, and even by international laws and conventions.

We tend to discuss the different forms of properties separately according to where their opportunities for achieving zero waste lie.

8.7.1 Unit Property

Depending on the function, unit properties can be divided into the following five categories: residential properties, commercial properties, industrial properties, government properties and properties for other purposes. The management of unit properties with different functions has different contents and requirements; at the same time, zero waste of unit properties is also the basis of zero waste of comprehensive integrated or properties of a larger scale. It is not difficult to understand that once each unit achieves zero waste, the whole will not be far behind.

(1)   Residential properties

Residential properties are buildings with residential functions for people to live and reside in, including residential communities, single residential buildings, apartments, villas, resorts, etc., and also include the basic common facilities and public shared sites that go with them. For zero waste in residential properties, the most important thing is waste sorting—this is because the demand and supply of residential life is basically constant, i.e. waste reduction at source is difficult to implement. The only way to better cooperate with municipal recycling as well as treatment and disposal is to sort waste properly (the more precise the better).

(2)   Commercial properties

Commercial properties, sometimes referred to as investment properties, are those properties that can be operated for a sustained growth return or that can continue to appreciate in value, which can be broadly divided into shop properties and office properties. Shop property refers to a variety of buildings used for shopping and related services; office property is the space of staff engaged in production, operation, consulting, service, etc. For both shop and office properties, the focus of zero waste is on front-end reduction—reducing the flow of all non-essential materials into the property area, and temporary materials are also required to be removed and taken out by the relevant units after use, so as to maintain the purity of shop and office properties as far as possible. Theoretically, the purer the commercial property, the closer towards zero waste it could be.

(3) Industrial properties

Industrial properties are buildings that provide space for human production activities, including light and heavy industrial buildings, and recently developed high-tech industrial buildings, as well as related research and development buildings and warehouses. The zero waste opportunity of industrial properties is closely related to the industrial sector to which they belong. The strict distinguishing of manufacturing waste from property waste can effectively avoid cross contamination of waste and thus increase the difficulty and cost of treatment and disposal. At the same time, industrial properties should provide storage and logistics facilities for industrial waste treatment and disposal.

(4) Government properties

With the socialization of logistics management in government agencies, their logistics management departments are transformed into corresponding government properties. In addition to the services included in residential properties, government properties also involve a variety of integrated services such as catering, conference, guest rooms and sports. There is nothing special about the implementation of zero waste in government properties, but it has a great symbolic meaning—government properties should make use of their special status to find ways to cooperate with municipal waste treatment and disposal units, and sum up their experience to serve as a model and reference for other types of properties.

(5) Other properties

Sometimes referred to as special properties, they include properties such as racetracks, golf courses, automobile fuel stations, airports, stations, terminals, highways, bridges, and tunnels. While these properties vary in type and generate distinctive types of waste, sometimes it is easy to achieve zero waste instead, as properties can be tailored to reduce waste at the source while actively seeking recycling outlets for a single type of waste items.

8.7.2 Comprehensive Properties

Depending on the function, comprehensive properties can be divided into two types: economic parks and residential areas.

8.7.2.1 Economic Parks

An economic park is an area designated by the government for centralized and unified planning, and the area is dedicated to a specific type of economy, form of business, company, etc. for unified management. According to their functions, economic parks can be broadly classified into the following categories, which have their own similarities and differences in zero waste practices.

(1) Industrial park

Industrial parks are specific areas that are dominated by industrial manufacturing companies. However industrial parks are positioned differently and have a completely different approach to zero waste.

Traditional industrial parks are collections of manufacturing factories in the same industry, and the materials in and out of the whole park are the same, and the park can basically be regarded as a large-scale enlargement of a single factory. In such an industrial park, the waste treatment and disposal of each factory is parallel, and the park should, according to its scale, unify the formulation of waste management method, build a unified waste treatment facility, and contact external waste treatment and disposal units, etc.

Shanghai's Wujing Industrial Zone, established in 1958, is one of these parks, where large chemical companies, such as the Shanghai Chlor-Alkali General Chemical Co., Ltd., Shanghai Coking and Chemical Cooperation and Shanghai Wujing Chemical Co., Ltd., concentrate their production of chemical products such as coke, gas, sulfuric acid, ammonia, urea, caustic soda, quartz and graphite products. What is shipped in are various chemical raw materials, and what is shipped out are chemical products from each factory. Although there are some shared services in the industrial zone, in general the waste is still treated and disposed of separately.

But some modern industrial parks have some innovative practices, where the park is no longer a superposition of manufacturing factories in the same industry, but a cluster of upstream and downstream enterprises. The whole park may have only one or two factories shipping in materials, and most other factories are using the products of those factories as raw materials, further processing and manufacturing new products; or they use the scraps or even waste from the upstream factories, recycling and processing it into new products. The waste treatment and disposal of each factory in this kind of industrial park is crossed, and the park should introduce upstream and downstream enterprises that match with each other from the early park planning period according to its vertical characteristics, and reasonably plan the production capacity, so that the scraps and waste of these factories can be basically absorbed by the enterprises in the park. In the end, only products are exported from the park, and no waste leaves the park. Industrial parks can also build their own waste incineration power plants to achieve zero waste and at the same time make up for the energy gap of the park as far as possible until self-sufficiency.

As one of the largest industrial projects in China during the "Tenth Five-Year Plan" period, the development and construction of Shanghai Chemical Industry Park introduced the advanced concept of "integration" of world-class large-scale chemical parks. Through the integration of product projects, public utilities, logistics, environmental protection and management services in the park, it has achieved professional integration, investment concentration and benefit intensification. In particular, the integration of product projects—the formation of a complete product chain by upstream products such as naphtha and ethylene, midstream products such as isocyanate and polycarbonate, and downstream products such as fine chemicals and synthetic materials—not only makes all the products entering utilized as much as possible, but also reduces the packaging waste and logistic waste among enterprises and factories (pipes are built to transport materials among factories). The affiliated hazardous waste incineration plant makes the waste harmless (waste piped to the incineration facility), and at the same time, generates power and heating for the park.

(2) Agricultural park

An agricultural park (sometimes called an agro-industrial park) is a specific area where agricultural production is the main focus. It is a relatively large geographical area set aside for the priority development of modern agriculture in an agricultural area with certain advantages in terms of resources, industry and location—guided by the government, operated by enterprises, and built and managed with the concept of an industrial park.

The waste generated in agricultural parks—agricultural waste, also known as agricultural litter—includes, by its composition, two main categories of fibrous plant waste (such as straw, stubble, weeds, fallen leaves, fruit shells, vines, branches, etc.) and livestock manure (also human feces and urine). From a macro balance point of view, these two types of waste are the material and energy difference between resource inputs and outputs in the agricultural production and reproduction loop. Since agricultural parks are built and managed according to the concept of industrial parks, they can promote zero waste in three ways: biogas composting, earthworms farming and agro-processing, as opposed to ordinary rural waste treatment and disposal.

The livestock manure and pen bedding (the main component is agricultural straw), or directly chopped straw mixed with the right amount of human and animal manure and urine for high-temperature compost, after a short period of fermentation to kill a large number of pathogenic bacteria, parasitic eggs, plant pests and weed seeds, etc., are put into the digester for fermentation to generate biogas. This treatment method provides both biogas and high-quality organic fertilizer.

As earthworms are rich in protein and are high-quality feed for poultry and fish, and that earthworm manure is a comprehensive organic fertilizer, agricultural straw, livestock manure and livestock bedding can be used as earthworm feed to promote artificial earthworm farming. Agricultural parks with conditions can also accept municipal kitchen waste as auxiliary fertilizer for earthworms, which can increase production capacity and solve the problem of outlets for municipal kitchen waste.

Most of the waste from agro-processing can also be used in an integrated manner. For example, waste from meat processing can be used to produce leather products, soap, animal glue, biological agents, down, bone meal, etc.; some residues from agricultural fields and orchards are raw materials for the production of crepe paperboard, soft fiberboard and paper, which can be used to manufacture fiberboard and recycled paper, as well as to further utilize the lignin and cellulose in them to manufacture chemical products.

Nowadays, many suburban agricultural parks are developed as agricultural demonstration parks, whose relatively good ecology and environment are important spatial carriers for people's leisure in the countryside. If the zero waste concept can be brought into such demonstration parks and formed into a comprehensive agricultural park integrating production and processing, science popularizing, and environmental protection based on agricultural production, it will certainly have a great positive impact on the zero waste in nearby cities and the countryside in general.

(3) Technology park

Technology parks are areas where high-tech research and development enterprises are the main focus, including software parks, high-tech parks, etc. A technology park can be approximated as a collection of R&D centers of various enterprises, universities and research institutes, so the waste from a technology park is also approximated as scaled-up laboratory waste.

As discussed from the previous Chap. 7, Sect. 6, due to the diversity of functions and variability of processes, laboratory waste types are also diverse and variable. The size of each laboratory or R&D center is still small, compared to a manufacturing plant, to treat and dispose of waste on its own—the efficiency is low while cost is high, whether it is off-gas, waste water or solid waste. Therefore, the key to zero waste in a technology park lies in the provision of a comprehensive platform for waste treatment and disposal by the local government, to centralize the waste from each laboratory or R&D center for treatment and disposal. This will share and reduce the cost, and effectively allow research institutes to focus on their research instead of being troubled by various compliance matters.

Of course, as a technology park, it can play a technical pioneering role in waste treatment and disposal. In addition to more accurate waste sorting, we can consider experimenting with smart waste treatment and disposal. Management softwares for waste collection and transport can also be piloted there, and applied to a larger area or even to a municipal scale after achieving milestone results.

(4) Logistics park

Logistics parks are areas where various products are distributed, traded and transferred as one, including port parks, trading parks, etc. Since logistics parks have very distinctive characteristics, there are also many innate advantages and conveniences for their zero waste implementation.

A collection of multimodal means of transport exists in logistics parks. Multimodal transport means are multimodal transportation, such as combined sea, rail, road and air transport. Hence the function of logistics parks are as integrated hubs. Although there are different types of transport modes, the park's function is essentially "trans-shipment" thanks to the universalization of logistics packaging, so that it generates little waste of its own and is relatively homogeneous and easy to manage.

8.7 Property and City

Logistics parks exist in the integration of multi-state operation methods. The logistics organization and service function of logistics park is reflected in the comprehensive and intensive characteristics of multiple operation modes, including warehousing, distribution, cargo consolidation and distribution, containerization, packaging, processing, trading and display of commodities. It is because of the intensification of operation methods that the total amount of waste in the park has more possibilities to be better controlled in the front and back operations.

Logistics parks exist as an option for multi-perspective city needs. The logistics park and the city development show an interactive relationship. How the logistics park can assist the city to rationalize its functions and meet the city's needs is another functional characteristic of the logistics park. Logistics parks can act as waste transfer hubs for nearby cities (or industrial parks) and serve the goal of zero waste in their territories with their strong hub function.

(5) Cultural and creative park

Cultural and creative parks are not special in terms of waste generation, but they are promising in terms of zero waste. Many cultural and creative products are made into brand-new products precisely through the secondary design of various wastes—unlike ordinary recycling, cultural and creative products are designed with new processes, so that certain wastes not only get a new life and get the environmental value they deserve, but also are injected with certain artistic value, or even trend-setting creativity.

In some cultural and creative parks, waste woolen products are designed and transformed into fashionable luggage fabric, waste glass products into avant-garde home decor, and waste electronic products into beautiful street sculptures… Cultural and creative parks in various countries and regions are actually promoting zero waste to the society through the power of culture and art.

8.7.2.2 Residential Communities

Residential communities are generally defined as places where citizens live in greater concentrations in cities and are of a certain size (covering an area much larger than a single residential area). A residential community also requires appropriate supporting facilities, such as schools, hospitals, markets, etc. Zero waste in residential communities is different from industrial parks, mainly because of the differences in individual waste generators (including families), which are very difficult to manage uniformly. The sorting and disposal of domestic waste, which is the main waste in residential communities, is the key to achieving zero waste in residential communities—and this alone requires reliance on higher-level administrative means and adequate facilities to support it, as well as the quality of the population groups.

Combining the opportunities and challenges of zero waste in industrial parks and residential communities, we naturally move over to the next sub-section: zero waste cities.

8.7.3　Zero Waste Cities (Waste-Free Cities)

Zero waste city, also known as "waste-free city", is a city development model that takes the new development concept of innovation, coordination, green, openness and sharing as its guide, and minimizes the environmental impact of solid waste by promoting the formation of green development and lifestyle, continuously promoting the reduction of solid waste at source and resource utilization, and minimizing the amount of landfill, and an advanced urban management concept.

As an important carrier of human living space, cities suffer from waste, which has attracted much attention from countries all over the world, and the realization of waste-free cities has now become the goal of more and more countries and cities in the planning of new or old upgrades. In fact, in the last 20 years since the concept of waste-free cities emerged globally, the international community has accumulated some relevant experience during the process.

The first eight cities in the world, which have explicitly proposed to build waste-free cities, are Vancouver in Canada, San Francisco in the United States, Capannoli in Italy, Ljubljana in Slovenia, Masdar in the United Arab Emirates, Sydney in Australia, Auckland in New Zealand and Kamikatsu in Japan, and their achievements have been recognized by the international community. Although the paths and measures taken in the process of building waste-free cities vary greatly depending on resource endowments, political systems, management systems, cultural habits, etc., what is common is that all these cities have set long-term and quantified "waste-free" goals, following the order of waste elimination, reduction, reuse, recycling, energy recovery, and landfill. They have also been improving their waste management systems and introducing professional management into the city.

On September 13, 2018, at the Global Climate Action Summit in San Francisco, California, 23 cities and regions of the C40 Cities Group (an international consortium of cities dedicated to addressing climate change, including member cities from China, the United States, Canada, the United Kingdom, France, Germany, Japan, South Korea, Australia, etc.) issued a declaration to advance urban "Zero Waste". Participating cities pledged that by 2030, compared to 2015, to

① Reduce domestic waste generation per capita by at least 15 percent.
② Reduce at least 50 percent in the amount of domestic waste landfilled and incinerated.
③ Increase diversion of waste to landfill and incineration to at least 70 percent.

In January 2019, the General Office of the State Council issued a pilot program for the construction of "waste-free cities", proposing to coordinate the management of solid waste in economic and social development, vigorously promote source reduction, resource utilization and harmless disposal, resolutely curb illegal transfer and dumping, explore the establishment of a quantitative indicator system, and systematically summarize the experience of the pilot program. In April of the same year, the Ministry of Ecology and Environment announced 11 pilot "waste-free cities": Shenzhen, Guangdong Province; Baotou, Inner Mongolia Autonomous Region; Tongling,

8.7 Property and City

Anhui Province; Weihai, Shandong Province; Chongqing (main city); Shaoxing, Zhejiang Province; Sanya, Hainan Province; Xuchang, Henan Province; Xuzhou, Jiangsu Province; Panjin, Liaoning Province; Xining, Qinghai Province; meanwhile, Xiong'an New Area in Hebei Province, Beijing Economic and Technological Development Zone, Zhongxin Eco-city in Tianjin, Guangze County in Fujian Province and Ruijin City in Jiangxi Province are also promoted as special cases to pilot "waste-free city".

China's waste-free cities have clearly defined six key tasks. First, to strengthen top-level design and leadership, and play a macro-guidance role of the government. Second, to implement green industrial production, and promote zero growth in the total amount of industrial solid waste storage and disposal. Third, to promote green agricultural production, and promote the full utilization of major agricultural waste. Fourth, to practice a green lifestyle, and promote the reduction of domestic waste at source and resource utilization. Fifth, to enhance the ability of risk prevention and control, and strengthen the comprehensive safety control of hazardous waste. Sixth, to stimulate the vitality of market players and cultivate new models of industrial development.

From this, it can be seen that in both developed and developing countries, the concept of zero waste cities or waste-free cities is inseparable from government education and guidance, and its practice is also inseparable from government promotion and support. Especially for cities in developing countries, due to the relatively backward industrial infrastructure and living habits of residents, before promoting the concept and practice of zero waste cities or waste-free cities, they need to firstly go through a stage of waste treatment and disposal "compliance". In simple terms, this means that industrial waste in cities is treated and disposed of in a compliant manner, and residential waste is collected and sorted in a compliant manner.

The compliance of industrial waste treatment and disposal is generally regulated by laws and regulations, while the sorting and collection of domestic waste depends almost entirely on the quality of urban residents. Of course, at the initial stage of implementing zero waste cities or waste-free cities, it is both necessary and practical to use administrative means and necessary economic leverage to restrain and help residents to improve their awareness. We can see from the two typical cases of Zurich in Switzerland and Shanghai in China the efforts and attempts made by different cities at different stages.

(1) Domestic waste classification and disposal in Switzerland

Switzerland has been sorting waste for more than 30 years. As early as in 1990, Switzerland introduced the first legislation on waste disposal. In addition, each of the 26 Swiss cantons has its own waste regulations under the general federal law, and the Zurich municipality publishes an instruction manual on waste sorting that is over 100 pages long! In Zurich, different types of waste are disposed of in different places, near and far. In addition to being disposed of in the community's garbage bins, some garbage has to be left at the doorstep for recycling, while others have to be taken to the appropriate recycling station by people themselves. Despite of the

100-page manual on waste sorting, residents will receive an annual "waste calendar" with specific times for recycling.

In some local communities, the more advanced sorting of organic waste was introduced a few years ago. Organic waste from the kitchen is disposed of in a green bin outside the building and is collected every Wednesday, and the green bins are cleaned and disinfected after the collection. The organic waste is then transported to a composting site in Zurich to be treated and disposed.

At first, Zurich encountered some resistance to the promotion and practice of "breaking the bag" of organic waste and then throwing it away. But later on, residents pooled their ideas to solve the problem—some people just dispose of their waste in a bowl in a bucket; supermarkets also sell organic garbage bins with a good seal for domestic use; or they buy small biodegradable plastic bags and dispose of them together with the organic waste inside.

In Zurich, white garbage bags, known as "Zurich bags", are more expensive and are used to dispose of dirty tissue, plastic bags and other garbage. A 17-L bag costs 0.85 CHF, a 35-L bag for 1.7 CHF, a 60-L bag for 3.1 CHF and a 110-L bag for 5.7 CHF! These are the bags that the Swiss government has priced to balance out the cost of garbage disposal—the "overpriced bags" are designed to encourage people to use them less and to be careful not to let the wrong kind of garbage get mixed in and take up valuable space.

Every two weeks or so, a man comes to the door of each building to collect paper waste. Before the collection date, it is tied up in very neat tofu blocks with special ropes, and the handles are left on top of the ropes, like "gifts", waiting for the workers to collect it efficiently. If the garbage is not sorted properly or disposed of on time, it is not collected and is left alone on the street. This indirect monitoring mechanism shames those who do not dispose of their garbage as they should. Over time, it becomes a habit for residents to properly sort and dispose of their garbage.

(2) Domestic waste classification and disposal in Shanghai

The city of Shanghai implemented the Shanghai Domestic Waste Management Regulations in July 2019. In the local regulations it reads:

① The standard of domestic waste sorting: the standard of domestic waste sorting directly affects the effectiveness of domestic waste sorting management. Shanghai's domestic waste sorting standards have undergone several changes, and in 2011, the "four types" of recyclable waste, hazardous waste, household food waste and residual waste were established and solidified in a government regulation in 2014. According to the opinions of various parties, the names and specific expressions of the four types of waste have been further clarified. First, the regulations state that household food waste is perishable waste, and residual waste is waste other than recyclable waste, hazardous waste and household food waste. Second, the common types of recyclable waste, hazardous waste and household food waste are listed, and in order to make it easier for the public to put them out at the initial stage and reduce the difficulty of identifying them, the regulations have adopted a simpler approach in listing the types. Third, it

8.7 Property and City

is clear that the sorting standards can be refined and adjusted according to the level of economic and social development and the characteristics of domestic waste, leaving room for further improvement in the future.

② Government management responsibilities: to promote the whole process of domestic waste management, governments at all levels and their relevant departments are duty-bound to do so. The regulation establishes a management model. First, at the municipal level, it specifies that municipal government should strengthen its leadership in the management of domestic waste in the city, and that the municipal Landscaping and City Appearance Administrative Bureau is the competent department for domestic waste management in the city, responsible for the organization, coordination, guidance and supervision of the relevant work, and clarifies the responsibilities of the relevant municipal departments. Second, at the district level, it's made clear that the district government is responsible for the domestic waste management in the district of its jurisdiction, and district Landscaping and City Appearance Administrative Bureau is responsible for execution. Third, at the street and town level, in line with the requirements of decentralization of management responsibilities, it is stipulated that township people's governments and street offices are responsible for the concrete implementation of related work. At the same time, also in the "planning and construction", "supervision and management" two chapters, it requires that government should develop domestic waste management planning, promote the construction of domestic waste treatment facilities, and to set up supervision and inspection system, improve the grid management, strengthen the performance review.

③ Promoting reduction at source: waste reduction at source is an important element in the comprehensive management of domestic waste, and is also a weak link and a difficult issue in promoting the whole process management of domestic waste at present. Laws such as the Circular Economy Promotion Law, the Cleaner Production Promotion Law and the E-commerce Law have corresponding requirements for promoting reduction at source, but most of them are advocacy provisions. In order to improve the rigidity of source reduction measures, the municipal government carried out several coordination processes during the drafting of the regulations, and the regulations put forward mandatory requirements for specific objects. Firstly, it is required to actively promote the reduction of product packaging and express delivery packaging. Secondly, it is stipulated that agricultural products markets and standardized wet market should be equipped with household food waste disposal facilities in accordance with the requirements. Thirdly, in terms of green office and green consumption, the use of disposable goods will be reduced as a focus point, stipulating that party and government departments and institutions shall not use disposable cups and utensils in their offices; hotels shall not take the initiative to provide disposable daily necessities in guest rooms; and food service providers and food delivery service providers shall not take the initiative to provide free disposable chopsticks, spoons and other tableware.

④ Waste sorting: sorting is the key link in the management of domestic waste, and is a prerequisite for the implementation of separate collection and separate transport together with separate disposal. The regulations provide for sorting in three aspects: first, it is clear that the units and individuals who generate domestic waste are the responsible subjects for sorting, and should put domestic waste into the corresponding collection containers. Second, it establishes a system of responsible persons for sorting management, distinguishing between different situations in units, residential areas and public places to determine the corresponding responsible persons for management and to clarify their rights and obligations. Third, collection containers in working locations, residential areas and public areas shall be regulated and standardized according to different situation.

⑤ Separate collection, transport and disposal: separate collection, transport and disposal are important between front-end sorting and end-use resource utilization. To solve the problems of mixing sorted waste in collection, transport and disposal, the regulations are comprehensively specified on separate collection, transport and disposal. The first is to clarify the separate ways of domestic waste collection and transport. The second is to strictly regulate the collection and transport behavior—the organization responsible for collection and transport must use special vehicles and ships to implement closed transport; mixing sorted waste is not allowed. The third is to stipulate for the main disposal ways of domestic waste—considering that Shanghai will basically achieve zero landfill of primary domestic waste in 2020, therefore, the regulations do not include landfill as the disposal method of domestic waste. The fourth is to establish "no sorting, no collection and transport; no sorting, no disposal" supervision mechanism, to ensure the achievement of the full sorting effect.

⑥ The development of recycling systems for recyclables: in order to improve the recycling rate of recyclable waste and promote the "integration of the two networks" of recycling and domestic waste sorting and collection system, the regulations put forward the following requirements for the construction of recycling systems for recyclable waste. First, the Landscaping and City Appearance Administrative Bureau is responsible for the construction of recycling systems, promoting the construction of "points, stations and yards" for recyclable waste, and working with relevant departments to formulate policies to support the recycling of low-value recyclable waste and foster the recycling service market. Second, encouraging the adoption of "Internet + " recycling and smart recycling, and encouraging social capital to participate in the construction of collection and transport facilities.

⑦ Waste utilization as resources: promoting waste utilization as resources of domestic waste is not only a practical need to achieve sustainable economic and social development, but also an inevitable requirement to carry out waste sorting. The regulations provide for the following: first, it is clear that development and reform departments should coordinate the formulation of the city's circular economy development policies and support resource utilization projects; second, it is clear that government departments should support the priority use of household food waste recovered products in public green areas and public welfare forest soil improvement work, and put forward requirements for the local and nearby resource utilization of household food waste; third, it is clear that municipal commerce and other departments are responsible for recyclable waste guidance and coordination of resource utilization activities, and makes provisions for the comprehensive utilization of heat and slag generated after residual waste incineration.

⑧ Social participation: the implementation of domestic waste sorting and management cannot be achieved without the joint participation and support of the whole society. The regulations propose a series of promotional measures: building a broad social mobilization system, establishing and improving a governance mechanism with the party organization of the residential (village) district as the leading core and the participation of all parties, encouraging social participation, industry participation and market participation, and incorporating the management of domestic waste sorting into awareness raising activities, etc.

⑨ The implementation of the regulations: the whole-process management of domestic waste is a systematic project that requires persistence and gradual progress. As for the difficulties that might come along with the regulations, the municipal government should study and propose a clear action plan to further increase its efforts to implement its provisions, so that the initiatives of reduction at source, sorting and management, and resource utilization can be put into practice. The Standing Committee of the Municipal People's Congress also carries out special supervision on the promotion of the full sorting and management of domestic waste, so as to jointly promote the management of domestic waste in Shanghai to a new level.

According to the Shanghai Landscaping and City Appearance Administrative Bureau, just two months after the implementation of the Shanghai Domestic Waste Management Regulations, the amount of recyclable waste reached 4,500 tons per day, a fivefold increase from the end of 2018; the amount of household food waste sorted out reached 9,200 tons per day, a 1.3-fold increase from the end of 2018. The significant increase in these figures means that a large amount of recyclable waste and household food waste have been separated from what used to be mixed together with residual waste. At the same time, residual waste disposal fell to 15,500 tons per day, a 26% reduction from the end of 2018.

The improvement in the level of domestic waste sorting will also "push" the municipal waste treatment and disposal capacity to improve. To cope with the implementation of the regulations, Shanghai has completed the standardization of about 20,000 sorting points and updated the signage of more than 40,000 road garbage bins. At present, Shanghai has configured and painted 1,092 household food waste trucks, 3,197 residual waste trucks, 80 hazardous waste trucks and 154 recyclable waste trucks, and built 9,609 recycling service points, 144 transport stations and 8 distribution yards. The sorting and collection system in Shanghai are basically in shape.

8.7.4 Nation-Wide Zero Waste

The further extension of the concept of zero waste cities or waste-free cities geographically will inevitably introduce the bold idea of zero waste countries. Although at today's economic and technological levels of human society, large countries with large populations are still quite far away from achieving zero waste, this does not prevent small and developed countries or regions from taking the lead when conditions allow.

A good example of a developed country is Singapore, which in November 2014 issued the Singapore Sustainability Blueprint 2015, which goes beyond the call for a waste management system and sets out a national vision of "moving towards zero waste"—a vision that seeks to reduce, reuse and recycle, to avoid the waste of food and raw materials, and to give a second life to all materials wherever possible.

At the same time, as a "Garden City", Singapore has enormous challenges in achieving this vision. First of all, Singapore's total national waste volume is 7,000 tons per day—one of countries with the highest per capita waste in the world and a huge waste base. Secondly, Singapore's waste recycling industry is not well developed, and it is difficult to invest on a large scale; its waste recycling is largely limited by the recycling capacity in the neighboring country Malaysia. Thirdly, due to the high reliance on incineration for a long time—though the waste amount can be reduced by more than 90% after incineration with energy output, but the final landfill of ash generated from incineration has made Pulau Semakau landfill site (consisting of sea islands and seawalls) gradually saturated, which urgently need to plan for new landfill sites. For Singapore, this country has to make more efforts in waste reduction at source and industrial layout in order to achieve zero waste.

Larger countries, such as Japan, which has almost perfect waste sorting, are continuing to promote the overall plan for building a circular economy society and cities, minimizing the consumption of natural resources and the burden on the environment by promoting the effective use and recycling of resources in the process of production, logistics, consumption and even disposal. For even larger countries and country unions, such as the European Union, a pioneer of circular economy society, have released the "Towards a Circular Economy: A Zero Waste Plan for Europe" and "Circular Economy Package", proposing that by 2030, the utilization rate of municipal waste will reach 65%, packaging waste reuse reaches 75%, municipal waste to landfill not over 10% and a ban on landfill of sorted waste, on top of all other zero waste targets.

So, for nation-wide zero waste, implementing or achieving zero waste requires more than just ideas and courage. It must be considered at several strategic levels, as follows.

(1) National need for legislative guarantee

Similar to all other national strategies, the implementation and enforcement of nation-wide zero waste needs to be supported by the law. Whether it is the Circular Economy Promotion Law (see Chap. 12, Sect. 3) or the Law on the Prevention and Control of

Environmental Pollution by Solid Waste, legal means can have effective constraints on all waste-generating processes, as well as effective incentives for waste treatment and disposal. With the law in place, compliance with the law, strict enforcement of the law and punishment on those against the law will follow.

(2) National need for mass balance

Same as the mass balance of a factory (described previously in Chap. 4, Sect. 1), a country should try to consider the mass balance within its entire territory. Theoretically,

$$R_{Total} + N_{Total} + I_{Total} = C_{Total} + M_{Total} + E_{Total} + W_{Net}$$

where, R_{Total} refers to total natural resources extracted and used; N_{Total} refers to total output of agriculture, forestry and fisheries; I_{Total} refers to total imported goods; C_{Total} refers to total infrastructure; M_{Total} refers to total industrial output; E_{Total} refers to total exported goods; W_{Net} refers to total net waste.

In order to reduce the total amount of net waste, at a national strategy level, the material efficiency of natural resources must be improved in parallel with the economic development and gross total increase. It is in line with the increase of the material efficiency in factories.

(3) National need for self-protection

While there is a Basel Convention that regulates the transboundary movement of hazardous wastes (described earlier in Chap. 5, Sect. 1), thereby protecting developing and underdeveloped countries, there is no international law that regulates the transboundary movement of ordinary wastes. Developing and underdeveloped countries may allow the import of recyclable waste for a certain period of time due to the needs of economic and industrial development at a given stage, but this requires three considerations. Firstly, there must be a limit on the amount of imports. Secondly, there must be a standard for the quality of waste allowed to be imported, no blind imports. Thirdly, there should be a time limit for the importation, with regulation and supervision. In short, reasonable import of recyclable waste is beneficial or even necessary for the economy and industry at certain times and under certain conditions, which can contribute to the nation-wide zero waste strategy; however, unrestricted import or simple "one-size-fits-all" absolute ban on import is harmful, which may increase the pressure of waste treatment and disposal at the national level.

Chapter 9
Zero Waste and Eco-Design

No matter in which industry, once the waste is generated during production and operation, it is quite challenging to achieve 100% zero waste through internal elimination, reuse and reduction, or external recycling, aerobic composting, anaerobic digestion and biofuel, including thermally processed with energy recovery.

As discussed on waste treatment and disposal technology previously, any waste diversion method will produce more or less secondary waste. Even though these secondary wastes can be harmless to direct landfill, meeting most national law, regu-lations and specifications, landfill is still landfill—a technical bottleneck is awaiting us if we continue to use such diversion method.

Is there any way for zero waste to go further? The correct answer is not in the waste treatment and disposal, downstream of production and operation, but in the upstream of them, which is, eco-design (also called green-design).

It is eco-design and zero waste together that constitute a complete concept of green manufacturing.

9.1 Eco-Design System

Eco-design refers to the activities of introducing environmental factors into product design and development in order to improve the environmental performance in the product life cycle and optimize its environmental impact. In the whole life cycle of the product, eco-design focuses on the environmental attributes of the product (dismantlability, recyclability, maintainability, reusability, and etc.) and takes them as the design objectives. While meeting the requirements of the environmental objectives, it also ensures the function, quality and basic life of the product.

For the environmental attributes of products in the eco-design system, the dismantlability is considered from the perspective of structural design, recyclability from material selection, maintainability (repairability) from service life, and reusability from the overall value.

These considerations are a little subjective, if without any unified standard, are difficult to be put into quantitative requirements and horizontal comparison. So technically, we put forward several corresponding concepts, which are dismantlability rate, recyclability rate, maintainability (repairability) rate and remanufacturability rate. Reusability, however, is closely connected to the damage rate or loss rate, which depends on the product quality (whole product and parts), as well as user habits, and will not be discussed here.

9.2 Design for Disassembly

9.2.1 *Dismantlable Design Definition*

The definition is to set up an easy dismantling theory and method in order to improve the maintenance (repairing), upgrading and recycling of products taking the product dismantlability as one of the design inputs, and fully considering the interconnections between dismantling and other product factors, using various technical means such as modeling, analysis, evaluation, planning, simulation, etc., under the premise of ensuring the product function.

9.2.2 *Dismantlable Design Criteria*

The criteria of dismantlable design can be considered from the aspects of material, parts, connection, structure, and information transmission.

(1) Material requirements

First of all, materials should be used with minimum variety during the design phase. When different materials have little difference in physical or chemical properties and can all meet the functional requirements, only one material should be used as much as possible.

Secondly, the principle of compatibility should be followed. Not only the types, but also the compatibility of materials should be considered in the design. If different materials are used for the same parts, materials with good compatibility shall be used as far as possible to facilitate recycling. For example, the compatibility between metal and plastic is poor, and they have to be separated first then recycled; but PC (polycarbonate) in plastics has good compatibility with ABS (acrylonitrile butadiene styrene terpolymer), which does not need sorting and can be recycled together.

Thirdly, materials should be as simple as possible. Except for functional requirements, the following materials or materials treated by the following processes should be avoided as far as possible in the design (such materials can only be separated by

9.2 Design for Disassembly

destructive dismantling, and the purity cannot be guaranteed, or even cannot be separated): incompatible materials mutually embedded in fasteners, connectors and reinforcements; electroplating, electrophoresis; spray and roll coating; screen printing and coating; incompatible inks and labels.

Finally, the principle of using hazardous, toxic and harmful substances should be followed. In the design, the hazardous, toxic and harmful substances (such as halides) should be used as little as possible or avoided. If they cannot be replaced due to limited conditions or functional requirements, the following measures should be taken: integration (convenient for centralized collection); protection (avoiding disassembly risk); inform (convey necessary information of hazardous, toxic and harmful substances to future dismantlers).

(2) Parts requirements

First of all, the principle of minimum usage should be followed. The type and quantity of parts determine the dismantling workload. The more the types and quantity, the more the connection, the longer the dismantling time and the worse the efficiency. Therefore, in the design process, the types and quantities of the parts should be minimized.

Secondly, we should follow the principle of modular design. As far as possible, the modular design is adopted for the parts to make the functions of each part relatively independent, so as to realize the non-destructive dismantling of the parts as far as possible.

Finally, we should follow the principle of standardization. In order to simplify the dismantling work, standardized parts should be used as far as possible.

(3) Connection requirements

First of all, the connection should be designed with easy dismantling. In the design, the convenience of dismantling should be fully considered, and the connection method that is easiest to dismantling should be designed or adopted as far as possible, such as plug-in and plug-in slots; welding, gluing, screwing and permanent fastening shall be avoided as much as possible.

Secondly, the number of fasteners and connectors should be minimized. In order to make the dismantling easy, time-saving and labor-saving, the number and types of fasteners and connectors at the dismantling parts should be as small as possible.

Finally, the fasteners and connectors should be standardized as much as possible, in order to reduce the types of dismantling tools and simplify the dismantling work.

(4) Structural requirements

Firstly, keep things simple. The connection of the structure, shape and physical body of the product should be clear in logic. The ergonomics in the process of dismantling should be also fully considered.

Secondly, the principle of shallowest depth. Any depth in the product should be designed as shallow as possible, so that the target parts can have easy access.

Finally, the principle of accessibility should be followed. In order to solve the problem of accessibility in the dismantling process, we should consider: visual accessibility, that is, when dismantling, we should be able to see the internal dismantling operation; physical accessibility, that is, when dismantling, the operator can directly or with the aid of tools touch the dismantling part; there should be enough space for dismantling operation, so as to facilitate the dismantling work. For example, enough wrench space should be reserved for the arrangement of bolts and nuts.

(5) Information transmission requirements

In order to improve the efficiency and safety of the dismantler, an effective communication channel should be established between the designer and the dismantler. For this reason, designers should adopt easy ways such as text and general graphics to convey relevant dismantler guidance information, such as material identification, material regeneration properties, direction of dismantling movement and applied force, logical order of dismantling, less obvious breaking point, hidden connection point, best cutting line and separation line, recommended dismantling tools, etc.

9.2.3 Dismantlable Design Evaluation

Dismantlable design is a dynamic process of evaluating, modifying, re-evaluating and re-modifying, until the design scheme meets the design requirements. The evaluation of dismantlable design is not only evaluating the simulation of dismantling process, but also the actual product dismantling process. The evaluation can provide effective feedback and help designers to improve the design, so as to further improve the dismantling performance of products.

The evaluation process of dismantlable design should include: defining the dismantling purpose, determining the target parts, selecting the evaluation index and evaluating.

(1) Dismantling purpose and target parts

The purpose and target parts of dismantling are different, so are the means and methods. When the product is in use, the purpose of dismantling is product maintenance (repairing) and upgrading. So, it is necessary that the target parts are dismantled without damaging other parts related. When the product is recycled in the end of its service life, the main purpose of dismantling is the reuse of the parts which are still qualified, separating parts containing hazardous, toxic and harmful substances, and obtaining rare and valuable materials. Dismantling can decrease the difficulty of material separation and improve the purity of recycling.

With the purpose of dismantling defined, the target parts to be dismantled should be identified, with requirement of their states after dismantling, which refers to whether they are damaged or have other physical or chemical changes. According to the purpose, the dismantling process could be simulated or actually carried out to evaluate the dismantlability.

(2) Evaluation index

The evaluation indexes related to dismantling process mainly include dismantling time, cost and environmental impact.

Dismantling time is the time required to remove all target parts. A part unit of a product may be composed of multiple connection modes, and the dismantling time of the part unit is the sum of the time consumed to separate all these connections. It includes basic dismantling time and auxiliary time. Basic dismantling time refers to the time taken to loosen the connector and separate the parts to be dismantled from the related connector; auxiliary time refers to the time spent on auxiliary work to complete the dismantling work, such as the time when the dismantling tool or human arm approaches the dismantling part, etc. In the process of dismantling, dismantling tools, workers' proficiency and structural complexity have different effects on the dismantling time, and the correction coefficient can be adjusted according to the specific situation. The determination of dismantling time should come from the collection, collation and analysis of actual dismantling data.

Dismantling cost refers to all expenses related to dismantling, like investment cost and labor cost. The investment cost includes the cost of dismantling site, tools and fixtures required for dismantling, the cost of tool positioning and fixture feeding device, the cost of identification and classification of removed materials, etc. Labor cost mainly refers to the wages of workers. The connection structure of the parts in the product is different, so is the dismantling difficulty and cost.

The environmental impact of dismantling process is mainly manifested as noise, energy consumption and pollutant emission. Dismantlable design should minimize the environmental impact of dismantling.

(3) Design evaluation

After selecting the evaluation index, relevant data for evaluation will be prepared. These evaluation indexes have both qualitative and quantitative indexes, which should be flexibly used according to different purposes in the evaluation of dismantlable design. They can be used alone or comprehensively.

9.3 Design for Recycling

Because recyclable design actually refers to the recycling of a certain product material, the first thing to consider is the recyclability of these materials (or recyclability rate from 0 to 100%)—Recyclability depends on the selection of recyclable materials at the early stage of the product design.

To avoid confusion in some definitions, it is necessary to clarify that the recyclable materials referred to here is in a narrow sense, excluding reusable parts or components, unless their materials are recyclable; it also does not include biodegradable materials, because biodegradation cannot regenerate materials, and its degraded materials are often quite different from the original materials; it does not include energy recovery materials—strictly speaking, those parts are burned as a last resort, not material recovery.

9.3.1 Process and Principle of Material Selection

The selection of materials is a very complex and comprehensive process, which is also the core and priority work of any product designer (design team). In short, material selection can be divided into the following five steps. As shown in Fig. 9.1.

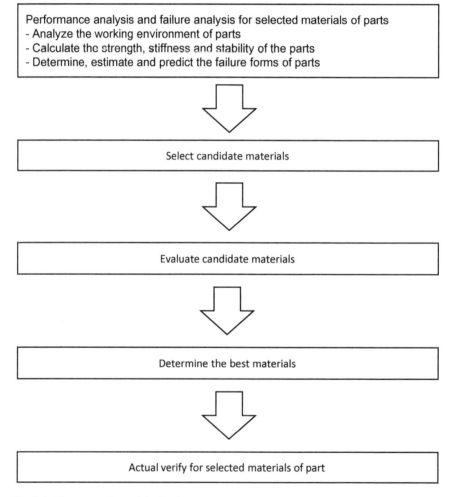

Fig. 9.1 Five steps of material selection

In addition, in the process of material selection, the selection and evaluation of materials should also follow certain basic principles, mainly including:

① Usability principle: the selected materials should meet the product function, product structure and working environment.
② Process principle: the feasibility and difficulty of material machining, and the technology of material acquisition process.
③ Environmentality principle: being easy for resource recovery, and making minimal environmental impact.
④ Economy principle: to ensure a reasonable total cost of products.

9.3.2 Basic Requirements for Selection of Recyclable Materials

The selection of recyclable materials should meet the following requirements: materials should not affect product's safety, performance and quality in order to achieve high recycling rate; while selecting the parts, reusability of parts should be given priority followed by the recyclability of materials, and finally the energy recovery of materials; in the manufacturing stage of the product, it should be considered to mark the material composition on the surface of the material, or the surface of the parts, or in the product manual, so as to facilitate the recycling at the end of the product life.

9.3.3 General Methods for Selection of Recyclable Materials

(1) Choose as few materials as possible

The fewer types of materials get used in products, the more conducive to the recycling of materials will be. Product parts should be made of a single recyclable material as much as possible, such as one same metal or the same plastic. If two or more kinds of plastics are needed, choose the ones with good compatibility. The recycling rate of incompatible mixed plastics in thermoplastic is very low and should be avoided as far as possible.

For parts with similar functional requirements or difficult to separate (using bonding, welding and other fastening methods), select materials of the same kind or high compatibility. For example, screws, fasteners and other connectors should be made of the same material as far as possible, and the material composition of the connector should be marked on the product or product manual. In addition, the surface coating or processing of metal or plastic parts, the paste of large pieces of stickers or foam on plastic parts, and the insertion of metal parts into plastic assemblies (unless they can be disassembled by ordinary tools) will reduce the recyclability of materials and should be avoided.

(2) Choose materials with high recycling rate

On the basis of the existing technology and on the premise of meeting the requirements of safety, function and cost, the materials with higher recycling rate should be selected, while the filling rubber and foaming materials with lower recycling rate should be avoided as much as possible.

When choosing plastic materials, try to choose thermoplastic materials rather than thermosetting materials. Under the existing production process, the recycling rate of thermoplastic is high, while the recycling rate of thermosetting plastic is very low, which can only be used for energy recovery.

(3) Choose materials with non or low toxicity and no or less harm

Harmful substances in materials will not only cause harm to consumers when they are using it, but also increase the difficulty of material recycling at the end of product life and reduce the utilization rate of resources. In order to facilitate the recycling, the materials without harmful substances or with low content of harmful substances should be selected.

(4) Choose recycled materials

Under the appropriate production process, the recycled materials made from a certain proportion of waste materials have basically the same physical and chemical properties as the original materials, which can meet most of the functional requirements. The alternative recycled materials include recycled metal, recycled plastic and recycled paper. The choice of recycled materials not only affirms the recyclability of previous products, but also means that the materials can still be recycled after the end of the service life of products. At the same time, it can reduce the material cost of products.

9.3.4 Calculation Method of Recyclability Rate

Recyclability rate is the percentage of the mass that can be recycled in the total mass of products. The recyclability rate of the whole product can be calculated according to each recyclable part and/or material:

$$R = \frac{\sum_{i=1}^{n} m_i}{M} \times 100\%$$

in which R refers to recyclability rate; m_i refers to the mass of category i recyclable parts and/or materials, in kg; n refers to total number of categories of recyclable parts and/or materials; M refers to the total mass of the product, in kg.

9.4 Design for Maintenance/Repairing

In fact, the so-called maintainable design in eco-design system is more widely called repairable design. It is a design concept based on dismantlable design and superior to recyclable design. This design concept comes from the repairability of the product itself, and ultimately serves the repairability of the product.

9.4.1 Several Definitions of Repairing

(1) Repairability

The ability of a product to maintain or restore the required functional state under a given condition when using certain procedures and resources for repairing.

(2) Repairing degree

Under the given conditions, the probability that the product can complete the scheduled actual repairing work in a certain time interval when using certain procedures and resources to carry out repairing.

(3) Repairing

A combination of all technical and management activities to maintain or restore a product to a specified function and state.

(4) Repairing plan

Description of the relationship among the repairing site level, repairing level and repairing activity level applied in product repairing.

(5) Repairing policy

The general method of providing repairing and repairing support, which is based on the objectives and principles of owners, users and customers.

9.4.2 Considerations in the Process of Repairable Design

The designer's responsibility is to achieve all kinds of work requirements including repairability under the constraints of time and cost. Therefore, repairability requirements should be stipulated from the beginning of the design process, and necessary repairability research should be carried out in the design process.

Design is an iterative process. For a high level of design, a comprehensive repairing outline is very important. A high level of design depends to a large extent on every subcontractor who manufactures the product. Therefore, it is necessary to include the subcontractor in the whole repairing outline in these designs. As shown in Fig. 9.2.

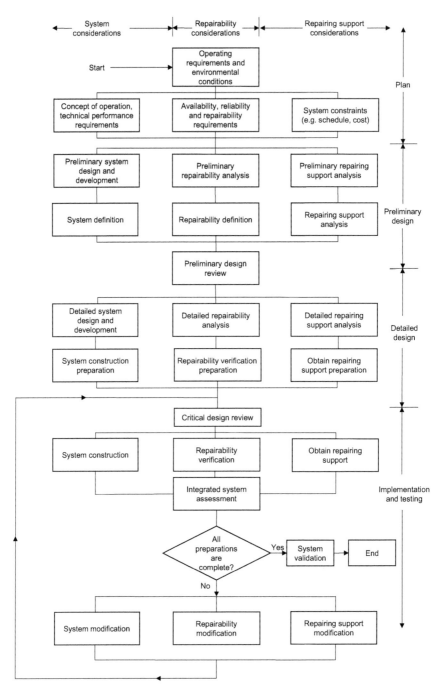

Fig. 9.2 Repairability research process

9.5 Design for Remanufacturing

Obviously, considering the repairability of the product carefully from the design stage will make the repairing more possible or easier. If it is the accidental damage repairing in the normal product service life, this kind of repairing can at least make the product reach its initial design life, keeping it from being scrapped in advance for recycling. If the product is repaired after the end of its normal service life, it can get a second "life" and avoid being recycled for the time being. In any case, it is conducive to zero waste.

Repairability may not necessarily increase the cost of design and manufacturing. The reasons can be considered from the following perspectives:

① Repairability inevitably requires the versatility and replaceability of the parts. Modular design, which meets such requirements, can greatly reduce the cost of design and manufacturing.
② Another inevitable result of repairability is the increased demand for product repairing services. There will be a market for easily damaged parts, from which companies can obtain additional profits from repairing services and parts sales.
③ One possibility brought by repairability is that a product of different generations can be owned by the same consumers at the same time, which objectively increases the market share of the product, and may indirectly drive the market of peripheral products or derivative products of the product due to customers' attachment. Examples are the Golf of Volkswagen and the iPhone of Apple. They all have three or four generations (even more) in the same time period thanks to their outstanding durability and repairability.

9.5 Design for Remanufacturing

The situation of remanufacturable design is more complicated than the previous ones. As discussed in the waste diversion method in Chapter 6, remanufacturing can be divided into two scenarios: product A returns to product A after remanufacturing the whole or parts; product A is redesigned and processed into product B. Although they are both remanufacturing, due to different purposes, the designs are completely different.

9.5.1 From A to A

In the first scenario, product A is designed with the knowledge that it will return to product A after being partially or wholly remanufactured. So, there are certain principles to follow:

(1) Dismantlability

No remanufacturing can't be realized without dismantling. But the dismantling for remanufacturing is not the same as individuals dismantling products using ordinary tools, instead, it's a large-scale technical dismantling of a batch of waste products in a special factory, using, for example, dismantling robots. Of course, machine dismantling is not the same as manual dismantling. Whether it's the heating of adhesive, or the turning of very fine screws, the robot's performance under the drive of the program is much better than that of human beings. With the precise control, the damage to parts is also much less than that of manual dismantling. Therefore, we must not confuse individual manual dismantling with professional dismantling purposed for remanufacturing and mistakenly think what individual can't dismantle is lack of dismantlable design.

(2) Versatility

The versatility of the parts is the same as that mentioned in repairability. Whether it is used for repairing or remanufacturing, the versatility of parts in the same generation or even different generations is very important. Remanufacturing from A to A requires a certain number of general-purpose parts as inventory, so as to ensure that the damaged or scrapped parts do not need to be repaired immediately during remanufacturing, but to be directly replaced with existing parts. Of course, the existing parts may be directly provided by the parts supplier, or they may be completely qualified parts (inspected, evaluated or certified) dismantled from another product A.

(3) Economic efficiency

Without certain economic feasibility, any kind of remanufacturable design is a failure. If large-scale dismantling and high-tech parts remanufacturing is more expensive than redesigning and manufacturing a new product, there is not a way out. Therefore, the remanufacturing from A to A will generally choose products with higher unit value, and the high-value parts that are relatively easy to be damaged and scrapped should be designed to be easily separated from the main body of the product. This remanufacturing has higher economic efficiency.

9.5.2 From A to B

In the second scenario, product A is designed without knowing what kind of remanufacturing will be carried out for it wholly or partially, or knowing what product B may be after remanufacturing. This puts forward great challenges and high requirements for remanufacturing designers.

It is generally believed that the principles of dismantlability, versatility and economic efficiency can still be observed in this kind of design scenario, to make sure at least the remanufacturing process will not be too complicated if the product B is the same category with product A after remanufacturing. However, it might be too naive to think so. Sometimes we have to admit that the lack of innovation often limits our thinking!

In remanufacturing design from A to B, we may not have to comply with dismantlability.

9.5 Design for Remanufacturing

If whole or part of product A can become a part of product B, and product B does not need to use the damaged or scrapped parts of product A, and the existence of these parts does not affect the volume and function of product B, there is no need to dismantle product A—it can be considered that the whole product A has been reused in part of product B.

In remanufacturing design from A to B, versatility may become less important.

Because A and B belong to completely different categories of products, it will work if the parts in product A useful to product B can play the function intended for product B. In other words, as long as there is the necessary physical connection (including data transmission) between A and B to make product A work, the versatility of product A itself is not important.

In the remanufacturing design from A to B, as long as there is innovation, the economic benefits may be radically changed.

If product A is totally or partially damaged and scrapped, its residual value is certainly less than that of a brand new product A. However, if we use the damaged and scrapped product A (one or more product A) to design and manufacture a new product B with higher profit, its value may be far greater than the sum of the residual value of one or more product A, or even greater than the direct manufacturing of product B with raw materials!

So, what are the principles we should consider in the remanufacturing design from A to B?

(1) Cross boundary design

Designers' thinking is often limited by the design of a certain kind of products. If they can think in a cross-border way, for example, designing industrial products as craft products, designing wearable products as home products, designing agricultural products as fashion products, etc., they can create product B by remanufacturing product A.

(2) Cross end design

It has never been said that product A can only be designed and remanufactured into a product B lower end than product A. On the contrary, a successful remanufacturing design is often to design product A into a higher end product B. The greater the contrast, the greater the profit margin in theory; its value lies in its design.

(3) Cross regional design

Different countries and regions, due to different histories and cultures, have different product value orientations. Designing damaged and scrapped product A as product B may have a flat response in the local market of product A, but great popularity and success in another country or region.

9.5.3 Calculation of Remanufacturing Rate

Whether from A to A or from A to B, there must be a standard to measure the design level of remanufacturing, so here is the concept of remanufacturing rate. Remanufacturing rate is usually for the parts with remanufacturable design. According to different application scenarios, the percentage of the total output of remanufactured parts used in the final product (A or B) in the corresponding total output is called output remanufacturing rate, and the percentage of the total output value of remanufactured parts used in the final product (A or B) in the corresponding total output value is called output value remanufacturing rate.

The output remanufacturing rate can be calculated by the following formula:

$$RR_{pq} = \frac{\int_0^T r(t)dt}{\int_0^T r(t)dt + \int_0^T m(t)dt}$$

where RR_{pq} denotes output remanufacturing rate; $m(t)$ the new product productivity at any time t, $\forall t \in [0, T]$, T is the specified calculation period of remanufacturing rate; $r(t)$ the productivity of remanufactured product at any time t, $\forall t \in [0, T]$.

If the value of products (including new products and remanufactured products) does not change with time, the output value remanufacturing rate can refer to the following formula:

$$RR_{pv} = \frac{P_r \int_0^T r(t)dt}{P_r \cdot \int_0^T r(t)dt + P_m \cdot \int_0^T m(t)dt}$$

where RR_{pv} denotes output value remanufacturing rate; P_m the value of single new product; P_r the value of single remanufactured product.

If the value of products (including new products and remanufactured products) changes with time, the output value remanufacturing rate can refer to the following formula:

$$RR_{pv} = \frac{\int_0^T P_r(t) \cdot r(t)dt}{\int_0^T P_r(t) \cdot r(t)dt + \int_0^T P_m(t) \cdot m(t)dt}$$

where RR_{pv} denotes output value remanufacturing rate; $P_m(t)$ the value of the new product at any time t, $\forall t \in [0, T]$, T is the specified calculation period of remanufacturing rate; $P_r(t)$ the value of remanufactured product at any time t, $\forall t \in [0, T]$.

9.6 Conclusion

When a product reaches the end of its service life, if the dismantlability is considered in the initial design, it can avoid being treated or disposed as waste; if the recyclability is considered in the initial design, it can avoid being sent to incineration or landfill because it is difficult to recycle; if the repairability is considered in the initial design, it can continue to play its value and avoid being abandoned after partial or overall repairing; if the remanufacturability is considered in the initial design, the product will be reborn and even get higher market value.

Eco-design has broken through the technical bottleneck of zero waste in the downstream of manufacturing from the upstream of manufacturing. Although it may not be able to help achieve 100% zero waste in all industries, it indeed is a great leap forward. It is also an introduction to material closed loop to be discussed later in the book.

Chapter 10
Reverse Logistics

Before discussing material closed loop, there is one more thing worth mentioning and that is reverse logistics.

In Chap. 9, dismantlability, recyclability, repairability, and remanufacturability take zero waste to a higher level from a product design perspective; and the realization of these properties requires first and foremost that the damaged or end-of-life product be returned to the manufacturing plant (only in rare cases can a simple repairing be made without returning to the plant). A commonly seen logistic direction is from the manufacturing plant to the consumer, which can be defined as forward logistics; then reverse logistics is needed for dismantling, recycling, repairing and remanufacturing.

10.1 Definition and Category

Reverse logistics is the process by which a business owner entrusts a third-party logistics company to deliver items from a user designated location to the business location, which can also be simply understood as the logistics activity triggered by the transfer of items from downstream to upstream in the supply chain.

The main ideas of reverse logistics can be summarized as follows.

① The reverse logistics process is driven by the product manufacturer and cannot be achieved by individuals.
② The settlement of reverse logistics costs is centralized between the manufacturer, the customer and the third-party logistics company.
③ Reverse logistics usually requires a strong ERP system (namely Enterprise Resource Planning) to support between the business owner and third-party logistics company.

The manifestations of reverse logistics are diverse, ranging from used packaging to processed computer equipment, returns of unsold goods to mechanical parts, etc. Reverse logistics is a process that begins with the recycling of used, obsolete or damaged products and packaging from the consumer and continues through the final disposal chain.

Although different experts and scholars have different definitions of reverse logistics, its main elements are consistent and can be summarized in four aspects.

① The purpose of reverse logistics is to recapture the use value of a discarded or defective product, or to dispose of the final waste properly.
② Reverse logistics are the flow of products, containers for product transport, packaging materials and related information, reversing them from the end of the supply chain along the channels of the supply chain to the respective nodes.
③ Reverse logistics activities include the recycling, sorting, testing, repairing, refurbishment, remanufacturing, final treatment and disposal of the above-mentioned objects.
④ Although reverse logistics is the physical flow of goods, like forward logistics, reverse logistics is accompanied by reverse capital flow and reverse information flow, etc.

There are different ways to classify reverse logistics according to different concerns. According to the channel of recycled items, reverse logistics can be divided into: reverse logistics for returning products and reverse logistics for recycling products. Reverse logistics for returning refers to the return of products due to the failure to meet downstream customers' requirements thus is returned to upstream suppliers, and its process is the opposite of the regular product flow; while reverse logistics for recycling refers to the logistics activity of recycling discarded products held by the final customer to the nodal enterprises in the supply chain.

Reverse logistics for returning and for recycling also correspond to reverse logistics in the narrow sense and in the broad sense, respectively. The narrow sense of reverse logistics is limited to the process of recalling products and parts to the production enterprise for various reasons; the broad sense of reverse logistics includes the content of waste logistics in addition to the narrow sense of reverse logistics, with the purpose of ultimately reducing the use of resources, and in order to achieve the goal of reducing the waste generated from production and consumption.

Reverse logistics in other bibliographies and literature, also appear as "returned logistics" or "intravenous logistics", but most of them, in fact, refer to the broad sense of reverse logistics.

10.2 Waste Logistics

The social significance of reverse logistics for returning is mainly at the level of commercial services, which itself is not directly related to zero waste; while reverse logistics for recycling often is called "waste logistics". As a special link in the value chain of manufacturing enterprises, waste logistics is similar to forward logistics in terms of packaging, loading and unloading, transport, storage, processing, but it also has its own distinctive characteristics.

(1) Dispersion

The timing, location, quality and frequency of waste logistics are unpredictable. Waste may be generated in production, distribution or domestic consumption, involving any sector, any individual, and occurring at any time of day and night in every corner of society. It is this multiplicity of characteristics that leads to its decentralized nature. However, it is not the case with forward logistics, whose basic form is the flow of products at regular time and place with regular quantities.

(2) Slowness

Waste logistics is small and diverse at the initial stage, and can only form a larger scale of flow if it is continuously pooled. Unlike normally produced and manufactured products, the generation of waste does not generate value immediately. It needs to be sorted, screened, processed and manufactured to gradually show its potential value, and this series of processes is relatively long. Forward logistics, on the other hand, is quick, and the drive to profit from the commodity will allow forward logistics to happen quickly and exhibit value in the hands of consumers.

(3) Hybridity

Waste is often highly mixed when it enters the reverse logistics system, with different values, materials, destinations and even regulatory requirements. It is usually only after a slow process of inspection, identification and sorting that the commingling of waste decreases with its different potential values. In the case of forward logistics, there is no commingling, and commodities are properly classified according to their value at the beginning of their design and manufacture, and are distinguished from each other in all necessary forms of packaging.

(4) Variability

Due to logistics development and policy regulation, waste logistics has a certain degree of uncertainty, with software and hardware being upgraded and modified at any time, and flow direction changing from location A-to-location B to location B-to-location A. These uncertainties directly increase the cost of waste logistics. But forward logistics, due to the relative stability of its commodities, is generally smooth and orderly, although various changes may occur according to market demand.

Based on these characteristics, dispersion of waste logistics can be addressed through better coordination and communication, slowness addressed by awareness raising and market development, hybridity addressed with more advanced engineering and technology, and variability addressed through the study of systematics and operations researches.

Obviously, since most waste logistics services in countries around the world today rely on government operations and are not sufficiently commercialized, relevant researches are inadequate, which need to get more attention from environmental protection and resource conservation academia.

10.3 Logistics Cost

Logistics costs are the expenses, expenditures, or the most basic costs related to logistics, and the costs of waste logistics are the operation costs related to waste. The study of waste logistics costs is the basis for waste logistics management and optimization. How to reduce the cost of waste logistics is a traditional topic. In the global context of environmental protection and resource conservation, how to maximize the economic benefit of enterprises involved in waste logistics is the most central issue in the process of promoting waste resource recovery by all national governments.

10.3.1 Cost Composition

Different criteria decide the cost of waste logistics. Taking logistics subject for example, it could be classified as logistics companies' own cost and delegation cost for third-party logistics company. But more practically, waste logistics costs can be classified according to the functions.

(1) Transport cost

It includes mainly waste operation labor cost, such as transport staff salaries and benefits; operation cost, such as operation vehicle fuel cost, depreciation, road transport management cost; and other cost like travel cost.

(2) Storage cost

It mainly includes the cost of constructing, purchasing or leasing waste-related sites and supporting facilities and equipment, and the cost arising from various types of temporary waste storage operations.

(3) Treatment cost

It mainly is the cost of basic treatment equipment, materials, labor and other cost necessary in the process to facilitate the transport of waste.

(4) Packaging cost

It mainly includes the cost of materials, machinery, technology and labor related to packaging, which is necessary in the waste transport process.

(5) Information management cost

It Includes travel expenses, meetings, interactions, software systems and other taxes incurred by the company for waste logistics management.

10.3.2 Costing

There is an "iceberg theory" in the general logistics costing, indicating that the cost could be calculated large or small based on different calculation methods and scope, as many of the costs are hidden. This is also true for waste logistics. When calculating the cost of waste logistics, the calculation criteria must first be clarified, including logistics scope, functional scope and accounting subject scope.

(1) Logistics scope

The logistics scope, as the name implies, refers to the distance between the starting and ending points of the logistics. The span from where it starts to where it ends (raw material origin, manufacturing plant, storage and transport, consumer, recycler, etc.) is quite wide, and a different spatial extent can lead to significant changes in waste logistics costing results.

(2) Functional scope

Functional scope refers to the different functions, such as transport, warehousing, distribution, packaging, handling, information management, etc. in the whole logistics process to be calculated. There will obviously be a considerable difference between the cost calculated with all functions included and the cost calculated with only the waste storage and transport functions.

(3) Accounting subject scope

The accounting subject scope is a matter of which accounts to include in the calculation. Usually, the accounting subjects will include expenses external to the enterprise such as freight expenses and storage expenses, as well as internal expenses such as labor, depreciation, repairs and fuel. The choice of which expense items to include in the costing object greatly affects the size of waste logistics costs. In order to facilitate comparisons between different waste logistics companies, or between different periods of time for a particular waste logistics company, the same accounting standards need to be used in calculating logistics costs as far as possible.

10.3.3 Cost Analysis

There are many methods of logistics cost analysis. With reference to common distribution center logistics cost analysis, waste logistics costs can be analyzed by both comprehensive and detailed analysis.

10.3.3.1 Comprehensive Analysis

After the total waste logistics costing, enterprises can calculate the following ratios, and then use these ratios to examine the changes in costs compared to the same period in the past, and also compared to other enterprises in the same industry.

(1) Logistics cost rate per unit weight (volume)

$$\text{Logistics cost rate per unit weight(volume)} = \frac{\text{Logistics cost}}{\text{Unit weight(volume)}} \times 100\%$$

The higher this ratio, the less elastic it is to the weight of the waste, but of course this ratio is more affected by changes in the amount of waste received and is therefore slightly inadequate as an assessment indicator.

(2) Logistics functional cost ratio

$$\text{Logistics functional cost ratio} = \frac{\text{Logistics functional cost}}{\text{Total logistics cost}} \times 100\%$$

This indicator can clarify the ratio of the cost of each logistics function, such as packaging, transport, storage, handling, distribution and processing, information and consulting, and logistics management, to the total cost of waste logistics.

10.3.3.2 Detailed Analysis

Through a comprehensive analysis, the changes in waste logistics costs and trends could be understood; however, we have to further classify the causes of cost changes according to functions, and analyze and compare various nuances with the past and other enterprises in the same industry through four types of indicators, in order to find the opportunities and plans for cost saving.

(1) Indicators on transport

$$\text{Loading ratio} = \frac{\text{Actual load}}{\text{Standard load}} \times 100\%$$

$$\text{Vehicle activation rate} = \frac{\text{Total number of activations per month}}{\text{Number of units owned}} \times 100\%$$

$$\text{Operation turnover rate} = \frac{\text{Total number of operations per month}}{\text{Number of units owned}} \times 100\%$$

$$\text{Monthly mileage per unit of vehicle} = \frac{\text{Total monthly mileage}}{\text{Number of units owned}}$$

10.3 Logistics Cost

$$\text{Unit mileage cost} = \frac{\text{Actual monthly mileage cost}}{\text{Total monthly mileage}}$$

where Mileage cost = repair fee + inner and outer tire fee + fuel fee

$$\text{Freight per unit of volume} = \frac{\text{Transport cost}}{\text{Total volume transported}}$$

(2) Indicators on storage activities

$$\text{Storage utilization rate} = \frac{\text{Waste storage area}}{\text{Total area}} \times 100\%$$

$$\text{Number of storage turns} = \frac{\text{Annual outgoing weight(volume)}}{\text{Average storage weight (volume)}}$$

(3) Indicators on loading and unloading activities

Unit work per man-hours
$$= \frac{\text{Total work}}{\text{Number of man-hours of loading and unloading operations}}$$

Number of man-hours of loading and unloading operations
$$= \text{Number of persons in operation} \times \text{Operation hours}$$

Loading and unloading efficiency
$$= \frac{\text{Standard umber of man-hours of loading and unloading operations}}{\text{Actual number of man-hours of loading and unloading operations}}$$

Loading and unloading equipment start-up rate
$$= \frac{\text{Actual loading and unloading equipment start-up time}}{\text{Standard loading and unloading equipment start-up time}}$$

Repair cost per unit of work
$$= \frac{\text{Repair cost of loading and unloading equipment}}{\text{Total work}}$$

Loading and unloading cost per unit of work
$$= \frac{\text{Loading and unloading cost}}{\text{Total work}}$$

(4) Indicators on logistics information activities

$$\text{Logistics information processing rate} = \frac{\text{Number of logistics information processed}}{\text{Number of standard logistics information processed}}$$

10.3.4 Cost Management

Regardless of the way to achieve zero waste, the economic benefits more or less will be generated on top of its social value; however, as a part of zero waste, the cost of waste logistics itself must be controlled and optimized in a scientific way.

(1) Standardization of technologies

Development of technical standards for all aspects of waste logistics—once standards are developed and unified, the interface between upstream and downstream waste logistics will become smooth and efficient; the standardization and compatibility of the entire industry will be enhanced as different waste logistics undertakings implement the same standards. The standardization of technology can help the whole waste logistics industry to reduce comprehensive costs. In addition, the standardization of waste logistics technology provides an enforceable yardstick for government monitoring and management.

(2) Enhancing supply chain management

The upstream and downstream supply chains of waste logistics need to coordinate various relationships, and in addition to the necessary standardization of technology, operations must also take into account the interests of all parties as much as possible to achieve efficiency in the entire supply chain. Many Fortune Global 500 companies are able to reduce logistics costs and thus increase their profitability through strong and efficient supply chain management.

(3) Leveraging information system

To achieve efficient trading relationships between waste logistics companies and other trading enterprises, the coordination, control and management of the entire logistics process must be accomplished with the help of modern information system constructions, especially the use of high technology such as the Internet to achieve networked services for all intermediate processes from the front end to the terminal. Obviously, the rapid development of logistics management information systems can also separate the costs of logistics previously mixed with other costs, especially complex costs like waste logistics. Such accurate calculation can facilitate the identification of cost reduction opportunities.

(4) Total process control theory

For an enterprise in the waste treatment and disposal chain, controlling its logistics costs is not only a matter for the enterprise, but also a matter for the local government and authorities to consider in a holistic manner. It should be developed in accordance with the development of the local industry and society, and supporting facilities for waste logistics should be constructed holistically, providing whole process information for enterprises in the upstream and downstream of the waste logistics. Only with the holistic management and coordination by the government, can manufacturing enterprises or special waste operation enterprises involved in waste logistics reduce the overall costs of the whole process.

(5) Improving logistics efficiency

With a certain amount of waste, the more efficient the logistics is, the shorter the logistics cycle will be. Less time means less cost, therefore the profit increases. The increased frequency and small-unit logistics requires that logistics companies should plan more vehicles, improve vehicle loading volume and transport operations. If cross-border logistics are involved, the efficiency of customs clearance at the border is also an important factor in limiting logistics efficiency. Waste-related logistics is more likely, due to the transport of waste (even resource-based waste), to be randomly inspected than common cargo. So, logistics companies should be absolutely compliant with the law and regulations, and if necessary, they can gain a pre-certification by third party in accordance with the relevant standards for inbound inspection, which can significantly improve the efficiency of waste clearance.

10.4 Drive and Development

Reverse logistics is driven, on the one hand, by manufacturing enterprises' need to take the necessary social responsibility for the treatment and disposal or comprehensive recovery of waste; on the other hand, by demand from upstream markets—after all, many components and parts are cheaper to reuse than to be newly manufactured, and the minerals in many wastes are also more abundant than the primary minerals. The economic value of repairing, refurbishment, remanufacturing, and refining of mineral raw materials is considerable, driving the rapid development of reverse logistics, of course including waste logistics.

Manufacturing enterprises can independently develop reverse logistics for products, components or raw materials related; suppliers of raw materials or components can also develop reverse logistics for their own customers; and third-party enterprises originally engaged in general logistics business can provide reverse logistics outsourcing services. Each of these development modes has its own characteristics, supplementing each other, and even cooperating for better development.

With reverse logistics gradually developed into more specialization and refinement, and manufacturing enterprises basically realizing zero waste, material closed loop can officially be introduced.

Chapter 11
Material Closed Loop

Closed loop is not a new concept. Playground laps are closed loops; PDCA (Plan Do, Check, Act) management is a closed loop; the four-dimensional Mobius Band is a closed loop. All these closed loops have something in common—it ends at its starting point after getting through some time or space; or there is neither a starting point nor an ending point in the definition of a closed loop; or simply that every point in a closed loop is both a starting point and an ending point.

Just as perpetual motion machines cannot exist in reality for not conforming to the second law of thermodynamics; neither can objects nor events in closed-loop motion spontaneously arise or circulate infinitely without an external energy injection. So, what exactly is the significance of material closed loop? How does it relate to material recycling? How does it work? And can its ultimate form lead to zero waste? Will it contribute to carbon neutral? We will then seek the answers to each of these questions.

11.1 Recycling and Closed Loop

A highly desirable state of resource use is one in which minerals are extracted, processed and manufactured into products, fully consumed by society (reused, repaired, refurbished, remanufactured, etc.) and eventually discarded, then completely broken down to the level of the initial raw material and re-enter into the industrial chain—unlike simple material recycling, which is undirected, material closed loop is directed.

So, compared to undirected material recycling, what are the characteristics of a directed material closed loop?

First, undirected material recycling is generally led by recyclers. After the recycler separates (physically) or breaks down (physically, chemically, biologically, etc.) the waste into its base materials (plastics, metals, etc.), it will return to the raw material market to participate in the material cycle at a certain value. So, the recycler does not care where the waste comes from (as long as the price is right), nor does he care what kind of customer will purchase the raw materials (as long as the price is reasonable), nor does he care what kind of product the customer will make from the raw materials after purchase (as long as it is not illegal). Because of this, recyclers are inevitably driven by profit to pick and choose waste with higher added value to recycle, rather than really focusing on all of it, especially the waste that has a greater impact on the ecology and environment.

Material closed loop is different. Directed material closed loop is generally manufacturer-driven. Manufacturers know exactly what raw materials they need to produce their products, and they know exactly which of these raw materials are easy to obtain from virgin sources and which are easy to obtain from recycled sources. Whenever possible, manufacturers are keen to have 100% of the materials in all waste products go back to their upstream raw material suppliers, preferably for free. So, manufacturer-led material closed loop is objectively most desirable for recycling their own products, which also includes waste with a high potential ecological and environmental impact.

Secondly, undirected material recycling does not have high requirement for recycling processes. It is because the recycler does not care what kind of customers will buy recycled materials, so it is generally in accordance with its own technical ability to choose the recycling process, as far as possible to find a balance between technical inputs and recycling profits. After all, recycled raw material can always find its buyer regardless of the process and quality, thus losing the drive for process improvement and stable quality.

But this is not the case for material closed loop. Since the manufacturer wants the material from the discarded product to go back to its upstream raw material supplier and continue to be used to supply its own production of the same product, the sophistication of the recycling process and the associated quality stability becomes important. The more advanced the process and the more consistent the quality, the more economical it is to return to the raw material; otherwise, poor or unstable quality will directly affect the subsequent processing and manufacturing, which is not as economical as sourcing the material from virgin sources.

Once again, undirected material recycling does not require much of logistics. As we learned in Chap. 10, material recycling is a relatively simple process in terms of its basic operation, although it falls under the scope of reverse logistics—the recycler collects the waste, processes it, and then distributes the value-added recycled material to the manufacturer's customers who need it. In this process, only the waste collection step is exactly reverse logistics, and the rest of the operation is exactly the same as forward logistics.

However, material closed loop works differently. The operation of material closed loop relies heavily on the implementation of full reverse logistics. In fact, there are two key points in the operation of material closed loop. The first is that in theory, only discarded in-house products (or waste from the manufacturing process of in-house products) are collected for raw materials recycling to the exclusion of other kinds of waste, even if they are the same materials; the second is that recycled raw materials are only sent upstream in the supply chain to continue to manufacture the same products of the same brand, rather than going to the market to sell for profit. It is not difficult to find that because of the exclusivity and non-marketability of material closed loop, the access to its reverse logistics is very narrow—if we compare this kind of logistics to a one-way bridge, it is not a big problem when the flow of people crossing the bridge is small; but when there are thousands of people to be selected to get across the bridge, and once arriving at the other side, they have to stay where they are, it would be quite a mess.

In addition, there is not much market regulation for undirected material recycling. As long as the recyclers comply with the requirements of local industrial, commercial and environmental regulations, and the quality of the recycled materials is not mixed up with that of virgin materials, the government will not intervene specifically, and may even issue supporting policies. This is quite understandable, after all, recyclers are making a positive contribution to ecological and environmental protection by treating and disposing of the waste.

But for material closed loop, because of the long supply chains of manufacturing in today's world, simple material recycling can be done locally, while the two logistics nodes for material closed loop are usually inter-territorial, or even cross-border. When one same waste is put in one place, the public and the media are often concerned about why and whether it will affect the local ecology and environment. When a recycled material passes through customs, which type of imported goods it is declared as, and whether it is a resource-based raw material or "foreign garbage" will attract additional attention from the regulatory authorities, which will lead to the enactment of regulations and special supervision.

Also, undirected material recycling cannot lead to total eco-design. As long as products are designed to be recyclable in their choice of materials, material recycling becomes possible. As discussed in Chap. 9, recyclability is still only a primary attribute of eco-design—recycling is better than incineration for energy recovery, but far worse than repairing and remanufacturing. If all discarded products were used for material recycling, then product design would not need to consider repairability and remanufacturability—two advanced attributes of eco-design that are not possible when manufacturers cannot obtain large quantities of their own discarded products for repairing and remanufacturing.

For material closed loop, when a discarded product returns to the manufacturer, repairing or remanufacturing to make it marketable again must be a priority from a manufacturing cost perspective—it becomes particularly important that the product was originally designed with repairability and remanufacturability; also, even if repairing or remanufacturing is not possible, only recyclability is considered, the manufacturer will still be able to fully realize the significance of eco-design at the beginning because it has considered the possible recycling process, combined with the target performance of the recycled material, the recycling rate, and recycled quality of the final material will be much higher than the general recycler.

At last, undirected material recycling does not fully reflect the Extended Producer Responsibility (EPR). Even if there are materials in the waste that can be recycled, it is worthwhile to recycle them, but this work, if done by the recycler, has little to do with the manufacturer. In other words, the manufacturer does not need to know what happens afterwards—whether it is actually recycled, incinerated, or landfilled, is unknown.

While in the case of material closed loop, for subsequent product manufacturing, the original manufacturer needs to know and be able to know where the waste is going, otherwise there is no way to close the loop; since they know where it is going, if the waste is not recycled or treated and disposed of in a compliant manner, the manufacturer also needs to take responsibility and solve the problem. When every manufacturer controls their own waste in a compliant manner, the entire industry chain will have a solid foundation for zero waste.

11.2 Regulatory Supervision

The previous chapter of reverse logistics mentioned waste logistics—waste logistics is the very basis of material closed loop, the purpose of which is to send certain waste products or waste from the manufacturing process of that product, in an organized and purposeful manner, to the raw material supplier of that product, and again into the manufacturing process of that product from the beginning.

In the discussion on the similarities and differences between material recycling and material closed loop, it is also mentioned that waste logistics are, and should be, subject to relevant laws and regulations. In Chap. 5 on waste management, the Basel Convention is one of the most important international conventions specifically for waste logistics, especially hazardous waste logistics.

Although the 1995 amendment to the Basel Convention explicitly prohibits the export of hazardous wastes from developed countries to developing countries for the purpose of final disposal, there are two details worth noting: one is the identification of hazardous wastes—if they are hazardous, they need to comply with the international convention, and if they are not hazardous, they don't need to comply; the other is final disposal—what is final disposal and what is not.

The answers to these two questions must be scientifically rigorous and, at the same time, dynamic as waste treatment and disposal technologies evolve. To address these two questions, the United Nations Environment Programme (UNEP) has established 14 Basel Convention Regional and Coordinating Centers (referred to as Basel Centers) around the world, whose basic functions are those of the regional centers identified by successive meetings of the Conference of the Parties to the Basel Convention, and also include training, technology transfer, provision of information, advisory services, awareness-raising activities, etc. Basel Centers will answer the above two questions and coordinate their implementation in accordance with the provisions of the Convention for countries and regions in the area.

If the so-called "waste" in material closed loop has a clear economic value, with logistics directed to a qualified processor that provides raw materials for a specified product, and the materials do not pose an obvious or potential hazard to the ecology and environment of the country or region involved during controlled transport and

11.2 Regulatory Supervision

processing, the "waste" should not be defined as "waste", not to mention hazardous waste (provided, of course, that there is proof and evidence of compliance).

Also comparing recycling we find that the environmental benefits of having "waste" products that cannot be reused, repaired, refurbished or remanufactured, along with the homogeneous materials cut and polished during the manufacturing process, directed back to the source of the specified product to be remanufactured as raw materials for that product, are significantly better than undirected recycling—since this is the case, material closed loop should not be considered as general disposal of waste (provided also that various process descriptions and lists of materials in and out of storage are prepared as proof and evidence of compliance).

In addition, Chap. 5 on waste management states that the governments of various countries and regions have formulated a series of laws, regulations and standards to positively guide waste logistics and material closed loop that are beneficial to the ecology and environment of the country, and to strictly restrict waste logistics that are detrimental to the ecology and environment of the country. In China, for example, the current Law on the Prevention and Control of Solid Waste Pollution has the following provisions.

> Chapter 1, General Provisions, Article 3, provides that:
>
> The State promotes a green approach to development and the development of cleaner production and a circular economy.
>
> The State advocates a simple and moderate, green and low-carbon lifestyle and guides the public to actively participate in the prevention and control of solid waste pollution.
>
> Chapter 1, General Provisions, Article 4, provides that:
>
> The prevention and control of solid waste pollution adheres to the principles of reduction, resource recovery and harmlessness.
>
> Any unit or individual should take measures to reduce the amount of solid waste generated, promote the comprehensive use of solid waste and reduce the hazardous nature of solid waste.
>
> Chapter 2, Supervision and Administration, Article 14, provides that:
>
> The department in charge of ecology and environment under the State Council shall, in conjunction with the relevant departments of the State Council, develop solid waste identification standards, identification procedures and national technical standards for the prevention and control of environmental pollution by solid waste in accordance with national environmental quality standards and national economic and technological conditions.
>
> Chapter 2, Supervision and Administration, Article 16, provides that:
>
> The department in charge of ecology and environment under the State Council shall, in conjunction with the relevant departments of the State Council, establish a national information platform for the prevention and control of pollution of the environment by hazardous wastes and other solid wastes, and promote the monitoring and information-based tracing of the entire process of collection, transfer and disposal of solid wastes.
>
> Chapter 2, Supervision and Administration, Article 22, provides that:
>
> The transfer of solid wastes out of the administrative region of a province, autonomous region or municipality directly under the Central Government for storage or disposal shall be applied for by the competent department of ecology and environment of the people's government of the province, autonomous region or municipality directly under the Central

Government from which the solid wastes are transferred. With the approval from the competent department of the ecology and environment of the people's government of the receiving province, autonomous region or municipality directly under the Central Government, the competent department of the ecology and environment of the people's government of the province, autonomous region or municipality directly under the Central Government shall transfer the solid waste within the prescribed time limit. No transfer shall take place without such approval.

The transfer of solid wastes for use out of the administrative region of a province, autonomous region or municipality directly under the Central Government shall be reported to the competent department of the ecology and environment of the people's government of the province, autonomous region or municipality directly under the Central Government from which the solid wastes are transferred for the record. The competent department of the ecology and environment of the people's government of the province, autonomous region or municipality directly under the Central Government from which the solid waste is transferred shall notify the competent department of the ecology and environment of the people's government of the province, autonomous region or municipality directly under the Central Government where it is received of the information and keep record.

Chapter 2, Supervision and Administration, Article 23, provides that:

The entry of solid wastes from outside the People's Republic of China for dumping, depositing and disposal is prohibited.

Chapter 2, Supervision and Administration, Article 24, provides that:

The State gradually realizes zero import of solid waste, which is organized and implemented by the competent department of the State Council for ecology and environment in conjunction with the competent departments of the State Council for commerce, development and reform, and customs.

Chapter 2, Supervision and Administration, Article 25, provides that:

If Customs finds that imported goods are suspected of being solid wastes, it may entrust professional institutions to carry out property identification and manage them according to the identification conclusions in accordance with the law.

Chapter 6 Hazardous Wastes, Article 89, provides that:

Prohibit the transboundary movement of hazardous wastes through the People's Republic of China.

Chapter 9, By-laws, Article 124, the meaning of terms is explained as:

Solid wastes are solid, semi-solid and gaseous objects and substances in containers that have lost their original use value or have not lost their use value but have been abandoned or discarded, as well as objects and substances that are included in the management of solid wastes under laws and administrative regulations, excluding those that have been processed in a harmless manner and meet the mandatory national product quality standards, do not endanger public health and ecological safety, or are determined not to be solid waste according to solid waste identification standards and identification procedures.

Hazardous wastes are solid wastes with hazardous characteristics that are listed on the national list of hazardous wastes or identified according to the national criteria and methods for the identification of hazardous wastes.

From the legal provisions, it is understood that in addition to strict control of transregional waste transfer, China will also gradually achieve zero import of solid waste; at the same time, it will develop solid waste identification standards and identification procedures to accurately screen out resource materials; in addition, it will encourage producers of products to carry out eco-design and establish a recovery system for used products to promote a circular economy.

Under such regulations, material closed loop not only have room to operate in compliance within the country, but can even receive policy support. But the cross-border situation is more complicated, as the material identification result must not be hazardous waste, even if it is ordinary resource-based waste—as long as it is waste, material closed loop cannot operate.

The strategic importance of such strict legislation is significant. On the one hand, it will put an end to the entry of solid waste from abroad for dumping, depositing and disposal under the guise of circular economy and material closed loop; on the other hand, gradually cutting off the offshore sources of solid waste will force all kinds of transformation of domestic resource-based waste—moving from zero import of solid waste to zero waste.

In short, the operation of material closed loop can only be truly ecologically and environmentally beneficial if it strictly adheres to the relevant laws and regulations.

11.3 Material Identification

At the legal and regulatory level, it can be seen that there is certainly no room for compliant material closed loop to operate as long as they are identified as solid waste, regardless of where they are and how resourceful they are. So, the identification of material closed loop, or conversely the identification of solid waste, directly determines the viability of material closed loop.

The identification of solid waste, in addition to the definitions in the legal and regulatory provisions, each country and region also has an identification process and technical standards to go with it. Taking China as an example, the identification process and technical standards for solid waste are mainly as follows.

11.3.1 Identification Procedures

The procedures of solid waste property identification mainly include commissioning and acceptance of identification, general identification, re-inspection, disagreement or objection handling, etc.

(1) Commission and acceptance of identification

When commissioning an identification, the commissioning party shall submit the following to the identification agency:

① Letter of request for identification services (need to state the reasons for identification);
② Identifying information on the origin of the goods produced;

③ Applications for re-inspection and identification should be submitted with a self-declaration and the test or identification material that has been carried out;
④ Other necessary information as required by the identification agency.

When the identification agency agrees to accept the commission, it shall inform the client of the cost and time required for the identification work.

(2) General identification

If it is one of the following scenarios, the client may commission an identification agency to identify whether a substance or article is solid waste and its category.

① Where it is difficult for Customs to make a decision on whether to include imported goods in the management of solid wastes due to the specificity of the substance or article properties, the Customs may commission an identification agency to identify the properties of solid wastes;
② Where the smuggled goods investigated by anti-smuggling department of Customs need identification of the properties of solid waste; where the competent ecology and environment authorities and other government agencies require identification of the properties of solid waste in the process of supervision and management;
③ Administrative departments and judicial authorities may commission identification agencies to identify the properties of solid waste after receiving administrative reconsideration or administrative litigation from consignees or their agents.

(3) Re-inspection

If the consignee or his agent disagrees with the Customs' inclusion of his imported goods into the scope of solid waste management, he may apply for re-inspection and identification, and the Customs will commission an identification agency to re-inspect and identify the solid waste properties. The re-inspection and identification shall be carried out at most once. The identification agency that has undertaken the task of identification of the goods will not accept the commission of re-inspection and identification in principle.

Re-inspection and identification of the commissioning party shall inform the re-inspection identification agency of Customs determination reference (inspection report or identification report) in writing; if the goods have been identified, the re-inspection agency shall notice the first identification agency of its acceptance of re-inspection and identification. If the commissioning party has not informed the re-inspection identification, its conclusions will be considered invalid. The identification agency shall indicate in the identification report that it is a re-inspection and identification.

(4) Disagreement or objection handling

If the conclusion of the re-inspection and identification is inconsistent with that of the first identification, or if there is serious disagreement between the relevant parties on the identification conclusion, or if there is no suitable identification agency to carry

11.3 Material Identification

out the identification, the relevant parties (such as Customs, judicial authorities, consignees or their agents, etc.) may submit a written application to the General Administration of Customs, which shall include the report on the identification of solid waste properties that has been carried out and other relevant materials, and shall state in writing the conclusions of each relevant party on the identification. The General Administration of Customs will consult the Ministry of Ecology and Environment on the application.

The Ministry of Ecology and Environment, in conjunction with the General Administration of Customs, shall organize and convene an expert meeting to study the matter, and the members of the expert group shall consist of experts recommended by the Ministry of Ecology and Environment and the General Administration of Customs; the personnel of the agency implementing the inspection and identification of the solid waste properties of the imported goods shall not be members of the expert group. The unanimous opinion reached at the expert meeting shall be the final result, and if it is difficult to reach a unanimous opinion at the expert meeting due to insufficient objective evidence, specific requirements for the next step need to be put forward, such as additional analysis of test data, and if another expert meeting needs to be held, the Ministry of Ecology and Environment shall determine the time and place.

11.3.2 Technical Regulation

(1) Sampling and analytical testing of samples

Collect representative samples (depending on the form and packaging of the goods), select analysis and testing items whose main purpose is to determine the origin and properties of the substances produced, and selectively conduct analysis and testing according to the characteristics of different samples, including but not limited to appearance characteristics, physical indicators, main components and content, chemical structure of the main substances, impurity components and content, typical characteristics indicators, processing performance, hazardous waste characteristics, etc.

The analysis and testing of samples should be in accordance with the relevant norms, and the laboratory management of the identification agency which is carrying out the analysis should be standardized and complete; when subcontracting is required for analysis and testing, priority should be given to laboratories with metrological certification, or to experienced professional laboratories.

(2) Sample property identification

① Compare and analyze the physical and chemical characteristics and properties of the identified samples with literature, product standards, etc. and, if necessary, consult with relevant industry experts to determine the basic process by which the identified samples were generated.

② The solid waste properties of the identified samples are determined according to the Identification Standards for Solid Wastes—General Rules (GB 34330—2017).
③ If the same identification sample or the same batch of identification samples is a mixture of solid waste and non-solid waste, an overall comprehensive judgment shall be made based on the analysis of the reasonableness of the source of the process or the source of generation, and strict requirements shall be imposed when it is found that harmful components are obviously mixed.

(3) On-site-spot identification

① The identification agent may carry out on-site identification of substances and articles that are not suitable for sending samples for identification.
② During on-site identification, all containers of the shipment to be identified shall be opened for inspection and the characteristics of the opened shipment shall be recorded and described.
③ On-site identification of the number of containers to be emptied and inspected shall not be less than 10% of the total number of containers; according to the on-site situation, the containers can be fully, half or 1/3 empty, in order to see and understand the overall condition of the goods, and characteristics of the emptied goods shall be recorded and described; if the goods are not too many and can be accurately inspected and understood without emptying the whole container, emptying the container can be unnecessary.
④ The percentage of goods emptied from the container to be opened for inspection shall be no less than 20% of the total goods emptied from the container; characteristics of the emptied and unpacked goods shall be described and recorded.
⑤ For on-site identification of solid wastes transported in bulk by sea and by land, 100% inspection shall be implemented, and no less than 10% of landing inspection shall be implemented.

(4) Identification report preparation

① The identification report shall contain the necessary identification information, such as the principal, the source of the sample, the customs declaration number, the time of receipt of the sample, the sample mark, the sample number, the description of the appearance of the sample, the basis of the identification work, the time of issuance of the identification report, the identification report number, etc., and the identification report may be appropriately simplified if it can be completed on the basis of on-site inspection.
② The identification report should be well prepared, clearly organized, with sound analytical arguments and clear property identification conclusions.
③ The identification report should be signed by at least the identification officer and the reviewer, with the official seal of the identification body.
④ When it is necessary to amend or supplement an identification report already issued, the original report issued shall be withdrawn and the necessary explanations shall be given in the re-issued identification report.

11.3.3 Identification Standard

In addition to using general solid waste determination criteria to distinguish and identify material closed loop, sometimes specific technical criteria for identification are used—if these criteria are met, a portion of the resource-based "waste" can often be exempted and become eligible material closed loop, rather than simply being determined as solid waste and lost to the material cycle.

The most common criteria for identifying resource-based "waste" currently focus on two main categories: recycled plastics and recycled metals.

There are many different kinds of recycled plastics. China is a major producer of recycled plastics, and national standards related to recycled plastics (pellets), which have been issued, are being developed or are under planning. These standards cover the five major general-purpose plastics [polyethylene (PE), polypropylene (PP), polyvinyl chloride (PVC), polystyrene (PS) and acrylonitrile–butadiene–styrene co-polymer (ABS)], as well as several other plastics commonly used in industry.

Plastics—Recycled Plastics—Part 1: General Rules
Plastics—Recycled Plastics—Part 2: Polyethylene (PE) Materials
Plastics—Recycled Plastics—Part 3: Polypropylene (PP) Materials
Plastics—Recycled Plastics—Part 4: Polyvinyl Chloride (PVC) Materials
Plastics—Recycled Plastics—Part 5: Acrylonitrile–Butadiene–Styrene (ABS) Materials
Plastics—Recycled Plastics—Part 6: Polystyrene (PS) Materials
Plastics—Recycled Plastics—Part 7: Polycarbonate (PC) Materials
Plastics—Recycled Plastics—Part 8: Polyamide (PA) Materials
Plastics—Recycled Plastics—Part 9: Polyethylene Terephthalate (PET) Materials

In addition, the national standard Classification and Code of Waste Plastics provides a unified and standardized definition of various resource waste plastics, the national standard Technical Specifications for Recycling of Waste Plastics provides clear technical requirements for waste plastics recycling process and enterprises, etc. These national standards are still being supplemented and revised.

There are many more types of recycled metals. Depending on the level of industrial development and subsequent manufacturing industries in each country and region, the standards implemented for metal recycling vary widely. The most common of these are copper and aluminum. Still taking China as an example, the following national standards have been issued, are being developed or are under planning.

Standards for recycled copper:

① Rods and bars of recycling copper and copper alloys;
② Recycling materials for copper;
③ Recycling materials for brass.

Standard for recycled aluminium:

① Recycling materials for cast aluminium alloys;

② Recycling materials for pure aluminium;
③ Recycling materials for wrought aluminium alloys.

In addition to this, China Non-Ferrous Metals Industry Association and other industry associations have issued some group standards on copper and aluminium. Of particular importance is that China has also issued the emission standards of pollutants for secondary copper, aluminum, lead and zinc, as a means of regulating the recycled metal industry in order to achieve the objective of no secondary pollution.

Like the relevant laws and regulations, these technical standards for identifying solid waste and material closed loop are not static. As the economy develops and science advances, either non-recyclable wastes become recyclable, or recycling processes that would have produced secondary pollution are upgraded so that those secondary pollutants are completely eliminated. Academically, there is no absolute boundary between solid waste and material closed loop; there are simply gaps waiting to be crossed at different times and in different places.

11.4 Economic Benefit and Environmental Benefit

The economic and environmental benefits of material closed loop, after ignoring the unavoidable and indeed negligible material losses, can both be assessed in terms of the energy consumption of the entire closed-loop industrial chain. The lower the energy consumption, the lower the cost to the whole industry chain is bound to be; at the same time, the lower the energy consumption, the lower the carbon emissions of the whole industry chain, the lower the impact on the ecology and environment, and more conducive to carbon neutral.

We again compare material recycling with material closed loop by calculating the energy consumption of the system under ideal conditions for a given material in a given product, through product discard and reverse logistics, in two different ways of recycling and closed loop, back to the original given product in the same physical state. Let's go back to the second law of thermodynamics from Chap. 3 and look at the difference in energy in terms of the enthalpy and entropy changes of the system.

The thermodynamic state parameter that characterizes the system energy in a given system is denoted by "enthalpy" (H). Enthalpy is a function of the state of the system, independent of the path of state change, and has a uniquely determined value as long as the state of the system is fixed. We assume that the system energy value of a material in a product is H_0.

The value of system energy change in the various steps of normal use, discard and reverse logistics is the enthalpy change, expressed as ΔH, and its differential expression is dH; the value of system disorder degree change is the entropy change, expressed as ΔS, and its differential expression is dS.

If the various steps (process) of normal material use, discard and reverse logistics are denoted as P, although these steps are scattered and uncertain, since they eventually return to the initial material state, system energy change can be written as a

11.4 Economic Benefit and Environmental Benefit

closed curve integral of the material enthalpy change from the initial state 0 through the path of P and back to the initial state.

$$\Delta E = \oint_0^P dH$$

According to the definition of Gibbs free energy (G), there is no reduced internal energy to do external work in the process we investigated, so the Gibbs free energy change $\Delta G = 0$. Combined with $\Delta G = \Delta H - T\Delta S$, we get $\Delta H = T\Delta S$, the differential expression is $dH = TdS$.

Combined with above, we have:

$$\Delta E = \oint_0^P dH = \oint_0^P TdS$$

Now we investigate two different P paths of material closed loop and material recycling, and write them as P_{MCL} and P_{MR}. In an ideal situation, the initial material M_0 in a product will undergo the following changes through the post-consumer material M_C:

$$P_{\text{MCL}} : M_0 \rightarrow M_C \rightarrow M_0$$

$$P_{\text{MR}} : M_0 \rightarrow M_C \rightarrow \sum_{u=1}^{\infty} M_{Ru} \rightarrow \sum_{u=1}^{\infty} M_{Rv} \rightarrow M_0$$

Among them, Ru means that the post-consumer material is recovered and dispersed to u states, while Rv means that the recovered and dispersed materials are recombined from different v states.

Under these two different paths, the energy changes of the system are as follows:

$$\Delta E_{\text{MCL}} = \oint_0^{P_{\text{MCL}}} TdS_{\text{MCL}}$$

$$\Delta E_{\text{MR}} = \oint_0^{P_{\text{MR}}} TdS_{\text{MR}}$$

In either case, for the sake of comparison, we can set the absolute temperature T to be the same and remain unchanged; at the same time, the system energy E is also a state function independent of the path of change, so in fact, we only need to compare dS_{MCL} and dS_{MR}.

It is obvious that P_{MR} is more disordered than P_{MCL}, and the entropy increase of material mixing process is higher (the microscopic state of material is more difficult to describe) due to the additional change of system from $\sum_{u=1}^{\infty} M_{Ru}$ dispersion to $\sum_{v=1}^{\infty} M_{Rv}$ recombination.

Therefore,

$$\mathrm{d}S_{\mathrm{MCL}} < \mathrm{d}S_{\mathrm{MR}}$$

$$\oint_0^{P_{\mathrm{MCL}}} T\mathrm{d}S_{\mathrm{MCL}} < \oint_0^{P_{\mathrm{MR}}} T\mathrm{d}S_{\mathrm{MR}}$$

Conclusion:

$$\Delta E_{\mathrm{MCL}} < \Delta E_{\mathrm{MR}}$$

So, in contrast to material recycling, material closed loop can reduce the overall energy consumption of the industrial chain associated with that material—the whole industry chain is more cost efficient and has lower carbon emissions—thus it has a lower ecology and environment impact.

In theory, material closed loop can have economic and environmental benefits for the entire industrial chain, and in reality, material closed loop will undoubtedly bring both economic and environmental benefits for product manufacturers.

① It is inevitably more cost efficient for a product manufacturer to obtain discarded products and scraps in the processing of that product at low or no cost, and send them to a raw material supplier, than for its raw material supplier to go through mining, processing and refining.
② Since discarded products and normal scraps are already qualified raw materials, in addition to the necessary cleaning and degreasing (generally lubricating and cutting oils from machining processes), the cost of manpower and equipment for material inspection is also reduced.
③ Since a series of primary and recycling processes are eliminated, potential secondary waste from these processes is also effectively avoided.
④ As mentioned in the previous difference analysis, manufacturers are concerned with the transformation between raw materials and waste—two different names for the same substance, throughout the "whole life" cycle of the products they manufacture, maximizing economic benefits while taking into account the Extended Producer Responsibility (EPR) and environmental benefits.

The inevitable result of balancing economic and environmental benefits is that material closed loop objectively lead to zero waste. Where is the waste when materials are all in a closed loop; and zero waste in turn drives material closed loop—if you don't want waste, find a way to send the "waste" back to the raw material suppliers! Zero waste and material closed loop are actually complementing each other.

11.5 Zero Waste, Carbon Neutral

Since material closed loop have clear economic and environmental benefits, they have a theoretical meaning of their existence; since regulations and technical supervision already exist, there is room for them to operate in practice. The ultimate goal of material closed loop is to achieve zero waste, and to boost carbon neutral. Why?

First, material closed loop have eliminated the concept of "waste" from their definition. Materials, at whatever stage, are materials in various forms, either mined, processed, manufactured, consumed, or recycled. In short, they are not discarded at all.

Secondly, material closed loop in order to maximize the value of materials in the operation, will not allow subjective loss and waste, but also will certainly objectively reduce the pollution caused to the environment in the whole chain, that is, will not produce a variety of secondary waste.

Finally, when all materials have closed the loop in their respective industries, if natural population growth is not taken into account, theoretically all humans will only need energy and no more material supply. According to the principles of thermodynamics, the contribution of human activities to the entropy reduction of the biosphere system on the Earth is minimized, which will help the biosphere system to maintain thermodynamic stability and the carbon neutral in human society—greatly reduce or even eliminate indirect carbon emissions from intermediate products consumption in the process of production or service.

Admittedly, the road to material closed loop is still very long—we don't know when and which materials will gradually be in a closed loop. But, we are confident that humankind is bound to take small steps towards this ultimate goal and outlook.

Chapter 12
On Circular Economy

The subject of circular economy is too large and not the focus of this book. However, as an inevitable direction and result of zero waste, it is necessary to discuss the various aspects of the circular economy and to analyze the contribution of zero waste to the circular economy with a few typical business models.

12.1 Background and Support

Circular economy, also known as "resource circular economy", is an economic development model characterized by resource conservation and recovery in harmony with the environment. The circular economy emphasizes the organization of economic activities into a feedback process of "resource—product—renewable resource". It is characterized by low extraction, high utilization and low discharge. All materials and energy can be used rationally and sustainably in this ongoing economic cycle, so as to reduce the impact of economic activities on the ecology and environment to the lowest possible level.

The fundamental purpose of a circular economy is to require the minimization of resource inputs in economic processes and the systematic avoidance and reduction of waste, with waste recycling only reducing the final volume of waste disposal. The importance of the "3R" principles of the circular economy—"Reduce, Reuse, Recycle"—is not juxtaposed; they are arranged in a scientific order:

Reduction belongs to the input side and aims to reduce the amount of material entering the production and consumption process;

Reuse belongs to the process and aims to extend the duration of products and services;

Recycle belongs to the output side and aims to resource the waste again to reduce the final disposal volume.

The priorities in dealing with waste are: avoidance of generation—recycling—final disposal. That is to say, firstly, we should give full consideration to saving resources, improving the utilization rate of resources per unit of product, preventing and reducing the generation of waste at the source of production; secondly, we should recycle the wastes that cannot be reduced at the source, so that they can be returned to the economic cycle; only when neither avoidance of generation nor recycling can be achieved is environment-harmless treatment of waste allowed. The highest goal of harmonizing environment and development is to achieve a qualitative leap from end-of-pipe treatment to source control, from waste utilization to waste reduction, and to fundamentally reduce the consumption of natural resources and thus the environmental load.

Circular economy is in line with sustainable development, emphasizing the harmonious coexistence of social and economic systems and natural ecology systems, and is a systematic project integrating economy, technology and society. The circular economy is not simply an economic issue, nor is it simply a technical issue or an environmental protection issue, but takes the coordinated relationship between human beings and nature as a guideline, simulates the mode of operation and laws of the natural ecology system, transforms social production from quantitative material growth to qualitative service growth, and pushes the whole society onto a civilized development path of production, affluent living and good ecology, which requires humanistic culture, institutional innovation, scientific and technological innovation, structural adjustment and other overall coordination of social development.

The implementation of a circular economy needs to be supported by a complete system, which includes:

(1)   Policy and legal support

The circular economy cannot start operating spontaneously without the support of policies and legal. Only if the state and society recognize the importance of the circular economy can the ideological limitations of enterprises and individuals be overcome and the measures of the circular economy be put in place.

(2)   Science and technology support

All reduce, reuse and recycle cannot be achieved without the development of sciences and technologies. "Pseudo" environmental projects without scientific proof abound; "pseudo" environmental theories without technical practice can be found everywhere. Only by starting with the objective laws of science and technology can we truly find opportunities for the development of a circular economy.

(3)   Financial investment support

Launching a circular economy requires national policies and laws, as well as a certain amount of financial investment. Many of these investments have long payback periods and the economic benefits are not visible in the short term, so in many cases project investments need to be strategically led by international or national development banks.

(4) Supervision and management support

There will always be companies or individuals who operate unscrupulously under the banner of the circular economy, so there is a need for both policy and legal support, as well as supervision and management by market regulators—effective supervision and management can help the circular economy model to develop healthily.

(5) Economic benefits support

The enterprises in the circular economy chain must be supported by stable economic benefits, must be profitable in the long term, and must continue to add value in order to ensure that the circular economy is sustained and widespread, and that investors recover their costs and invest more in the same project, or find new circular economy projects to invest in.

12.2 Development Concept

The circular economy, as a scientific concept of development and a new model of economic development, has been universally recognized worldwide. Its main concepts are expressed in the following aspects.

(1) New system outlook

A cycle is a process of movement within a certain system, and the system of a circular economy is a large system composed of elements such as people, natural resources and science and technology. The circular economy concept requires that people are no longer outside this large system when considering production and consumption.

(2) New values outlook

When considering nature, the circular economy concept treats it as the basis on which human beings live and as an ecosystem that needs to maintain a virtuous cycle; when considering science and technology, it takes full account of its ability to repair the ecosystem and make it environmentally beneficial; and when considering the development of human beings themselves, it attaches greater importance to the ability of human beings to live in harmony with nature and to promote the all-round development of human beings.

(3) New production outlook

The circular economy concept requires that the carrying capacity of natural ecosystems be fully considered in production, that natural resources be conserved as much as possible, that the efficiency of their use be continuously improved, that resources be recovered and that virtuous social wealth be created. At the same time, production also requires the use of renewable resources to replace non-renewable resources as far as possible.

(4) New consumer outlook

The circular economy concept advocates moderate and hierarchical consumption of materials, taking into consideration the resourcefulness of waste while consuming and establishing the concept of circular production and consumption; at the same time, the circular economy concept calls for restricting the production and consumption of disposable products made from non-renewable resources through tax and other administrative means.

12.3 Legal Difference

In the 1970s in developed countries, although people did not yet have a clear concept of circular economy legislation, Germany, Japan, the United States and the European Community (the predecessor of the EU) enacted some laws that dealt with the idea of circular economy, such as the Waste Disposal Act enacted in Germany in 1972, the Waste Disposal Act published in Japan in 1970, the Resource Conservation and Recycling Act in 1976, and the Waste Directive adopted by the European Community in 1975, were the germ of circular economy legislation. These pieces of legislation objectively set out what we mean by circular economy legislation today and initially embodied the legislative requirements for safeguarding and developing a circular economy.

By the early 1990s, with the gradual clarification of the idea of developing a circular economy, the issue of circular economy legislation was naturally brought up. True circular economy legislation was marked by the enactment of Germany's Circular Economy and Waste Disposal Act (27 September, 1994), followed by Japan's Basic Law for the Establishment of a Circular Society. China's Circular Economy Promotion Law has been in force since 1 January, 2009, and was amended and published for implementation on 26 October, 2018.

Germany, Japan and China, which are representative of circular economy legislation in the world, have all established the 3R principles of Reduce, Reuse and Recycle, Extended Producer Responsibility (EPR) systems and waste recovery systems in different forms in their legal provisions; however, there are obvious differences between the three countries' circular economy legal systems in terms of legislative models, management systems, producer responsibility and waste recovery systems.

(1) Legislative model

Germany's circular economy legislation was developed on the basis of the waste legal system, adopting a monolithic legislative model that integrates the disposal and utilization of waste; Japan's circular economy legislation was developed on the basis of the legal system for waste disposal and for the promotion of the efficient utilization of resources, adopting a legislative model that uses the basic circular law as the framework law to unify the two; China's circular economy legislation was developed on the basis of the comprehensive utilization of resources China's circular economy legislation is based on the policy system of comprehensive utilization of resources and draws on the experience of developed countries' circular economy legislation—it differs from both Germany's monolithic model (in addition to the Circular Economy Promotion Law, China also has the Law on Prevention and Control of Solid Waste Pollution) and Japan's basic law model (the basic law encompasses the whole process of management of the material cycle of reduction, efficient utilization and harmless disposal). This is the whole process of managing the material cycle, and its goal is to unify the waste disposal law and the law on the promotion of the efficient utilization of resources, whereas China's circular economy legislation focuses on the conservation and comprehensive use of resources and does not include the content of harmless disposal.

(2) Management system

In both Germany and Japan, the legislation on circular economy stipulates that the environment department is the competent authority for circular economy, which is related to the fact that the legislation on circular economy in both countries mainly focuses on waste; the legislation on circular economy in China covers a broader scope, including the rational development and efficient use of resources, the total control of water and land use, as well as the promotion of circular production methods and industrial restructuring, etc. China's circular economy authority is in fact a horizontal and vertical cross-cutting authority, namely the National Development and Reform Commission (NDRC).

(3) Producer responsibility

As a form of legal principle, China's Law on the Promotion of Circular Economy stipulates that the extended producer responsibility is borne by the producer; as a specific institutional form, the obligation of the producer to pay the treatment and disposal fund is clearly stipulated in the relevant regulations of each industry (e.g. the Regulations on the Administration of the Recycling of Waste Electrical and Electronic Equipment). This is similar to Germany, but also has some difference. In Germany, producers are broadly defined as "those who develop, produce, process, sell or dispose of products" and are subject to product liability for the purpose of achieving a circular economy; in China, extended producer responsibility is concentrated on producers, while the role of trading companies and consumers is minimal.

(4) Waste recovery system

Germany and Japan have established public recovery systems or private recovery systems for waste under institutional arrangements, forming a stable and standardized recovery system and ensuring a high resource recovery rate—since the recovery systems operate under strict control of administrative regulation, the operation costs are relatively high; China's recovery system is more complex, showing a diversified structure of recovery channels, among which the private recovery system plays a leading role—since resource recovery is paid recovery, administrative regulation is weak and it operates entirely by market forces, so the operation costs are relatively low, while there are problems such as unregulated recovery behavior and unstable recovery levels.

12.4 Innovation Model

The "lure" of the circular economy has often led us to think outside the box and take a disruptive approach to finding a way out to zero waste—we look at several innovative models that are rapidly developing in the twenty-first century to explore new opportunities for zero waste in the circular economy.

12.4.1 Commercial Leasing

A lease is simply the act of a lessor giving the right to use an asset to a lessee for an agreed period of time in return for rent. Commercial leasing is a new way to acquire equipment or products by a leasing company that purchases the equipment or products when the enterprise or individual needs them and then subleases them to the enterprise or individual.

The idea of commercial leasing, for the (manufacturing) enterprise, lies in the fact that profits can only be generated through the use of an asset—not by owning it; for the (consumer) individual, lies in the fact that I don't have to own a product, but I can use it if I like it—I only pay for the right to use it.

If society were to accept the commercial leasing model, it would open a completely different window to zero waste. As enterprises and individuals no longer own a certain equipment or product, the concept of "abandonment" will not arise in the lessees of enterprises and individuals. Even on the lessor side, i.e., the leasing company that purchased the equipment or product, not only will the equipment or product be "fully" reused among enterprise customers and individual users as much as possible for the sake of maximizing economic benefits, but also will spare no effort to use repairing and refurbishment methods to extend the life of the equipment or product as long as possible, and will send the equipment or product to recycling and remanufacturing for a second life after it has completely lost its rental value.

The leasing market in many industries is extremely hot today. The main areas involved in commercial leasing in terms of size, from large to small generally include: real estate leasing, aviation leasing, car leasing, construction machinery leasing, book leasing, clothing leasing, outdoor sporting goods leasing, etc. The industry penetration is quite extensive.

Real estate rentals really don't have much to do with zero waste. Real estate, whether bought or rented, does not build and demolish its building too often; multiple rentals and secondary (multiple) renovations instead generate a lot more construction waste.

Aviation leasing is on the rise in the world. By acquiring the right to use an aircraft through leasing, the airline operator (carrier) can not only save the huge investment in the initial purchase of the aircraft, but also have the flexibility to choose a replacement aircraft type to meet the market demand. The form of leasing aircraft can significantly increase the comprehensive service life of a certain type of aircraft, thus relatively delaying the abandonment of aircraft due to the obsolescence of old models.

Car leasing is much more common and widespread in the world. The vast majority of enterprises and individuals who own cars do not use them very much and spend much of their time "idling" in parking garages or parking lots. Leasing is a more rational way to use cars, leaving repair, maintenance and end-of-life disposal to more professional car rental companies, again with the aim of increasing utilization and reducing the number of abandoned vehicles.

Leasing of construction machinery generally occurs during mega construction projects. Engineering enterprises generally do not go for special procurement of construction machinery for a particular project even a very big one, but use leasing. This saves on fixed asset investment, and secondly, there are no problems such as idling and scrapping of equipment.

Book rentals have been around for ages. In ancient times, books were collectible, so people bought them, and after reading them they would rather put them away than lend them easily. Nowadays books have become increasingly electronic and, like other audio-visual publications, there is little point in owning and collecting them—since they are only for reading, learning and entertainment, it is better to rent them than to buy them, saving money without regretfully throwing them away as trash when moving and cleaning.

Clothing rentals, while loved by some and disliked by others, and often lacking effective market regulation (mainly from a health and hygiene perspective), have become a major means of clothing waste diversion, along with donations. Not to mention the rental of theatre and performance costumes, I'm sure many of you have experienced renting dresses and wedding gowns for your wedding photos. For clothing that are needed extremely occasionally, renting is a wonderful way to avoid discarding.

Outdoor sporting goods, as specialized personal equipment, don't generally need to be purchased and equipped by the individual, as long as they are not professional athletes. In particular, special equipment for hiking, skiing and camping can be rented at your destination, so there is no need to take up a space at home in the city and abandon it after just using it a few times a year.

12.4.2 Sharing Economy

Sharing economy, usually refers to a new economic model based on strangers and the existence of temporary transfer of the right to use goods for the main purpose of obtaining certain benefits. Its essence is to integrate various social resources, such as idle goods, labor, education and health care, which are otherwise unrelated to each other, to serve consumers with greater efficiency.

The most important feature of the sharing economy is an information technology-based marketplace platform created by a third party (which can be a commercial institution, organization or government), through which individuals exchange idle goods, share their knowledge and experience, or raise funds for a company or an innovative project; the sharing economy platform serves as a link between supply and demand, through the design of applications, dynamic algorithms and pricing.

The five elements of the sharing economy are: idle resources, access, connectivity, information, and mobility. The key to the sharing economy is how to achieve optimal matching, achieve zero marginal cost, and solve the bottlenecks of established technologies and systems. The development of the sharing economy is a process of disintermediation and reintermediation.

Disintermediation: the emergence of the sharing economy breaks the dependence of workers on commercial organizations, and they can provide services or products directly to end users.

Reintermediation: individual service providers, although detached from commercial organizations, need access to (mobile) Internet sharing economy platforms in order to reach the demand side more widely.

Today the sharing economy has become an important force within the social services industry. In transportation, space, entertainment and financial services, well-known sharing economy companies are emerging, including UBER for travel sharing, WeWork for office sharing, Airbnb for accommodation sharing, VaShare for vacation sharing, Steam for video game sharing, Eatwith for food sharing, Prosper for money sharing, etc.

The benefits of the sharing economy are obvious under certain context—while saving society's resources, it can also theoretically directly avoid or reduce the production of various wastes.

(1) Creating or perpetuating the value of resources

The sharing economy allows idle resources, from not being used to being fully used, in which case it can be given added or continued value. Added value refers to the value that is added to an object's original value—the use of a given goods by its owner generates a certain value, and by sharing it, others, who do not own the goods, generate added value in the process of enjoying the right to use it; continued value refers to, an idle resource owned by an individual in the sharing economy can be transferred from the hands of those who do not need it, to the hands of those who need it, so that it can be used again. For a specific good, the owner of its property rights changes, and the new owner of the property rights continues to own the goods and generates continued value in the subsequent use.

Through the sharing economy, items that might otherwise be discarded can be kept and reused to avoid wasting excess resources, while reducing the amount of waste. On the other hand, bartering and second-hand trading platforms will also enable people to buy fewer new products, which will not only reduce the waste caused by the vicious cycle of over-consumption and over-production, but also promote simple and green living, which is beneficial to the ecology and environment, and will definitely promote sustainable development in the long run.

12.4 Innovation Model

(2) Improving efficiency in the use of resources

In the age of consumption, everyone may have some unused items hoarded in their homes, but lack of a platform in the past made it impossible to effectively revitalize unused resources to know who has what needs and when. The sharing economy provides platforms that allow both supply and demand to quickly and effectively discover each other and connect, enabling sharing and greatly enhancing the efficiency of resource flows. In addition, the sharing economy unlocks the potential benefits of unused goods, as the owner of the resource, the demander and the platform that connects the supply and demand sides can share the potential benefits and improve the efficiency of the group without the need for significant resources such as time and manpower.

The sharing economy therefore allows social resources to be used fully, thereby reducing the waste caused by the production of redundant products; it increases the efficiency of the use of resources per unit, while the total amount of social resources remains the same.

However, there are advantages and disadvantages, and the sharing economy is not exempt from this. If both oversupply and platform abuse are not well managed and controlled, they will not only be detrimental to zero waste, but will even accelerate the generation of all kinds of waste.

(3) Oversupply

Some of the goods that can be shared in the sharing economy are already available in social resources and can be shared directly on the corresponding platform; however, it is usually found in the process of sharing that these shareable goods are not sufficient, so it is necessary to produce and replenish these goods specifically. Once production is involved, the unplanned disadvantages of capital are exposed—the businessman, in pursuit of low costs and high profits, will not take into account the actual demand and thus produce blindly, which inevitably lead to excessive supply over demand. So, what was intended to be a full use of idle goods turns out to be the production of more idle goods, resulting in an oversupply, and in some extreme cases, they become waste directly without being used or consumed. The "crazy" development of bicycle-sharing in China over a period of time (many bicycles were sent directly to the so-called "bicycle graveyard" without being used for a long time) is a typical negative example. Instead of reducing waste (bicycles that are scrapped after normal personal use), they consume social resources and directly "produce" waste. How heartbreaking!

Therefore, the supply of goods involved in the sharing economy still requires some planning and government supervision in terms of laws, regulations and standards. It is better to undersupply sharing goods than to oversupply.

(4) Platform abuse

The sharing economy relies on sharing platforms to match resources with demand, and a certain number and quality of platforms can match the supply side of goods with the demand side of goods. However, the demand side often finds that there are a large number of "so-called" platforms of varying quality, which are full of useless commodity information; at the same time, information about a shareable commodity appears repeatedly on different platforms, often with inaccurate and asymmetric information, causing a lot of confusion to the demand side. Both of these negative results are due to platform abuse, and instead of providing sharing goods well, such platforms cause a waste of information resources (junk data in fact), which in turn brings about a waste of shared goods—and a disguised abandonment of shared goods.

So just like the supply of sharing goods, there should be some regulation and restriction on the sharing platform. The government should unify the establishment of platforms, or unify the standards for the establishment of platforms, and unify the database behind the platforms. Sharing platforms should be few and precise, not many and varied.

12.4.3 Cloud Technology

Cloud technology is a general term for network technology, information technology, integration technology, management platform technology and application technology based on the application of cloud computing business model. The emergence and development of cloud technology also brings a new engine to the circular economy and zero waste, a new opportunity that is unprecedented, and makes it possible to integrate people and nature.

(1) Technology features

Virtualized computing—which means that computing components run on a virtual rather than a real basis, can expand the capacity of hardware, simplify the software reconfiguration process, reduce the overhead associated with software virtual machines and support a wider range of operating systems. Software applications can be isolated from the underlying hardware through virtualization technology, which when applied to CPUs, operating systems, servers, etc., is tantamount to saving local hardware as a physical condition, providing a possibility for zero waste of certain electronic products.

Distributed storage—cloud computing systems consist of a large number of servers serving a large number of users at the same time, so cloud computing systems use distributed storage to store data and use redundant storage to ensure data reliability. The redundant approach replaces supercomputers with low-equipped machines through task decomposition and clustering, which saves the investment and maintenance costs of high-performance hardware, and eliminates the need to discard various major and auxiliary materials in the process of upgrading and disusing equipment.

Big data encryption—cloud computing behind unified storage and computing makes it easy to achieve confidential processing of big data. Compared to traditional computing and storage technologies, which have to employ a lot of mechanical and physical secrecy facilities and confidentiality measures due to the need to encrypt various data and programs locally, which will instantly turn into waste once they are cracked. The data encryption schemes of cloud computing are like the vaults of the

12.4 Innovation Model

central banks of various countries and there is absolutely no possibility of the local safes being abandoned due to cracked passwords.

(2) Technology applications

Cloud mailboxes—while traditional emails use physical memory to store communication data, cloud computing allows emails to be checked and sent using resources in the cloud, and individual or enterprise users can access their emails from anywhere, on any device and at any time, eliminating all kinds of potential due to the elimination of individual physical memory of e-waste.

Cloud call—cloud call center is a call center system based on cloud computing technology. Enterprises do not need to buy any software and hardware systems, only need to have personnel, sites and other basic conditions. They can quickly own a call center while the hardware and software platform, communication resources, routine maintenance and services are provided by the server provider. Cloud call application avoids the infrastructure construction of various territorial call centers, thus making various regular upgrades of telecom-type waste no longer exist.

Cloud gaming—cloud gaming is a cloud-based approach to video gaming. In the cloud gaming mode of operation, all games are run on the server and the rendered game graphics are compressed and delivered to the users through the network. Under this operation mechanism, host manufacturers will become network operators, they do not need to invest heavily to develop, manufacture and sell high-performance game hosts, but only need to take a small part of the money to upgrade their own servers; users' game devices do not need any high-end processors and graphics cards, but only need basic video decompression capabilities, and in principle, they can integrate game consoles with the hardware of TVs through the function of game set-top boxes, thus reducing the use and disposal of screen-based electronics.

Cloud education—cloud education means that the streaming platform for educational resources is deployed using a distributed architecture, with streaming functional components such as recording systems or live streaming systems configured in the classrooms of established schools. In this way, the teaching reality can be transmitted in real time to the global live server in the management center of the streaming platform, while the recorded school can also upload and store the recorded content to the streaming storage server in the information center for future retrieval, on-demand, evaluation and various other applications. Cloud education reduces the demand for land requirement to build schools, as well as reduces the waste that is inevitably generated by operating a large social public place like a school.

Cloud conferencing—cloud conferencing is an efficient, convenient and low-cost form of video conferencing based on cloud computing technology. Users can quickly and efficiently share voice, data files and video synchronously with teams and customers around the world by simply performing easy-to-use operations through an Internet interface, while the complex technologies of data transmission and processing in the meeting are operated by cloud conferencing service providers to help users. Cloud conferencing solves much more than the waste problems associated with large and small meeting venues and various conference services, but also significantly reduces unnecessary traffic carbon emissions by avoiding travel.

12.4.4 Blockchain Technology

Blockchain is a new application model of computer technology such as distributed data storage, peer-to-peer transmission, consensus mechanism, and encryption algorithm. Blockchain involves many scientific and technological issues such as mathematics, cryptography, Internet and computer programming, etc. From the application perspective, it is a distributed shared ledger and database with the characteristics of decentralization, immutability, full traceability, collective maintenance, openness and transparency. Blockchain can solve the problem of information asymmetry and achieve trust collaboration and consistent action among multiple subjects.

The following features of blockchain technology, if fully and rationally applied in a circular economy society, could bring a qualitative leap forward in waste management.

(1) Decentralization

Blockchain technology does not rely on additional third-party governing bodies or hardware facilities, there is no central control, except for the self-contained blockchain itself, and through distributed accounting and storage, individual nodes enable self-verification, delivery and management of information. Decentralization is the most prominent and essential feature of blockchain, and it is this feature that makes it possible for our society not to need any kind of waste information and management body.

(2) Openness

The blockchain technology base is an open source, except for the private information of the parties to the transaction which is encrypted, the data of the blockchain is open to all, and anyone can query the blockchain data and develop related applications through the open interface. So, the information of the whole system is highly transparent. The openness makes the generation of waste transparent as well, and the responsibility of waste producer becomes clear.

(3) Independence

Based on consensus norms and protocols (various mathematical algorithms such as Hash algorithms), the entire blockchain system is not dependent on other third-parties and all nodes are able to automatically and securely verify and exchange data within the system without any human intervention. Independence allows for various supervision of waste without the influence of any other institution or individual.

(4) Security

As long as one cannot control 51% of all data nodes, one cannot manipulate and modify network data with impunity, which makes the blockchain itself relatively safe from subjective and deliberate data changes. Security makes it impossible to tamper with information about waste generation and transfer, especially hazardous waste generation and transfer.

12.4 Innovation Model

(5) Anonymity

Unless required by legal norms, technically speaking alone, the identity information of each block node does not need to be made public or verified, and information transfer can take place anonymously. Obviously legal norms can and even should require information about waste generators to be made public and verified for administrative oversight.

Today's blockchain technology is already primed to drive new developments in the circular economy in a number of social sectors.

Monetary and financial sectors—blockchain has potentially huge applications in monetary and financial sectors such as international exchange, letters of credit, equity registration and stock exchanges. Applying blockchain technology to the financial industry can eliminate third-party intermediary links, enable direct peer-to-peer docking, and complete transaction payments quickly and inexpensively. In theory and in practice blockchain technology can completely replace all kinds of physical currency transactions, saving a lot of materials and energy needed because of physical currency transactions.

IoT and logistics sectors—blockchain can also be well integrated in the IoT and logistics sectors. With blockchain it is possible to reduce logistics costs, trace the production and delivery process of items, and improve the efficiency of supply chain management. Blockchain combined with big data solutions can lead to a more directional expansion between the decentralized base users of the smart IoT, reducing the waste of social resources while optimizing material efficiency.

Ecology and environment investment sectors—the data stored on the blockchain, which is extremely reliable and tamper-proof, is just right for use in the development of ecology and environment investment. Information on investment projects, details of funds, flow of funds, project returns, etc., need to be transparently and openly publicized for social monitoring, but also need to protect the privacy of relevant organizations and individuals, and blockchain applications can precisely meet these specific requirements to ensure the healthy and orderly operation of ecology and environment investment projects.

Chapter 13
Circular Economy Standard and Certification

All aspects of circular economy, in addition to the corresponding laws and regulations support, are the same as ordinary things, which need to follow some executable standards, as well as the third-party certification under the framework of these standards.

In some specific implementation links of circular economy, such as the transfer and disposal of wastes (especially hazardous wastes), the country will formulate mandatory standards. Most of the rest are voluntary activities of an enterprise or group for sustainable development. The country will not formulate mandatory standards, but there will be some voluntary standards for the industry to refer to.

Non-governmental organizations or independent third-party organizations will also compile and promulgate some evaluation standards related to circular economy. In the practice of circular economy, leading enterprises usually refer to these standards and request a third-party organization to certify the enterprise itself or its behavior when all necessary conditions are met, so as to confirm their leading position in the sustainable development of the industry.

As a well-known international independent third-party organization, UL (Underwriters Laboratories Inc.) has promulgated a series of standards (procedures) focusing on circular economy in recent decades with its own research results. Although these standards (procedures) cannot cover all the contents of circular economy, they are self-consistent and representative. They examine the proposition of circular economy from dimensions of products, factories and enterprises.

13.1 Product Circularity

In the standard of UL circular economy system, the standard (procedure) applicable to the evaluation of recycling and recovery in products is UL 2789 Calculation of Estimated Recyclability Rate, UL 2809 Recycled Content, and UL 2990 By-Product Synergy. At the same time, other ASTM standards and EN (CEN/CENELEC) standards are directly used to evaluate the content of compostable materials and the conversion rate of anaerobic digestion.

(1) UL 2789 Calculation of Estimated Recyclability Rate

This procedure incorporates the use of methods for measuring recyclability discussed in IEC/TR 62635–2012 Guidelines for end-of-life information provided by manufacturers and recyclers and for recyclability rate calculation of electrical and electronic equipment.

This procedure provides instructions on how to perform basic disassembly of a product and sort into different material fractions, which shall be weighed in order to calculate recyclability rate. For the purposes of this procedure, the following fractions are considered recyclable: batteries, metals, plastics, mixed electronics (PWB, wire, flex, LCD), and glass.

This procedure requires at least one representative product, which does not have to be fully functional, and which, preferably, can be destroyed during disassembly shall be submitted for testing. Basic tools, such as screwdrivers, cutters, and needle-nose pliers may be used. A small laboratory balance capable of measuring to nearest 0.1 g shall be used.

The goal of disassembly is to sort the parts into the following fractions of material: batteries, metals, plastics, mixed electronics (PWB, wire, flex, LCD), glass and non-recyclables. Disassembly does not have to continue indefinitely, but shall continue until approximately 90% of the weight of the product has been classified into the groups indicated above.

1) Plastic part recyclability determination

Plastic parts shall be considered recyclable if the following criteria are met:

① <10% of the surface area is coated with paint, metallization, glue, or other non-plastic materials;
② <5% of the part or assembly is made of a different material or different type of base plastic;
③ There are no metal inserts that are not easily removed with a quick pull of a tool.

2) Metal part recyclability determination

① Parts that are composed of >75% ferrous metals are considered recyclable. A quick test for this is attraction to a permanent magnet.
② Non-ferrous metals, including aluminum, magnesium, zinc and other non-magnetic metals are also recyclable. Note that copper-based parts shall be included in the electronics fraction.

3) Mixed electronics (PWB, wire, flex, LCD's displays) recyclability determination

① The basis of recycling this fraction is presence of copper, along with the precious metals as gold, silver, platinum, palladium and other high value metals.
② Other metals shall be grouped with their respective fractions.

13.1 Product Circularity

4) Glass part recyclability determination

Glass components including display windows or lenses not permanently attached to displays are recyclable.

5) Calculation of product recyclability rate

Each fraction collected shall be weighed and masses recorded in Table. 13.1. And the recyclability could be calculated:

$$\text{Recyclability} = \frac{\text{Sum of Recyclable Masses of Each Set of Parts(Row7)}}{\text{Total Product mass(Row1)}} \times 100\%$$

Table. 13.1 Calculation of product recyclability rate

Disassembly fraction number	Mass (nearest 0.1 g)
1. Total weight of product (and battery)/g	
2. Weight of battery	
3. Weight of recyclable plastic parts	
4. Weight of recyclable metal parts	
5. Weight of circuit boards, displays, and other electronic components	
6. Weight of glass display windows or lenses if separated	
7. Sum of Row 2 through Row 6. This is mass recyclable	
8. Divide Row 7 by Row 1. This is estimated % recyclability rate	

This part of the procedure follows the guidelines in IEC/TR 62635 for the determination of estimated recyclability rate. The product is documented as described and sent to a recycler for assessment. The recycler then assesses the recyclability of the product based on the base components, reports the mass and material of the component. The report from the recycler also includes the material recycling categories used for the product and the expected rate of recycling using that recycling route.

Data compiled by the recycler on the mass of recyclable components in the product and the recycling rate for the material(s) or recycling method(s) is used to calculate the recyclability rate using the following formula:

$$\text{Recyclability Rate} = \frac{\text{Sum of Recyclable Masses of Each Part}}{\text{Total Product Mass}} \times 100\%$$

$$= \frac{\sum (m_i \times \text{RCR}_i)}{m_{\text{Total}}} \times 100\%$$

where m_i refers to the mass of ith part, RCR_i refers to the recycling rate of the ith part in the corresponding end-of-life treatment scenario, and m_{Total} refers to the total product mass.

(2) UL 2809 Recycled Content

This procedure outlines the measurement of pre-consumer and/or post-consumer "Controlled Source" material content in raw materials, manufactured products and components of manufactured products that contain any total pre-consumer and/or post-consumer content. Controlled Source material includes recycled content, by-product synergy, reused components, refurbished components, ocean plastic or any other specified source of controlled material. Both segregated supply chain management of materials and mass balance accounting system are included in the procedure.

The manufacturer shall provide full product composition specifications for each product submitted. Product composition specifications, must, at minimum, include detailed information on all raw materials and recycled content that goes into the final product. The facilities within the scope of the claim shall submit documentation necessary for verifying the proposed claim(s). In addition, the following specific documentation should be submitted:

① Manufacturing site address for all validated products;
② Manufacturing process flowchart and/or description;
③ Recycled content supplier declarations;
④ Bill of materials for the products being evaluated with recycled content calculations;
⑤ Production Records from source material to final product.

About segregated supply chain management, each process beginning with the original separation of the defined material from other materials to the final product manufacturing process, must have a system for management of material content. In general, the system must provide enough documentation to demonstrate assurance of the goals of the management system.

About mass balance, each organization using an allocation system for tracking controlled content shall clearly designate the system and system boundary. A system is defined by the boundary and the movement of materials within the boundary. The boundary is where the materials flow into or out of the system. The system can be defined by a physical boundary or group of physical boundaries which are connected through shipment of materials between the boundaries. Some example system boundaries are:

① A single facility where all material exchanging taking place;
② A site which has multiple buildings connected by pipelines which interchange feedstock between the buildings;
③ A group of sites which are geographically distant and exchange feedstock through either pipelines, railcar or truck.

The content shall be calculated using the following equation:

$$\text{Controlled Source Content\%} = \frac{\text{Mass of Controlled Source Material Content}}{\text{Mass of Finished Product}}$$

13.1 Product Circularity

The manufacturer shall submit the requested documentation necessary for verifying the proposed claim.

① The manufacturer shall undergo a facility on-site audit by an approved auditor from a certified auditing service to ensure compliance with this procedure and the criteria within. For closed loop claims supplier sites shall also undergo a facility on-site audit to ensure compliance with the chain of custody requirements of the procedure.

② As part of an annual review, the manufacturer must complete a recycled content annual review declaration and return it to the designated compliance manager along with any requested documentation to confirm on-going compliance with the recycled content environmental claim.

Three scenarios for acceptable recycled content claim wording:

① Recycled content claim wording

[Product/actual product name/packaging] contains a [minimum/average] of $XX\%$ [pre/post-consumer] recycled content.

[Product/actual product name/packaging] contains a [minimum/average] of $XX\%$ recycled content, consisting of $XX\%$ recycled [raw material/component].

[Product/actual product name/packaging] contains a [minimum/average] of $XX\%$ recycled [raw material/component].

Include footnote in the final report stating total recycled content: [Product/actual name/packaging] contains a [minimum/average] of $XX\%$ recycled content, consisting of $XX\%$ recycled [raw material/component].

[Product/actual product name/packaging] contains $XX\%$ pre-consumer and $XX\%$ post-consumer recycled content.

② Closed loop system claim wording

[Product/actual product name/packaging] contains a [minimum/average] of $XX\%$ [pre/post-consumer] closed-loop recycled content.

[Product/actual product name/packaging] contains a [minimum/average] of $XX\%$ closed-loop recycled content, consisting of $XX\%$ recycled [raw material/component].

[Product/actual product name/packaging] contains a [minimum/average] of $XX\%$ recycled [raw material/component].

Include footnote in the final report stating total closed loop recycled content: contains a [minimum/average] of $XX\%$ closed loop recycled content, consisting of $XX\%$ recycled.

[Product/actual product name/packaging] contains $XX\%$ pre-consumer and $XX\%$ post-consumer closed-loop recycled content.

③ Allocation based recycled content claim wording

[Product/actual product name/packaging] contains a [minimum/average] of *XX*% [pre/post-consumer] recycled content using [allocation/mass balance] system.

[Product/actual product name/packaging] contains a [minimum/average] of *XX*% recycled content, consisting of *XX*% recycled [raw material/component] using [allocation/mass balance] system.

Product/actual product name/packaging] contains a [minimum/average] of *XX*% recycled [raw material/component] using [allocation/mass balance] system.

Include footnote in the final report stating total recycled content: [Product/actual name/packaging] contains a [minimum/average] of *XX*% recycled content, consisting of *XX*% recycled [raw material/component] using [allocation/mass balance] system.

[Product/actual product name/packaging] contains *XX*% pre-consumer and *XX*% post-consumer recycled content using [allocation/mass balance] system.

(3)   UL 2990 By-Product Synergy

This procedure describes the process for validating "By-Product Synergy" environ-mental claims for a network with two or more facilities from diverse industries prac-ticing by-product synergy, and calculations of waste diversion as well as by-product synergy content in final product. These facilities reduce the need for virgin-source materials, divert waste from landfills, and localize the supply chain thus providing substantial environmental benefits.

For by-product that is not appeared in the final product manufactured at recipient, the by-product resource (such as water, energy, or a certain type of material) that is saved via by-product network may be validated. For by-product that is appeared in the final product manufactured at recipient, the final product may claim an average or minimum amount (or percentage) of by-product synergy content.

This procedure is divided into two sections: the first is focused on the measurement of waste diversion via by-product synergy; the second is optional—calculation of by-product synergy content in a final product via by-product synergy.

1)   Assessment of waste diversion

Facilities shall provide sufficient documentation for all materials (including leftover materials, by-products, and waste) and/or energy being exchanged, sold, or passed free of change between facilities within the by-product synergy network in order to demonstrate specific by-product synergy practices. Only materials that are unwanted by-products or wastes from supplier that can be used as a primary resource with no (or very little) processing at recipient will qualify for validation. By-product materials from suppliers that would need additional processing to be able to be used as an input resource at recipient will not qualify for the "By-Product Synergy" claim. Processing methods such as chemical processing or heating that will change the physical properties of received materials are not acceptable. By-product materials from suppliers that only a small proportion can be used as a primary resource and the majority ($\geqslant$60% by weight) cannot be used at recipient will not qualify for the "By-Product Synergy" claim.

This procedure provides for waste to be exchanged, sold or circulated between sites within the by-product synergy framework free of charge. The total amount of by-product material used by the recipient through the by-product synergy framework, including surplus material, excess energy, by-products and waste, shall be measured and recorded as waste transfer.

2) Calculation of by-product synergy content

For by-product that is appeared in the final products manufactured at recipient, the amount of by-product synergy material used in a single final product should be measured and recorded as mass of by-product synergy content. The percentage of by-product synergy content shall be calculated using the following equation:

$$\text{By-Product Synergy Content\%} = \frac{\text{Mass of By-Product Synergy Content}}{\text{Mass of Final Product}}$$

Four acceptable claim wordings are:

<XX tons> of by-product synergy [by-product material name] have been used at [Recipient's name] annually for the [product/ actual product name] production;

<XX tons> of [virgin-source materials] have been substituted at [recipient's name] annually via by-product synergy;

<XX kW·h> of [waste energy] have been recovered and used at [recipient's name] via by-product synergy;

[Product/actual product name] contains a [minimum/average] of $XX\%$ by-product synergy [waste material name] content.

13.2 Facility Circularity

In the standard of UL circular economy system, the standard (procedure) applicable to the evaluation of waste streams for facility is UL 2799 Zero Waste to Landfill. Based on the practice of different industries, UL 2799 can also be used to evaluate the waste streams for organizations or events beside of facility within the specified time and space.

UL 2799 belongs to the second type of typical self-environment claim in ISO 14000 system, which conforms to the relevant requirements of ISO 14021. According to the procedure, waste refers to the material flow that does not belong to the valuable final product, while diversion is to avoid or reduce the generation of waste through the reduction, recycling, reuse, or composting, etc., so as to reduce the amount of waste directly simply sent to landfill—so-called waste landfill diversion, which can be effectively calculated and evaluated.

According to the procedure, the waste generated by a designated facility in a certain time and space is equal to the diverted waste, plus the landfill waste, plus the

Mandated waste material—materials that are required by law, ordinance, or regulation to be disposed of via thermal technology or landfill that is outside of the control of the generator and where other waste minimization options do not exist.

According to calculation of diversion rate, four levels of claim are shown in Table. 13.2.

There are two acceptable claim wordings:

[Entity's facility name] has achieved zero waste to landfill operations, 100% diversion, with *XX*% thermal processing with energy recovery.

[Company's facility name] has achieved a landfill diversion rate of *XX*%.

Table. 13.2 UL 2799 designation

Designation	Diversion rate (including WTE) (%)	Maximum WTE recovery rate (%)	Landfill rate (including thermal processing without energy recovery and additional WTE that exceeds 10% threshold) (%)
Certified landfill diversion rate	<90	–	–
Zero waste to landfill silver	90~94	≤4	≤10
Zero waste to landfill gold	95~99	≤9	≤5
Zero waste to landfill platinum	100	≤10	0

waste that is burned without generating energy. The detailed diversion calculation formula is (m is calculated by weight):

$$\eta\% = \frac{m_{eliminate} + m_{reduce} + m_{reuse} + m_{recycle} + m_{composting} + m_{anaerobic} + m_{biofuel}}{m_{total\ discarded\ material} - m_{mandated}}$$

13.3 Corporate Circularity

Among the standards of UL circular economy system, UL 3600 Corporate Circularity is the standard (outline) applicable to the evaluation of comprehensive circular degree of enterprises. In fact, the outline is not a new independent standard, but a selective integration of several existing UL product level and facility level circularity standards, and then a calculation formula based on importance weight is established to consider and evaluate the comprehensive level of a sustainable development enterprise in circular economy.

13.3 Corporate Circularity

The scope of an assessment can be set against one of three general supply chain boundaries:

① Scope 1 includes performance of directly owned and operated company assets;
② Scope 2 includes Tier 1 suppliers, those suppliers who supply parts or services directly to the company including contract manufacture of the company's products;
③ Scope 3 include impacts from the full lifecycle of the products, sites and companies participating in the supply chain, delivery and use of the product.

List of symbols and meanings in Table. 13.3.

UL 2799 shall be used to calculate the circularity rate for entities (facilities, sites or operations):

$$\text{Mass Discarded Material } (m_{dm}) = m_{recycle} + m_{compost} + m_{anaerobic}$$
$$+ m_{reuse} + m_{reduce} + m_{TWER} + m_{biofuel} + m_{mandated} + m_{landfill} + m_{thermal}$$

$$S_{circularity} = S_{reduce} + S_{reuse} + S_{recycle} + S_{by\text{-}product} + S_{biochem} + S_{composting} + S_{anaerobic} + S_{biofuel}$$

All products are evaluated individually and calculations within the standards are applied to each product before results from multiple products are combined. All sources of materials, parts, and components making up the product and product primary package must be included so that the total adds up to 100%. The percent for design and percent for content are averaged to get a combined product circularity rate.

$$C_{rate} = C_{reuse} + C_{recycle} + C_{closed} + C_{bio}$$
$$D_{rate} = D_{reuse} + D_{recycle} + D_{closed} + D_{bio} + D_{compost} + D_{anaerobic}$$
$$P_{circularity} = \frac{D_{rate} + C_{rate}}{2}$$

As for the fact of the Corporate Circularity, the outline requires that the comprehensive level of circular economy of the enterprise be reflected by calculating the waste diversion rate of the whole enterprise and the product circularity of all product lines.

Corporate Diversion Rate
$$= \frac{\text{Materials Diverted for Whole Company}}{\text{Materials Discarded for Whole Company}}$$

Product Portfolio Circularity
$$= \frac{\sum_{\text{All Products}} (\text{Product Circularity} \times \text{Mass Product Shipped})}{\text{Mass All Product Shipped to Market}}$$

Table. 13.3 Site (entities) waste diversion

Site (entities) waste diversion	
S_{reduce}	Discarded material which is reduced rather that discarded as a percent of total discarded material
S_{reuse}	Percent material reused rather than discarded as a percent total discarded material
$S_{recycle}$	Percent material sent for recycling rather than being discarded
$S_{by\text{-}product}$	Percent material send to another site to be used as a raw material for production of new product
$S_{biochem}$	Percent material sent for recovery of biochemicals rather than being discarded
$S_{composting}$	Percent material send to composting rather than being discarded
$S_{anaerobic}$	Percent material sent for anaerobic digestion rather than being discarded
$S_{biofuel}$	Percent material sent for use as a source material for biofuels rather than being discarded
Product content	
C_{reuse}	Percent reused material in a product
$C_{recycle}$	Percent material in a product from recycled sources
C_{closed}	Percent material in a product from closed cycle recycled sources
C_{bio}	Percent material in a product from biobased sources
C_{rate}	Sum of material from reused, recycled, closed cycle recycled and biobased sources in percent
Product design	
D_{reuse}	Percent material in a product designed to be reused
$D_{recycle}$	Percent material in a product designed to be recycled
D_{closed}	Percent material in a product designed to be closed cycle recycled
D_{bio}	Percent material in a product designed to be used as a source of biochemicals at end of life
$D_{compost}$	Percent material in a product designed to be composted
$D_{anaerobic}$	Percent material in a product designed to be anaerobically digested
D_{rate}	Sum of designed to be reused, recycled, closed cycle recycled, extracted for biochemicals, composted or anaerobically digested
Circularity score	
$P_{circularity}$	The Product Circularity score calculated as an average between content and design scores
$S_{circularity}$	Percent of discarded material from a site which is reused, reduced, recycled, sent for by-product synergy, biochemical extraction, composting, anaerobic digestion or biofuel processing

$$\text{Corporate Circularity} = \frac{\text{Corporate Diversion Rate} + \text{Product Portfolio Circularity}}{2}$$

The outline does not include the calculation of greenhouse gas emissions and energy use related to the facts of circular economy, so it only studies the circular economy from the perspective of material flow, and needs to supplement the content of energy consumption and transformation in order to further improve the assessment method of circularity.

With the continuous research and development, all the UL standards mentioned above are not invariable. Like all other international standards and national standards, they will be revised to meet the needs of the times.

Chapter 14
Zero Waste Philosophy and Environmental Ethics

Humankind have been exploring the theories and practices of zero waste, while asking themselves simple questions like:

Given the fact that the way to zero waste is full of challenges, why do we produce waste in the first place?

Are we humans existing for the fun of producing waste and then eliminating it?

Is the increase of waste volume always in proportion to the increase of human population? Is the increase of waste varieties always exponential along with human technology development?

…

This kind of questions starts to perplex more and more people, when they find that the answer to technology and engineering questions may lie in philosophy and ethics.

14.1 Zero Waste Philosophy

Philosophy is systematic theories of the worldview and the methodology. The worldview is to study and learn about the nature of the world, the fundamental laws of development, and the essential relationship between the human thoughts and the existence; and the methodology is the basic method for humans to know about the world. The methodology is the function of the worldview, while the worldview decides the methodology.

In essence, philosophy is a system of logical views of the universe. It is the quest for essential issues like the nature of the universe, the fundamental laws of all kinds of things' evolution and development in the universe, and what humans are in the universe, etc. It can of course be used to study the strategic questions of zero waste.

The relationship between the subject and the object is known as the fundamental question in philosophical studies. Using philosophical methodology to study the waste of human beings should firstly identify the subject and the object; then find out how the subject decides the object and how the object influences the subject. As obvious as it could be, humankind is the subject while the waste is the object. Human activities produce the waste, and the existence of waste brings down, or even spoils the quality of human living environment.

There are many schools in philosophical researches, which interconnect and at the same time oppose each other. We can study and discuss the interactions between humans (the subject) and waste (the object) from the views of some main philosophical schools.

14.1.1 Taoism

The basic concept of Taoism is "Tao", which is considered to be the origin of the universe and the rules governing the movements and behaviors of every object in the universe. Tao is what Taoists use to explore the relationship among nature, society and human life. Taoists promotes to follow the rules of nature with little human interference, and to keep harmony with the nature. Taoism is omnipotent and eternal, with dialectical thoughts and atheistic tendencies.

To follow the rules of nature with little human interference is not to be passive and do nothing. Instead, it is to follow the laws and rules of nature and take actions accordingly. As a result, the waste produced by human activities should not just be discarded and landfilled, but be solved by way of nature—humans should limit the desire of excessive consumption, and at the same time, use methods already existed in the nature, such as biological method, to treat and dispose of waste in order to reduce secondary pollution. As the key viewpoint of Taoism, humans to live in harmony with nature means that humans, the subject, should take actions to get the balance with the waste in nature, which is produced by humans themselves. The omnipotence of Taoism can be understood that all waste can be used in one way or another; and the eternity of Taoism can mean that (within certain time and space), waste and natural resources recycle eternally.

As the biggest achievement of speculative philosophy, the Tao concluded by Laozi is the highest abstraction of the nature of the world, and the highest condensation of the laws of things' movement. Transforming into the opposite direction is the law of Tao's movement—if entropy of nature is the Tao of humankind, the development of entropy is inevitably opposite to the development of humankind. Only when human lives harmoniously with nature (without producing waste), and when entropy is not increased or decreased can human society reach relative stability. Nature and human beings are also in constant change, as in everything there are always two contradictory opposites, which will turn into each other at all times, just like existence and absence, difficulty and ease, life and death, progress and retreat, etc. Natural resources and human waste are of this kind as well—they exist because of each other's existence and they transform into each other from time to time.

14.1.2 Confucianism

Confucianism explores the understanding of heaven and the relationship between men and heaven, and makes comparison and choice among the different kinds of men-heaven-relationship. From there, Confucianism starts to build its fundamental worldview. In the eyes of the Confucianism, through diligence and creation, the meaning and value of men's existence can be paralleled with that of heaven and earth.

Confucianism is originated from "the doctrine of Confucius and Mencius". It focuses on self-cultivation and ethics, with "benevolence and righteousness"—the harmonious relationship between one and another—lying at its core. The harmonious relationship is not only referring to the allocation of materials and resources between people, but also the allocation of rights and obligations. People have rights to share materials and resources, the same as they have obligations to deal with waste together. The more a person or a country enjoys the material resources, the more responsibilities they should carry on their shoulders. And that will be harmonious.

Science and technology and its applications are also a focus of Confucianism, as it could work with less effort but produce a much higher yield. The harmony of a society depends on its technologies' material efficiency and energy efficiency. Greater material efficiency and energy efficiency mean less waste produced per capita.

"Those who don't have a foresight for the future will be trapped by immediate problems", this is clearly stated in Confucianism, and it can apply to a person and a society. If we human beings don't have a thoughtful plan for the increasing amount of waste generated, we will have to face the trouble it brings about at certain stage—unfortunately, it is already a reality in some countries and regions. We can only hope that it's not too late for us to take actions.

14.1.3 Marxist Philosophy

Dialectical materialism, materialistic dialectics, and dialectical-materialist epistemology are important components of Marxist philosophy. Marxist philosophy believes that the material world moves, changes and develops according to its innate laws. It reveals that the fundamental cause of the development of things lies in their internal contradictions. Things always have two contradictory sides which are in unity and in struggle. This nature drives things to develop from lower to higher levels. Therefore, the law of contradiction, namely the law of unity of opposites, is the most fundamental law of the movement, change and development of the material world.

Dialectical materialism is the study of the nature of the world from a dialectical point of view, i.e. the study of "what" is the nature of the world. The four principles can easily lead us to the following conclusions about waste:

① The principle of the form of material existence—diversion is a way of waste existence; time and space are a way for waste in diversion to exist.
② The principle of practical essence—the diversion of waste features direct realism and subject initiative.
③ The principle of the essence of consciousness and proactivity—humans, who are striving for a better existence, are willing to make efforts toward zero waste.
④ The principle of the unity of the world—natural resources and human waste are actually in unity.

Materialistic dialectic answers how the world works. And from that perspective, we can conclude the following:

① Universal connection—human waste is universally and deeply connected with natural resources.
② Extent—the content of recycled materials and material closed loop as well as the diversion rate of waste is a critical indicator of zero waste.
③ Mutual change law of quality and quantity—when waste is accumulated to a certain quantity, it is pollution; when waste can be diverted to a certain quantity, it is resource.
④ Dialectic negation—waste should not be easily judged or negated unless it is on scientific basis.
⑤ The development of the unbalance between two opposite sides—the demand for resources and waste diversion is constantly unbalanced and in dynamic development in given time and space.

Dialectical materialist epistemology answers the question of "how to know the world" by focusing on the three cores of practice, cognition, and truth, as well as the principle of dialectical relationship between practice and cognition, the law of cognition. Thus, we have the following conclusions:

① Dialectical relationship between practice and knowledge—only through the practice of waste diversion can we better understand the nature of waste.
② The dialectical development of cognition—recognize that the principles and techniques of waste diversion requires time and it couldn't happen overnight.
③ The materialism and dialectics to test truth—to test whether waste can be diverted (as resources), it needs to be studied from objective factual results.
④ Dialectical relationship between truth and value—waste diversion may not be able to demonstrate economic value in the short term, but in the long run, it will definitely manifest ecological, environmental, as well as social value.

14.2 Environmental Ethics

Ethics, just like metaphysics, logic, epistemology and aesthetics, is a subordinate discipline of philosophy. The essence of ethics is the science of moral principles, the systematization and theorization of moral ideas and perspectives. Or rather, ethics is the study of human moral problems as the object.

14.2 Environmental Ethics

The basic question to be answered in ethics is the relationship between morality and interests, that is, the relationship between "the right thing to do" and "the benefits". This question has two further ones: the relationship between economic interests and morality—who determines whom and whether morality has a negative effect on the economy; the relationship between individual interests and the overall interests of the society—who is subordinate to whom. Obviously, different answers to this basic question determine the principles and norms of various moral systems, as well as the criteria and orientations for judging various moral activities.

Environmental ethics is an emerging comprehensive science between ethics and environmental science. The birth of environmental ethics is the product of the social need to harmonize the relationship between human beings and the living environment system and to achieve a sustainable development after their sharp confrontation. Environmental ethics aims to solve the contradiction between human beings and the living environment system.

To solve human waste problem under the framework of environmental ethics is to firstly understand the principles of environmental ethics and then to find a reasonable solution from ethical and legal perspectives.

14.2.1 Environmental Ethics Principles

(1) Environmental justice

Justice is the balance between rights and obligations. It requires those who have enjoyed a certain right to fulfill relevant obligations. Environmental justice is the justice in environmental affairs, including the justice for allocation and participation: the justice for allocation is to focus on the allocation of environment related cost and benefit. The society should fairly allocate the benefit brought about by zero waste. At the same time, any individual or organization that produces waste should provide necessary funds or compensation for waste treatment and disposal. The justice for participation means that every person has the right to directly or indirectly participate in the making of environment related laws and regulations. The society should be open for all parties to express their views about waste treatment and disposal so that the interests of all waste-related parties can be treated reasonably.

(2) Intergenerational equality

Intergenerational equality is an extension of the ethical principle that all people are equal. Equality of rights is the core requirement of the principle of equality. The present generation enjoys the basic right to live in a good ecological environment. Same rights should be enjoyed by future generations. So while creating a high quality life, the present generation should not sacrifice the quality of living for future generations, nor should the present generation only consider their own production and consumption while leaving the waste problem for future generations to solve. It is a basic human moral obligation not to leave a waste-filled environment to future generations.

(3) Respecting nature

Respect for nature is the inevitable outcome as science and rationality develops to a certain extent. Modern system science and environmental science have already told us that humans are an integral part of the ecological system of nature. Different parts in the system are interconnected, just as the fate of humankind is closely connected with other lives in the system. They prosper all together, or lose together. Man to throw waste into nature is disrespect for themselves. Man to hurt other lives with waste produced will indirectly hurt themselves. And the linear transformation of resources into waste will surely affect the balance between man and nature.

14.2.2 The Content of Environmental Ethics

Environmental ethics, as a science that studies moral phenomena arising from the interaction between human beings, society and nature, is as complex and extensive as other environmental issues concerning waste—it contains the following two main aspects:

(1) To resolve conflicts

Man is a creature with subjective and proactive behaviors, his action is generally to achieve his own survival interests. That's why man only cares about the material and energy needed for his own survival, and will not actively care about environmental issues such as waste. Society is composed of individual human beings, and the goals and interests of the society in survival and development as a whole may not fully coincide with individual human beings. Society can't be concerned only with the material and energy needed for humans, but also with the reserves of natural resources and the negative effects of waste. How to reconcile this contradictory relationship is the first element of the study of environmental ethics.

(2) To maintain balance

Nature, as the object of environmental ethics, obeys all the laws of physics known to man, including the second law of thermodynamics. There are still a large number of unknown laws of the universe, and humans are not yet able to cope with all kinds (and we do not even know which ones there will be yet) of natural retaliation due to excessive consumption of natural resources. At present humans can only regulate the integration of waste and natural environment in a very limited manner. How to develop the limited regulation into a long-term balance can be the second element of environmental ethics studies.

14.2.3 Environmental Ethics and Environmental Legal System

Environmental ethics is a science, and what is researched is a method. The implementation and enforcement of the method can't depend entirely on morality in human society—at least at current stage, human society still has to rely on the environmental legal system in order to achieve zero waste. Many waste-related laws and regulations have been discussed in previous chapters, and here we will focus on the relationship between environmental ethics and environmental laws.

(1) To provide guidance

Environmental ethics emphasizes that human beings are an organic part of the natural order of the Earth's biosphere, that human beings are inseparable from other organisms, that they are common components of the Earth's ecosystem. They depend on each other, constrain each other and evolve together. The purpose of the environmental legal system is to protect the balance and development of this multifaceted system by legal means. So we can say that the study of environmental ethics guides the development of the environmental legal system.

(2) Be the foundation and core

Any legal society must have a certain moral foundation and core values, otherwise the implementation of the legal system will be difficult due to the lack of necessary public support. Same for the environmental legal system. Only when the concept of environmental ethics is deeply rooted in people's hearts through publicity and education, and people agree with the correctness and necessity of this concept and no longer feel that human beings can do whatever they want to the environment, can all legal measures play a certain deterrent role. At the same time, all potential environmental violations will be disliked and resisted by the public.

(3) Applications

The concept of environmental ethics can only be embodied and function well with specific legal provisions. Ethics can form public opinion to criticize and condemn environmental damages. But it can't correct the situation. Moreover, once the environment is damaged, criticism and condemnation is ineffectively pale. Only when the legislature puts environmental ethics into the form of law through the legislative process can we ensure that all environmental protection work can be carried out effectively to achieve sustainable development.

14.2.4 Case Studies

It is only in recent decades that the research and discussion on waste has reached the height of philosophy and ethics. In fact, although the wastes generated by general industrial manufacturing and human life have caused many problems, none of them is more worthy of reflection than the following kinds of wastes from the perspective of environmental ethics.

(1) War waste

Human history has seen countless wars, large and small. In the cold weapon era, there was little waste left behind, except for the bodies of the unfortunate fallen soldiers and the stones and dirt under the broken walls. These would soon disappear completely into nature (archaeological finds are treasures, not waste). However, with the advent of the hot weapon era, the waste of war suddenly became much more diverse.

Landmines, if not detonated in wartime, become the number one waste product after war. Landmines are quite an inexpensive defensive weapon, costing only about 3 USD on average. But, even if there were no new wars around the world (which is only a human dream), the 110 million mines already in the ground would cost about 33 billion USD just to be removed. Since no one takes care of those "abandoned" mines (and about 2.5 million newly increased a year), the number of casualties caused by mines is almost 70 people a day, mostly civilians. The number of wildlife killed and injured by mines is even greater... But the good thing is that the international conventions have completely banned the use of landmines. The only thing unknown is who will actually comply in wars.

Davis Monthan Air Force Base in Tucson, Arizona, the U.S., is a well-known "aircraft graveyard" that houses retired military aircraft for scrapping. The base is a 2,600-acre, 35 billion USD worth facility where approximately 4,200 obsolete and worn-out warplanes are kept. More than 80% of the aircraft will eventually end up here, and 350,000 pieces of steel can be recovered if necessary. 20% of the parts and even the entire aircraft are repaired, upgraded and rebuilt to return to new war zones. The waste, with such "repair", "refurbishment" and "reuse" intending to kill humans themselves, would be better off in landfills.

Decommissioned nuclear warheads are definitely a "hot potato". The end of the Cold War between the United States and Russia and the conclusion of the Nuclear Non-Proliferation Treaty have resulted in the creation of tens of thousands of "obsolete" nuclear warheads in the world, and this number will continue to grow as nuclear-armed states upgrade their arsenals. Current disposal of waste nuclear warheads is mainly based on two U.S. approaches. One is to use the highly enriched U-235 (more than 90%) in the warheads as fuel for nuclear-powered aircraft carriers or submarines after removing the fuses, and the other is to convert the highly enriched or low-enriched U-235 into fuel for nuclear power plants. Unfortunately, the first option is still a military one, and either the first or the second option would still end up generating the problem of depleted uranium nuclear waste (see Chap. 7 about nuclear waste). Mankind cannot help but ask themselves: if we had known, why would we have done it in the first place?

The environmental ethics of war waste is closely linked to the ethics of war. Humankind does not completely eliminate war, I am fearful that all kinds of war waste, known and unknown, will continue to bring endless nightmares to humankind.

14.2 Environmental Ethics

(2) Space junk

We have come to realize that there should be no waste in the universe, nor should there be waste on the Earth originally. With human activities in the Earth's surface biosphere has left waste on the land, in the oceans, and in the atmosphere, now space near the Earth has gradually become unclean. Space debris is useless man-made objects in orbit around the Earth, including debris from artificial satellites, paint chips, dust, up to the wreckage of entire spacecraft.

Figure 14.1 shows three diagrams of artificial satellites and spacecraft (including wreckage) in near-Earth orbit for different years, and Fig. 14.2 shows the current distribution of artificial satellites and spacecraft (including wreckage) in far-Earth orbit. According to NASA (National Aeronautics and Space Administration), there are about 4,000 operational or scrapped satellites and rocket remnants in Earth orbit, in addition to about 6,000 pieces of space debris that can be seen and tracked. There are even more than 200,000 pieces of space debris with a diameter of more than one centimeters. Most of them operate at a speed of more than 20,000 km/h. They pose a constant threat to the safety of the satellites themselves, the space shuttle, and the International Space Station; what's more troubling is the fact that space debris collides frequently with each other to create more debris, which can cause an ever-growing problem.

The world's major Space Powers are currently taking a number of measures to try to solve the problem of space debris, mainly through observation, tracking and protection to avoid collisions, and through capture and cleanup to bring them back into the atmosphere to burn up, etc. International regulations also stipulate that countries should consider how to effectively protect against small debris collisions when designing their vehicles, and that newly launched vehicles, after their missions are completed, should have the ability to leave their normal orbits and return to the atmosphere on their own for burning up.

Another concern is that not only in Earth orbit, but also on the Moon today, human waste is left behind: the Apollo program "dropped" about 70 tons of devices and

Fig. 14.1 Artificial satellites and spacecraft in near-Earth orbit

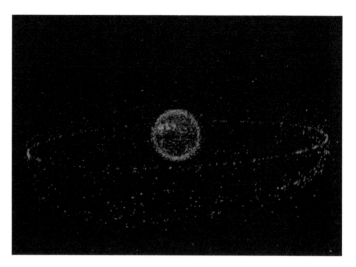

Fig. 14.2 Artificial satellites and spacecraft in far-Earth orbit

instruments on the Moon, and the unmanned spacecraft of other lunar exploration nations have "dropped" about 100 tons of various equipment. It is not difficult to imagine that as the lunar landing project continues, there will be more and more waste on the surface of the Moon, and it will be difficult for the Moon to remain clean forever.

It might be fortunate that although human spacecraft have already been on the Moon and other planets and have left waste in those places, humans haven't been able to explore the depths of the Earth, which means no human waste being left under the crust—even if there was, it would be completely destroyed by the high temperature and pressure there and instantly turned into the Earth's minerals.

(3) Marine debris

Marine debris refers to persistent, man-made or processed solid waste in the marine and coastal environment, mainly including floating debris, beach debris and seabed debris. All analysis and studies have shown that the largest proportion and most harmful of marine debris is ocean plastic.

The plastic debris floating on the sea is mainly plastic bags and bottles, accounting for about 60% of the total floating debris. The plastic washed aground on the beach is mainly plastic bags and fast food boxes, accounting for 75% or so of the total beach debris; the plastic debris accumulated on the seabed is mainly plastic bags and broken fishing nets, accounting for about 40% of the total seabed debris. The ocean is full of plastic.

There are three main sources of ocean plastic, namely, plastic on land flowing into the ocean through surface runoff, plastic dumped into the ocean during sailing activities and plastic cargo falling into the water due to large and small maritime accidents.

According to the French newspaper *Le Figaro*, in 2013, about 1.5 million animals fell victim to plastic debris in the ocean. Ocean plastic has a huge impact on animals: fish in the ocean eat plastic, which is often fatal to them; other species that feed on marine fish, including birds, whales, turtles, etc., are indirectly impacted or killed; harmful substances in plastic, through the food chain, eventually return to the human table as well, affecting human health again.

Currently, the main concentration of ocean plastic is in the North Pacific Ocean between California and Hawaii, covering an area of 3.5 million square kilometers. This super plastic pile will continue to grow at a rate of 80,000 square kilometers per year. The outlook is quite worrying.

Although the world has seen the problem of ocean plastic, and many NGOs are crying out for help, the solution to the problem would still be a pipe dream unless the rate of plastic production and the use of plastic products is reduced and the amount of plastic on land decreases.

The ocean is where the life started, and may as well be where it ends.

14.3 The Future of Humankind

No matter how the waste changes, or when zero waste is achieved, humankind is moving toward the future—in fact, according to special relativity, the future of humankind has already occurred in the timeline, but the people in our time haven't yet reached this spatial and temporal node so that they haven't seen it yet.

Let's make a rational speculation on what humans and their waste will look like. The first possibility is that human society is highly developed in science and technology with material efficiency at almost 100%. Humans hardly produce waste, and man and nature are perfectly integrated, developing harmoniously together.

The second possibility is that human society as a whole is highly developed and there is no waste in local areas or even on the entire surface of the Earth, while all waste is sent back to nature below the Earth's crust or returned to the universe in far-away space. Humans live and work in peace on the surface of the Earth and in the biosphere of near-Earth space.

Thirdly, the speed of human society in treating and disposing of waste isn't able to keep up with the speed of waste generation, and human beings are besieged by waste until they cannot stand on the Earth and have to migrate to or colonize other planets, just to repeat the story of waste on the Earth.

The fourth possibility is that, before human society finds the best solution for waste treatment and disposal, technology is not sufficient enough to support the mass departure of human beings from the Earth. Eventually, the extractable resources are completely exhausted, and the Earth is completely covered by waste. Human civilization unfortunately becomes (perhaps once again) "prehistoric" on the Earth.

Objectively speaking, the first possibility is too ideal, and the chances are fat; the fourth possibility is too pessimistic, and better not to be realized. The key to the remaining second and third possibilities lies in the race between humans and time—if humans act quickly enough, we may get the more positive result as the second one; but if humans are slow, we may end up in the third passive situation.

That is to say, humans still have half of initiative for the future of man and waste. On one hand, scientific and technological development should be boosted through more investment in order to recycle all kinds of waste as soon as possible; on the other hand, we should slow down the speed of social consumption by changing people's mindset and awareness through publicity and education, so as to produce as little waste as possible. Only in this way can we get a chance in the race against time and win a ray of hope for human civilization.

As with all kinds of awareness-raising, all social resources need to work and take actions together, whether it's in traditional schools, in the media, or in all kinds of literary and artistic expressions. The goal is common—to protect the one and only Earth, with zero waste.

Or we could give these actions a coinage name—Wasteless.

Appendix

Appendix 1 ASTM Standards Related to Waste

ASTM E829-16 Standard Practice for Preparing Refuse-Derived Fuel (RDF) Laboratory Samples for Analysis.

ASTM E776-16 Standard Test Method for Determination of Forms of Chlorine in Refuse-Derived Fuel.

ASTM D4844-16 Standard Guide for Air Monitoring at Waste Management Facilities for Worker Protection.

ASTM D6051-15 Standard Guide for Composite Sampling and Field Subsampling for Environmental Waste Management Activities.

ASTM D5513-15 Standard Practice for Microwave Digestion of Industrial Furnace Feed Streams and Waste for Trace Element Analysis.

ASTM E2421-15(2021) Standard Guide for Preparing Waste Management Plans for Decommissioning Nuclear Facilities.

ASTM D5088-15a Standard Practice for Decontamination of Field Equipment Used at Waste Sites.

ASTM F917-14 Standard Specification for Commercial Food Waste Disposers.

ASTM F1899-14(2019) a Standard Specification for Food Waste Pulper Without Waterpress Assembly.

ASTM D6234-13(2020) Standard Test Method for Shake Extraction of Mining Waste by the Synthetic Precipitation Leaching Procedure.

ASTM D5658-13 Standard Practice for Sampling Unconsolidated Waste from Trucks.

ASTM D5681-13 Standard Terminology for Waste and Waste Management.

ASTM D4979-12 Standard Test Method for Physical Description Screening Analysis in Waste.

ASTM D4982-12 Standard Test Methods for Flammability Potential Screening Analysis of Waste.

ASTM D3987-12(2020) Standard Practice for Shake Extraction of Solid Waste with Water.

ASTM D4981-12 Standard Test Method for Screening of Oxidizers in Waste.

ASTM D5058-12(2020) Standard Practices for Compatibility of Screening Analysis of Waste.

ASTM F1150-11 Standard Specification for Commercial Food Waste Pulper and Waterpress Assembly.

ASTM C1133/C1133M-10(2018) Standard Test Method for Nondestructive Assay of Special Nuclear Material in Low-Density Scrap and Waste by Segmented Passive Gamma-Ray Scanning.

ASTM D5792-10(2015) Standard Practice for Generation of Environmental Data Related to Waste Management Activities: Development of Data Quality Objectives.

ASTM C1207-10(2018) Standard Test Method for Nondestructive Assay of Plutonium in Scrap and Waste by Passive Neutron Coincidence Counting.

ASTM D5057-10 Standard Test Method for Screening Apparent Specific Gravity and Bulk Density of Waste.

ASTM D5284-09(2017) Standard Test Method for Sequential Batch Extraction of Waste with Acidic Extraction Fluid.

ASTM D5198-09 Standard Practice for Nitric Acid Digestion of Solid Waste.

ASTM D4793-09 Standard Test Method for Sequential Batch Extraction of Waste with Water.

ASTM C1563-08(2017) Standard Test Method for Gaskets for Use in Connection with Hub and Spigot Cast Iron Soil Pipe and Fittings for Sanitary Drain, Waste, Vent, and Storm Piping Applications.

ASTM C1174-07 (2013) Standard Practice for Prediction of the Long-Term Behavior of Materials, Including Waste Forms, Used in Engineered Barrier Systems (EBS) for Geological Disposal of High-Level Radioactive Waste.

ASTM D4547-06 Standard Guide for Sampling Waste and Soils for Volatile Organic Compounds.

ASTM F1673-2002 Standard Specification for Polyvinylidene Fluoride (PVDF) Corrosive Waste Drainage Systems.

ASTM D5608-01(2006) Standard Practices for Decontamination of Field Equipment Used at Low Level Radioactive Waste Sites.

ASTM D6311-98(2014) Standard Guide for Generation of Environmental Data Related to Waste Management Activities: Selection and Optimization of Sampling Design.

ASTM D5928-1996(2010)e1 Standard Test Method for Screening of Waste for Radioactivity.

ASTM D5368-1993(2006) Standard Test Methods for Gravimetric Determination of Total Solvent Extractable Content (TSEC) of Solid Waste Samples.

ASTM D5233-92 (2009) Standard Test Method for Single Batch Extraction Method for Wastes.

ASTM D5231-92 (2008) Standard Test Method for Determination of the Composition of Unprocessed Municipal Solid Waste.

ASTM D5232-92(2003) Standard Test Method for Determining the Stability and Miscibility of a Solid, Semi-Solid, or Liquid Waste Material.

ASTM D5013-89 (2009) Standard Practices for Sampling Wastes from Pipes and Other Point Discharges.

ASTM D4843-88(2009) Standard Test Method for Wetting and Drying Test of Solid Wastes.

Appendix 2 ANSI Standards Related to Waste

ANSI/NFPA 82-2013 Standard on Incinerators and Waste and Linen Handling Systems and Equipment.

ANSI Z245.2-2013 Stationary Compactors—Safety Requirements for Installation, Maintenance and Operation.

ANSI Z245.5-2013 Baling Equipment—Safety Requirements for Installation, Maintenance, Modification, Repair and Operation.

ANSI Z245.1-2017 Mobile Wastes and Recyclable Materials Collection, Transportation, and Compaction Equipment.

ANSI/AAMI ST15883-3: 2012 Washer-disinfectors—Part 3: Requirements and tests for washer-disinfectors employing thermal disinfection for human waste containers.

ANSI/ASTM F810-2012 Specification for Smoothwall Polyethylene (PE) Pipe for Use in Drainage and Waste Disposal Absorption Fields.

ANSI/ASTM F2390-2012 Specification for Poly(Vinyl Chloride) (PVC) Plastic Drain, Waste, and Vent (DWV) Pipe and Fittings Having Post-Industrial Recycle Content.

ANSI/ASTM F1150-2011 Specification for Commercial Food Waste Pulper and Waterpress Assembly.

ANSI/ANS40.37-2009 Mobile Low-Level Radioactive Waste Processing Systems.

ANSI/ASTM F2618-2009 Specification for Chlorinated Poly(Vinyl Chloride) (CPVC) Pipe and Fittings for Chemical Waste Drainage Systems.

ANSI Z245.41-2008 Facilities for the Processing of Commingled Recyclable Materials — Safety Requirements.

ANSI Z245.30-2008 Waste Containers — Safety Requirements.

ANSI/AHAM TC-1-2007 Method for Measuring Performance of Household Trash Compactors.

ANSI/ASME PTC34-2007 Waste Combustors with Energy Recovery.

Appendix 3 CEN Standards Related to Waste

CEN/TS 15864:2015 Characterization of waste—Leaching behaviour test for basic characterization—Dynamic monolithic leaching test with continuous leachant renewal under conditions relevant for specified scenario(s).

CEN/TS 16660:2015 Characterization of waste—Leaching behaviour test—Determination of the reducing character and the reducing capacity.

CEN/TS 14429:2015 Characterization of waste—Leaching behaviour test—Influence of pH on leaching with initial acid/base addition.

EN 16174:2012 Sludge, treated biowaste and soil—Digestion of aqua regia soluble fractions of elements.

EN 16167:2012 Sludge, treated biowaste and soil—Determination of polychlorinated biphenyls (PCB) by gas chromatography with mass selective detection (GC-MS) and gas chromatography with electron-capture detection (GC-ECD).

EN 15935:2012 Sludge, treated biowaste, soil and waste—Determination of loss on ignition.

EN 16169:2012 Sludge, treated biowaste and soil—Determination of Kjeldahl nitrogen.

EN 16168:2012 Sludge, treated biowaste and soil—Determination of total nitrogen using dry combustion method.

CEN/TS 1566-2:2012 Plastics piping systems for soil and waste discharge (low and high temperature) within the building structure—Chlorinated poly(vinyl chloride) (PVC-C)—Part 2: Guidance for assessment of conformity.

EN 13965-2:2010 Characterization of waste—Terminology—Part 2: Management related terms and definitions.

EN ISO 15883-3:2009 Washer-disinfectors—Part 3: Requirements and tests for washer-disinfectors employing thermal disinfection for human waste containers.

EN 15308:2008 Characterization of waste—Determination of selected polychlorinated biphenyls (PCB) in solid waste by using capillary gas chromatography with electron capture or mass spectrometric detection.

EN 14582:2016 Characterization of waste—Halogen and sulfur content—Oxygen combustion in closed systems and determination methods.

EN 15169:2007 Characterization of waste—Determination of loss on ignition in waste, sludge and sediments.

EN 15347:2007 Plastics—Recycled Plastics—Characterisation of plastics wastes.

EN 15012:2007 Plastics piping systems—Soil and waste discharge systems within the building structure—Performance characteristics for pipes, fittings and their joints.

CEN/TS 15364:2006 Characterization of waste—Leaching behaviour tests—Acid and base neutralization capacity test.

EN 12920:2006 + A1:2008 Characterization of waste—Methodology for the determination of the leaching behaviour of waste under specified conditions.

EN 14803:2006 Identification and/or determination of the quantity of waste.

EN 12574-3:2017 Stationary waste containers—Part 3: Safety and health requirements.

EN 15002:2015 Characterization of waste—Preparation of test portions from the laboratory sample.

EN 14346:2006 Characterization of waste—Calculation of dry matter by determination of dry residue or water content.

CEN/TR 15310-2:2006 Characterization of waste—Sampling of waste materials—Part 2: Guidance on sampling techniques.

CEN/TR 15310-3:2006 Characterization of waste—Sampling of waste materials—Part 3: Guidance on procedures for sub-sampling in the field.

CEN/TR 15310-4:2006 Characterization of waste—Sampling of waste materials—Part 4: Guidance on procedures for sample packaging, storage, preservation, transport and delivery.

CEN/TR 15310-5:2006 Characterization of waste—Sampling of waste materials—Part 5: Guidance on the process of defining the sampling plan.

EN 15192:2006 Characterisation of waste and soil—Determination of Chromium (VI) in solid material by alkaline digestion and ion chromatography with spectrophotometric detection.

EN 14735:2005 Characterization of waste—Preparation of waste samples for ecotoxicity tests.

EN 13493:2005 Geosynthetic barriers—Characteristics required for use in the construction of solid waste storage and disposal sites.

EN 14899:2005 Characterization of waste—Sampling of waste materials—Framework for the preparation and application of a Sampling Plan.

CEN/TR 15018:2005 Characterization of waste—Digestion of waste samples using alkali-fusion techniques.

EN 14345:2004 Characterization of waste—Determination of hydrocarbon content by gravimetry.

EN 14039:2004 Characterization of waste—Determination of hydrocarbon content in the range of C_{10} to C_{40} by gas chromatography.

EN 12940:2004 Footwear manufacturing wastes—Waste classification and management.

EN 13427:2004 Packaging—Requirements for the use of European Standards in the field of packaging and packaging waste.

EN 13965-1:2004 Characterization of waste—Terminology—Part 1: Material related terms and definitions.

EN 13370:2003 Characterization of waste Analysis of eluates Determination of Ammonium, AOX, conductivity, Hg, phenol index, TOC, easily liberatable CN^-, F^-

EN 12457-4:2002 Characterisation of waste—Leaching—Compliance test for leaching of granular waste materials and sludges—Part 4: One stage batch test at a liquid to solid ratio of 10 L/kg for materials with particle size below 10 mm (without or with size reduction).

EN 13657:2002 Characterization of waste—Digestion for subsequent determination of aqua regia soluble portion of elements.

EN 13656:2002 Characterization of waste—Microwave assisted digestion with hydrofluoric (HF), nitric (HNO_3) and hydrochloric (HCl) acid mixture for subsequent determination of element.

EN ISO 8099-1:2018 Small craft—Waste systems—Part 1: Waste water retention.

EN ISO 8099-2:2021 Small craft—Waste systems—Part 2: Sewage treatment systems.

EN 12740:1999 Biotechnology—Laboratories for research, development and analysis—Guidance for handling, inactivating and testing of waste.

Appendix 4 BSI Standards Related to Waste

BS EN 14405:2017 Characterization of waste—Leaching behaviour test—Up-flow percolation test (under specified conditions).

BS EN 12574-3:2017 Stationary waste containers—Part 3: Safety and health requirements.

BS EN 12574-2:2017 Stationary waste containers—Part 2: Performance requirements and test methods.

BS EN 15308:2016 Characterization of waste. Determination of selected polychlorinated biphenyls (PCB) in solid waste by gas chromatography with electron capture or mass spectrometric detection.

BS EN 13257:2016 Geotextiles and geotextile-related products—Characteristics required for use in solid waste disposals.

BS EN 14582:2016 Characterization of waste—Halogen and sulfur content—Oxygen combustion in closed systems and determination methods.

CEN/TS 16660:2015 Characterization of waste—Leaching behaviour test—Determination of the reducing character and the reducing capacity.

BS EN 15002:2015 Characterization of waste—Preparation of test portions from the laboratory sample.

BS EN 14429:2015 Characterization of waste—Leaching behaviour test—Influence of pH on leaching with initial acid/base addition.

BS EN 14997:2015 Characterization of waste—Leaching behaviour test—Influence of pH on leaching with continuous pH control.

BS EN 16424:2014 Characterization of waste—Screening methods for the element composition by portable X-ray fluorescence instruments.

BS PD CEN/TS 16675:2014 Waste—Test methods for the determination of the monolithic status of waste to be landfilled.

BS PD CEN/TR 13801:2014 Plastics piping systems for soil and waste discharge (low and high temperature) within the building structure—Thermoplastics—Recommended practice for installation.

BS EN 16457:2014 Characterization of waste—Framework for the preparation and application of a testing programme—Objectives, planning and report.

BS EN 16377:2013 Characterization of waste—Determination of brominated flame retardants (BFR) in solid waste.

BS EN 13492:2018 Geosynthetic barriers—Characteristics required for use in the construction of liquid waste disposal sites, transfer stations or secondary containment.

BS EN 13493:2018 Geosynthetic barriers—Characteristics required for use in the construction of solid waste storage and disposal sites.

BS EN 16123:2013 Characterization of waste—Guidance on selection and application of screening methods.

BS EN 15933:2012 Sludge, treated biowaste and soil—Determination of pH.

BS EN 15936:2012 Sludge, treated biowaste, soil and waste—Determination of total organic carbon (TOC) by dry combustion.

BS EN 15935:2012 Sludge, treated biowaste, soil and waste—Determination of loss on ignition.

BS EN 16166:2012 Sludge, treated biowaste and soil—Determination of adsorbable organically bound halogens (AOX).

BS EN 16167:2012 Sludge, treated biowaste and soil—Determination of polychlorinated biphenyls (PCB) by gas chromatography with mass selective detection (GC-MS) and gas chromatography with electron-capture detection (GC-ECD).

BS EN 15934:2012 Sludge, treated biowaste, soil and waste—Calculation of dry matter fraction after determination of dry residue or water content.

BS EN 16168:2012 Sludge, treated biowaste and soil—Determination of total nitrogen using dry combustion method.

BS EN 16169:2012 Sludge, treated biowaste and soil—Determination of Kjeldahl nitrogen.

BS EN 16173:2012 Sludge, treated biowaste and soil—Digestion of nitric acid soluble fractions of elements.

BS EN 16174:2012 Sludge, treated biowaste and soil—Digestion of aqua regia soluble fractions of elements.

BS EN 16179:2012 Sludge, treated biowaste and soil—Guidance for sample pretreatment.

BS EN 16192:2011 Waste—Guidance on analysis of eluates.

BS EN 15875:2011 Characterization of waste—Static test for determination of acid potential and neutralisation potential of sulfidic waste.

BS EN 13071-3:2019 Stationary waste containers up to 5,000 L, top lifted and bottom emptied—Part 3: Recommended lifting connections.

BS EN 13965-2:2010 Characterization of waste—Terminology—Part 2: Management related terms and definitions.

BS EN ISO 15883-3:2009 Washer-disinfectors—Part 3: Requirements and tests for washer-disinfectors employing thermal disinfection for human waste containers.

BS EN 15169:2007 Characterization of waste—Determination of loss on ignition in waste, sludge and sediments.

BS EN 15216:2007 Characterization of waste—Determination of total dissolved solids (TDS) in water and eluates.

BS EN 15309:2007 Characterization of waste and soil—Determination of elemental composition by X-ray fluorescence.

BS EN 13071-1:2008 Stationary waste containers up to 5,000 L, top lifted and bottom emptied—Part 1: General requirements.

BS EN 15527:2008 Characterization of waste—Determination of polycyclic aromatic hydrocarbons (PAH) in waste using gas chromatography mass spectrometry (GC/MS).

BS EN 13071-2:2008 + A1:2013 Stationary waste containers up to 5,000 L, top lifted and bottom emptied—Part 2: Additional requirements for underground or partly underground systems.

BIP 2117:2008 The Waste Electrical and Electronic Equipment Directive—Requirements and implementation.

BS EN 15012:2007 Plastics piping systems—Soil and waste discharge systems within the building structure—Performance characteristics for pipes, fittings and their joints.

BS EN 15347:2007 Plastics—Recycled Plastics—Characterisation of plastics wastes.

BS EN 15132:2006 Container shells for mobile waste containers with a capacity up to 1,700 L—Performance requirements and test methods.

BS EN 15192:2006 Characterisation of waste and soil—Determination of Chromium (VI) in solid material by alkaline digestion and ion chromatography with spectrophotometric detection.

BS PD CEN/TR 15310-1:2006 Characterization of waste—Sampling of waste materials spectrophotometric—Part 1: Guidance on selection and application of criteria for sampling under various conditions.

BS PD CEN/TR 15310-3:2006 Characterization of waste—Sampling of waste materials spectrophotometric—Part 3: Guidance on procedures for sub-sampling in the field.

BS PD CEN/TR 15310-4:2006 Characterization of waste spectrophotometric Sampling of waste materials spectrophotometric—Part 4: Guidance on procedures for sample packaging, storage, preservation, transport and delivery.

BS PD CEN/TR 15310-5:2006 Characterization of waste—Sampling of waste materials spectrophotometric—Part 5: Guidance on the process of defining the sampling plan.

BS PD CEN/TR 15310-2:2006 Characterization of waste—Sampling of waste materials—Part 2: Guidance on sampling techniques.

BIP 2102:2006 Environment management report—Focus on Waste Management.

BS EN 14899:2005 Characterization of waste—Sampling of waste materials—Framework for the preparation and application of a Sampling Plan.

BS DDCEN/TS 15364:2006 Characterization of waste—Leaching behavior tests—Acid and base neutralization capacity test.

PD CEN/TR 15018:2004 Characterization of waste—Digestion of waste samples using alkali-fusion techniques.

BS 5906:2005 Waste management in buildings—Code of practice.

BS EN 14735:2005 Characterization of waste—Preparation of waste samples for ecotoxicity tests.

BS EN 12940:2004 Footwear manufacturing wastes—Waste classification and management.

BS EN 14345:2004 Characterization of waste—Determination of hydrocarbon content by gravimetry.

BS EN 14039:2004 Characterization of waste—Determination of hydrocarbon content in the range of C_{10} to C_{40} by gas chromatography.

BS ISO 14850-1:2004 Nuclear energy—Waste-packages activity measurement—High-resolution gamma spectrometry in integral mode with open geometry.

BS EN 13427:2004 Packaging—Requirements for the use of European Standards in the field of packaging and packaging waste.

BS EN 13965-1:2004 Characterization of waste—Terminology—Material related terms and definitions.

BS EN 60335-2-16:2003 + A2:2012 Household and similar electrical appliances—Safety— Particular requirements for food waste disposers.

BS EN 12506:2003 Characterization of waste—Analysis of eluates—Determination of pH, As, Ba, Cd, Cl$^-$, Co, Cr, Cr(VI), Cu, Mo, Ni, NO$_2^-$, Pb, total S, SO$_4^{2-}$, V and Zn.

BS EN 13370:2003 Characterization of waste—Analysis of eluates—Determination of Ammonium, AOX, conductivity, Hg, phenol index, TOC, easily liberatable CN$^-$, F$^-$.

BS EN 13593:2003 Packaging—Paper sacks for household waste collection—Types, requirements and test methods.

BS EN 13657:2002 Characterization of waste—Digestion for subsequent determination of aqua regia soluble portion of elements.

BS EN 13656:2002 Characterization of waste. Microwave assisted digestion with hydrofluoric (HF), nitric (HNO$_3$), and hydrochloric (HCl) acid mixture for subsequent determination of elements.

BS EN 12457-4:2002 Characterisation of waste—Leaching—Compliance test for leaching of granular waste materials and sludges—Part 4: One stage batch test at a liquid to solid ratio of 10 L/kg for materials with particle size below 10 mm (without or with size reduction).

BS EN 12457-3:2002 Characterisation of waste—Leaching—Compliance test for leaching of granular waste materials and sludges—Part 3: Two stage batch test at a liquid to solid ratio of 2 L/kg and 8 L/kg for materials with high solid content and with particle size below 4 mm (without or with size reduction).

BS EN 12457-2:2002 Characterisation of waste—Leaching—Compliance test for leaching of granular waste materials and sludges—Part 2: One stage batch test at a liquid to solid ratio of 10 L/kg for materials with particle size below 4 mm (without or with size reduction).

BS EN 12457-1:2002 Characterisation of waste—Leaching—Compliance test for leaching of granular waste materials and sludges—Part 1: One stage batch test at a liquid to solid ratio of 2 L/kg for materials with high solid content and with particle size below 4 mm (without or with size reduction).

BS EN 13137:2001 Characterisation of waste—Determination of total organic carbon (TOC) in waste, sludges and sediments.

EN ISO 8099-1:2018 Small craft—Waste systems—Part 1: Waste water retention.

BS EN 12740:1999 Biotechnology—Laboratories for research, development and analysis—Guidance for handling, inactivating and testing of waste.

BS EN 12461:1998 Biotechnology—Large scale process and production—Guidance for the handling, inactivating and testing of waste.

EN 12920:2006 + A1:2008 Characterization of waste—Methodology for the determination of the leaching behaviour of waste under specified conditions.

BS 5832:1980 Specification for compacted waste containers for lift-off vehicles.

BS 2889:1967 Method for the determination of trash content of cotton and for trash and lint content of waste intended for spinning, by the Shirley analyser.

BS 3813-1:1964 Specification for incinerators for waste from trade and residential premises—Capacities between 50 lb/h and 1,000 lb/h.

Appendix 5 DIN Standards Related to Waste

DIN EN 16170:2017 Sludge, treated biowaste and soil—Determination of elements using inductively coupled plasma optical emission spectrometry (ICP-OES); German version EN 16170:2016.

DIN EN 16171:2017 Sludge, treated biowaste and soil—Determination of elements using inductively coupled plasma mass spectrometry (ICP-MS); German version EN 16171:2016.

DIN EN 14582:2016 Characterization of waste—Halogen and sulfur content—Oxygen combustion in closed systems and determination methods; German version EN 14582:2016.

DIN EN 15308:2016 Characterization of waste—Determination of selected polychlorinated biphenyls (PCB) in solid waste by gas chromatography with electron capture or mass spectrometric detection; German version EN 15308:2016.

DIN EN 15863:2015 Characterization of waste—Leaching behaviour test for basic characterization—Dynamic monolithic leaching test with periodic leachant renewal, under fixed conditions; German version EN 15863:2015.

DIN EN 14997:2015 Characterization of waste—Leaching behaviour test—Influence of pH on leaching with continuous pH control; German version EN 14997:2015.

DIN EN 14429:2015 Characterization of waste—Leaching behaviour test—Influence of pH on leaching with initial acid/base addition; German version EN 14429:2015.

DIN EN 16424:2015 Characterization of waste—Screening methods for the element composition by portable X-ray fluorescence instruments; German version EN 16424:2014.

DIN 19742:2014 Soil quality—Determination of selected phthalates in sludge, sediment, solid waste and soil after extraction and determination using gas chromatography mass spectrometry (GC-MS).

DIN EN 16457:2014 Characterization of waste—Framework for the preparation and application of a testing programme—Objectives, planning and report; German version EN 16457:2014.

DIN 30745:2014 Radio-frequency identification of waste containers by transponder technology using frequencies below 135 kHz and 868 MHz; Text in German and English.

DIN CEN/TS 16023:2014 Characterization of waste—Determination of gross calorific value and calculation of net calorific value; German version CEN/TS 16023:2013.

DIN EN 16377:2013 Characterization of waste—Determination of brominated flame retardants (BFR) in solid waste; German version EN 16377:2013.

DIN CEN/TS 16201:2013 Sludge, treated biowaste and soil—Determination of viable plant seeds and propagules; German version CEN/TS 16201:2013.

DIN CEN/TS 16181:2013 Soil, treated biowaste and sludge—Determination of polycyclic aromatic hydrocarbons (PAH) by gas chromatography (GC) and high performance liquid chromatography (HPLC); German version EN 16181:2018.

DIN EN 13071-2:2013 Stationary waste containers up to 5,000 L, top lifted and bottom emptied—Part 2: Additional requirements for underground or partly underground systems; German version EN 13071-2:2019.

DIN CEN/TS 16202:2013 Sludge, treated biowaste and soil—Determination of impurities and stones; German version CEN/TS 16202:2013.

DIN EN 13493:2013 Geosynthetic barriers—Characteristics required for use in the construction of solid waste storage and disposal sites; German version EN 13493:2018.

DIN CEN/TS 15937:2013 Sludge, treated biowaste and soil—Determination of specific electrical conductivity; German version CEN/TS 15937:2013.

DIN EN 840-6:2013 Mobile waste and recycling containers—Part 6: Safety and health requirements; German version EN 840-6:2020.

DIN EN 840-4:2013 Mobile waste and recycling containers—Part 4: Containers with 4 wheels with a capacity up to 1,700 L with flat lid(s), for wide trunnion or BG- and/or wide comb lifting devices—Dimensions and design; German version EN 840-4:2020.

DIN EN 16168:2012 Sludge, treated biowaste and soil—Determination of total nitrogen using dry combustion method; German version EN 16168:2012.

DIN CEN/TS 15864:2012 Characterization of waste—Leaching behaviour test for basic characterization—Dynamic monolithic leaching test with continuous leachant renewal under conditions relevant for specified scenario(s); German version CEN/TS 15864:2015.

DIN CEN/TS 15862:2012 Characterisation of waste—Compliance leaching test—One stage batch leaching test for monoliths at a fixed liquid to surface area ratio (L/A) for test portions with fixed minimum dimensions; German version CEN/TS 15862:2012.

DIN EN 15936:2012 Sludge, treated biowaste, soil and waste—Determination of total organic carbon (TOC) by dry combustion; German version EN 15936:2012.

DIN EN 16179:2012 Sludge, treated biowaste and soil—Guidance for sample pretreatment; German version EN 16179:2012.

DIN EN 15935:2012 Soil, waste, treated biowaste and sludge—Determination of loss on ignition; German version EN 15935:2021.

DIN EN 15934:2012 Sludge, treated biowaste, soil and waste—Calculation of dry matter fraction after determination of dry residue or water content; German version EN 15934:2012.

DIN EN 16173:2012 Sludge, treated biowaste and soil—Digestion of nitric acid soluble fractions of elements; German version EN 16173:2012.

DIN EN 15933:2012 Sludge, treated biowaste and soil—Determination of pH; German version EN 15933:2012.

DIN EN 16174:2012 Sludge, treated biowaste and soil—Digestion of aqua regia soluble fractions of elements; German version EN 16174:2012.

DIN EN 16166:2012 Sludge, treated biowaste and soil—Determination of adsorbable organically bound halogens (AOX); German version EN 16166:2012.

DIN EN 16169:2012 Sludge, treated biowaste and soil—Determination of Kjeldahl nitrogen; German version EN 16169:2012.

DIN CEN/TS 1565-2:2012 Plastics piping systems for soil and waste discharge (low and high temperature) within the building structure—Styrene copolymer blends (SAN+PVC)—Part 2: Guidance for the assessment of conformity.

DIN CEN/TS 1455-2:2012 Plastics piping systems for soil and waste discharge (low and high temperature) within the building structure—Acrylonitrile-butadiene-styrene (ABS)—Part 2: Guidance for the assessment of conformity; German version CEN/TS 1455-2:2012.

DIN EN 60335-2-16:2012 Household and similar electrical appliances—Safety—Part 1: General requirements (IEC 60335-1:2010, modified + COR1:2010 + COR2:2011 + A1:2013, modified + A1:2013/COR1:2014 + A2:2016 + A2:2016/COR1:2016); German version EN 60335-1:2012 + AC:2014 + A11:2014 + A13:2017 + A1:2019 + A2:2019 + A14:2019.

DIN 86210-1:2012 Replenishment with operating materials and disposal of fluid waste from seagoing vessels—Part 1: Hose fittings for hose assemblies, testing and maintenance up to PN10; Text in German and English.

DIN CEN/TS 16188:2012 Sludge, treated biowaste and soil—Determination of elements in aqua regia and nitric acid digests—Flame atomic absorption spectrometry method (FAAS); German version CEN/TS 16188:2012.

DIN CEN/TS 16177:2012 Sludge, treated biowaste and soil—Extraction for the determination of extractable ammonia, nitrate and nitrite; German version CEN/TS 16177:2012.

DIN CEN/TS 16182:2012 Sludge, treated biowaste and soil—Determination of nonylphenols (NP) and nonylphenol-mono- and diethoxylates using gas chromatography with mass selective detection (GC-MS); German version CEN/TS 16182:2012.

DIN CEN/TS 16178:2012 Sludge, treated biowaste and soil—Determination of linear alkylbenzene sulfonates (LAS) by high-performance liquid chromatography (HPLC) with fluorescence detection (FLD) or mass selective detection (MS); German version CEN/TS 16189:2012.

DIN CEN/TS 16183:2012 Sludge, treated biowaste and soil—Determination of selected phthalates using capillary gas chromatography with mass spectrometric detection (GC-MS); German version CEN/TS 16183:2012.

DIN CEN/TS 16190:2012 Soil, treated biowaste and sludge—Determination of dioxins and furans and dioxin-like polychlorinated biphenyls by gas chromatography with high resolution mass selective detection (HR GC-MS); German version EN 16190:2018.

DIN EN 13965-2:2011 Characterization of waste—Terminology—Part 2: Management related terms and definitions; Trilingual version EN 13965-2:2010.

DIN EN 13071:1 Stationary waste containers up to 5,000 L, top lifted and bottom emptied—Part 1: General requirements; German version EN 13071-1:2019.

DIN EN ISO 15883-3:2009 Washer-disinfectors—Part 3: Requirements and tests for washer-disinfectors employing thermal disinfection for human waste containers (ISO 15883-3:2006); German version EN ISO 15883-3:2009.

DIN EN 12920:2008 Characterization of waste—Methodology for the determination of the leaching behaviour of waste under specified conditions; German version EN 12920:2006+A1:2008.

DIN EN 15527:2008 Characterization of waste—Determination of polycyclic aromatic hydrocarbons (PAH) in waste using gas chromatography mass spectrometry (GC-MS); German version EN 15527:2008.

DIN EN 13592:2008 Plastics sacks for household waste collection—Types, requirements and test methods; German version EN 13592:2017.

DIN EN 15012:2008 Plastics piping systems—Soil and waste discharge systems within the building structure—Performance characteristics for pipes, fittings and their joints; German version EN 15012:2007.

DIN EN 15216:2008 Environmental solid matrices—Determination of total dissolved solids (TDS) in water and eluates; German version EN 15216:2021.

DIN EN 15309:2007 Characterization of waste and soil—Determination of elemental composition by X-ray fluorescence; German version EN 15309:2007.

DIN EN 14346:2007 Characterization of waste—Calculation of dry matter by determination of dry residue or water content.

DIN EN 14735 Characterization of waste—Preparation of waste samples for ecotoxicity tests; German version EN 14735:2005.

DIN CEN/TS 15364:2006 Characterization of waste—Leaching behaviour tests—Acid and base neutralisation capacity test; German version CEN/TS 15364:2006.

DIN EN 14803:2006 Identification and/or determination of the quantity of waste; German version EN 14803:2020.

DIN EN 14899:2006 Characterization of waste—Sampling of waste materials—Framework for the preparation and application of a sampling plan; German version EN 14899:2005.

DIN EN 13965-1:2005 Characterization of waste—Terminology—Part 1: Material related terms and definitions.

DIN EN 14039:2005 Characterization of waste—Determination of hydrocarbon content in the range of C_{10} to C_{40} by gas chromatography; German version EN 14039:2004.

DIN EN 14345:2004 Characterization of waste—Determination of hydrocarbon content by gravimetry; German version EN 14345:2004.

DIN EN 12940:2004 Footwear manufacturing wastes—Waste classification and management; German version EN 12940:2004.

DIN CEN/TS 14405:2004 Characterization of waste—Leaching behaviour test—Up-flow percolation test (under specified conditions); German version EN 14405:2017.

DIN EN 13593:2003 Packaging—Paper sacks for household waste collection—Types, requirements and test methods; German version EN 13593:2003.

DIN EN 13656:2003 Soil, treated biowaste, sludge and waste—Digestion with a hydrochloric (HCl), nitric (HNO_3) and tetrafluoroboric (HBF_4) or hydrofluoric (HF) acid mixture for subsequent determination of elements; German version EN 13656:2020.

DIN EN 13657:2003 Characterization of waste—Digestion for subsequent determination of aqua regia soluble portion of elements in waste; German version EN 13657:2002.

DIN EN 12457-3:2003 Characterization of waste—Leaching—Compliance test for leaching of granular waste materials and sludges—Part 3: Two stage batch test at a liquid to solid ratio of 2 L/kg and 8 L/kg for materials with high solid content with particle size below 4 mm (without or with size reduction); German version EN 12457-3:2002.

DIN EN 12457-1:2003 Characterization of waste—Leaching; Compliance test for leaching of granular and sludges—Part 1: One stage batch test at a liquid to solid ration of 2 L/kg with particle size below 4 mm (without or with size reduction); German version EN 12457-1:2002.

DIN EN 12457-2:2003 Characterization of waste—Leaching; Compliance test for leaching of granular and sludges—Part 2: One stage batch test at a liquid to solid ratio of 10 L/kg with particle size below 4 mm (without or with size reduction); German version EN 12457-2:2002.

DIN EN 12457-4:2003 Characterization of waste—Leaching; Compliance test for leaching of granular waste materials and sludges—Part 4: One stage batch test at a liquid to solid ratio of 10 L/kg for materials with particle size below 10 mm (without or with limited size reduction); German version EN 12457-4:2002.

DIN EN 13137:2001 Characterization of waste—Determination of total organic carbon (TOC) in waste, sludges and sediments.

DIN VEN V13801:2001 Plastics piping systems for soil and waste discharge (low and high temperature) within the building structure—Thermoplastics—Recommended practice for installation; German version CEN/TR 13801:2014.

DIN EN ISO 8099:2001 Small craft—Waste systems; German version EN ISO 8099:2018.

DIN 30742-1:1995 Waste disposal engineering—Waste containers for liquid and solid special waste—Part 1: Containers with a capacity from 60 L to 240 L made from metal material.

DIN 30743:1995 Waste disposal engineering—Loading aid for the storage and transportation of waste containers for special wastes.

Appendix 6 AFNOR Standards Related to Waste

NF X30-406-2016 Characterization of waste—Halogen and sulfur content—Oxygen combustion in closed systems and determination methods.

NF X30-495-2014 Characterization of waste—Screening methods for the element composition by portable X-ray fluorescence instruments.

NF X30-443-2014 Waste—Laboratory determination of the coefficient of permeability of a saturated material—Flexible wall permeameter with constant hydraulic gradient.

NF T54-017-1-2014 Plastics piping systems for soil and waste discharge (low and high temperature) within the building structure—Unplasticized poly(vinyl chloride) (PVC-U)—Part 1: specifications for pipes, fittings and the system.

NF X30-492-2014 Characterization of waste—Framework for the preparation and application of a testing programme—Objectives, planning and report.

NF X30-472-2014 Household and related waste—Characterisation of sorting rejects.

NF X30-425-2014 Waste—Determination of the permeability coefficient of field by a varying load test in a covered boring.

NF G38-176-2013 Geosynthetic barriers—Characteristics required for use in the construction of solid waste storage and disposal sites.

NF G38-173-2013 Geosynthetic barriers—Characteristics required for use in the construction of liquid waste disposal sites, transfer stations or secondary containment.

NF H96-115-2-2013 Stationary waste containers up to 5000 L, top lifted and bottom emptied—Part 2: additional requirements for underground or partly underground systems.

NF P40-202-2013 Building works—Calculation rules for sanitary installations and rainwater draining off—Part 1: design and calculation for looped networks. Part 2: waste and black water draining. Part 3: rain water draining.

NF X30-504-2013 Healthcare waste with infectious risk—Good practices for collecting risk infections health care waste.

NF X30-424-2013 Waste—Determination of the permeability coefficient of land by constant load infiltration test in a borehole.

NF X30-483-2013 Characterization of waste—Guidance on selection and application of screening methods.

NF H96-110-6-2013 Mobile waste and recycling containers—Part 6: safety and health requirements.

NF X31-040-2013 Sludge, treated biowaste, soil and waste—Determination of total organic carbon (TOC) by dry combustion.

NF X30-418-2012 Waste—Determination of the vertical permeability coefficient of a land using the open-type double-ring infiltrometer test.

NF C73-816/A2-2012 Household and similar electrical appliances—Safety—Part 2–16: particular requirements for food waste disposers.

NF X31-082-2012 Sludge, treated biowaste and soil—Guidance for sample pretreatment.

NF X31-037-2012 Sludge, treated biowaste and soil—Determination of Kjeldahl nitrogen.

NF X31-033-2012 Sludge, treated biowaste and soil—Determination of pH.

NF X31-211-2012 Characterization of waste—Leaching test of a solid waste material initally massive or generated by a solidification process.

NF X31-045-2012 Sludge, treated biowaste and soil—Digestion of nitric acid soluble fractions of elements.

NF X31-043-2012 Sludge, treated biowaste and soil—Digestion of aqua regia soluble fractions of elements.

NF X30-420-2012 Waste—Determination of the vertical permeability coefficient of a land through testing using a closed type, single ring infiltrometer—Constant load and variable load test.

NF X31-038-2012 Sludge, treated biowaste, soil and waste—Calculation of dry matter fraction after determination of dry residue or water content.

NF X30-485-2012 Characterization of waste—Analysis of eluates.

NF X30-478-2011 Characterization of waste—Static test for determination of acid potential and neutralisation potential of sulfidic waste.

NF M60-323-2011 Nuclear energy—Nuclear fuel cycle technology—Waste—Guide for pre-analysis dissolution of effluents, waste and embedding matrices.

NF M60-335-2011 Guideline standard for the analysis of 15 items of interest for the chemical characterisation of radioactive waste.

NF X30-011-2-2010 Characterization of waste—Terminology—Part 2: management related terms and definitions.

NF X30-510-2010 Terminology of health care waste.

NF X30-502-2010 Packaging for medical care waste—Dental amalgam waste packaging—Tests and specifications.

NF X30-500-2009 Packaging for medicinal care waste—Boxes and small collectors for perforating waste—Specifications and tests.

NF X30-507-2009 Packaging for medical waste—Medical waste—Cardboard box with inner bag for infectious medical waste.

NF H96-118-2008 Selective waste collection containers—Old engine oil containers, non-movable when loaded and during service—Specifications and testing.

NF X30-421/IN1-2008 Characterization of waste—Methodology for the Determination of the leaching behaviour of waste under specified conditions.

NF X30-446-2008 Characterization of waste—Determination of polycyclic aromatic hydrocarbons (PAH) in waste using gas chromatography mass spectrometry (GC/MS).

NF H96-115-1-2008 Stationary waste containers up to 5,000 L, top lifted bottom emptied—Part 1: general requirements.

NF X30-453-2008 Characterization of waste—Determination of selected polychlorinated biphenyls (PCB) in solid waste, by using capillary gas chromatography with electron capture or mass spectrometric detection.

NF X30-432-2008 Waste—Steels stemming from sorting of domestic and related waste—Methods for assessing the bulk density and cohesion of batch-packaged steels and for assessing the magnetic metal content of bulk steels prior to packaging.

NF T50-806-2008 Plastics—Recycled Plastics—Characterisation of plastics wastes.

NF M60-327-2008 Nuclear energy—Nuclear fuel technology—Waste—Determination of released tritium from radioactive waste packages.

NF M60-329-2008 Nuclear energy—Nuclear fuel technology—Waste—Determination of the plutonium alpha activity in effluents or solid waste by alpha spectrometry.

NF X30-480-2007 Characterization of waste—Determination of total dissolved solids (TDS) in water and eluates.

NF H34-090/IN1-2007 Plastics sacks for household waste collection—Types, requirements and test methods.

NF X30-506-2007 Health care waste—Packaging for infectious liquid health care waste—Specifications and tests.

NF M60-455-2007 Nuclear energy—Nuclear fuel technology—Scaling factor method to determine the radioactivity of low—and intermediate-level radioactive waste packages generated at nuclear power plants.

NF X30-462-2007 Characterization of waste and soil—Determination of elemental composition by X-ray fluorescence.

NF X30-463-2007 Characterization of waste—Determination of loss on ignition in waste, sludge and sediments.

NF X30-501-2006 Packaging for medicinal care waste—Bags for soft infections risk-generating waste—Specifications and tests methods.

NF X30-400-2006 Characterisation of waste—Sampling of waste materials—Framework for the preparation and application of a sampling plan.

NF M60-313-2006 Nuclear energy—Soxhlet-mode chemical durability test—Application to vitrified matrixes for high-level radioactive waste.

NF X30-455-2015 Characterization of waste—Preparation of test portions from the laboratory sample.

NF X30-413-2006 Waste—Constitution of a sample of household waste contained in a waste collection vehicle.

NF X30-452-2006 Characterization of waste—Preparation of waste samples for ecotoxicity tests.

NF M60-322-2005 Nuclear energy—Nuclear fuel cycle technology—Waste—Determination of iron 55 activity in effluents and waste by liquid scintillation after prior chemical separation.

NF X30-465-2005 Characterization of waste—Leaching behaviour test—Up-flow percolation test (under specified conditions).

NF X30-405-2005 Characterization of waste—Determination of hydrocarbon content in the range of C_{10} to C_{40} by gas chromatography.

NF X30-505-2004 Packaging for medical care waste—Health care waste—Plastic barrel and jerrycans for infections risk health care waste.

NF X30-449-2004 Characterization of waste—Determination of hydrocarbon content by gravimetry.

NF G62-700-2004 Footwear manufacturing wastes—Waste classification and management.

NF X30-011-1-2004 Characterization of waste—Terminology—Part 1: material related terms and definitions.

NF X30-503-2016 Healthcare waste—Reduction of microbiological and mechanical risks from potentially infectious and other comparable healthcare waste by disinfection pretreatment appliances.

NF H11-014-2003 Packaging—Paper sacks for household waste collection—Types, requirements and test methods.

NF J22-910-2001 Small craft—Toilet waste retention systems.

Appendix 7 National Mandatory and Recommended Standards Related to Waste

(1) Mandatory Standards

GB 16933—1997 Acceptance criteria for near surface disposal of radioactive waste.
GB 14500—2002 Regulations for radioactive waste management.
GB 34330—2017 Identification standards for solid wastes General rules.
GB 13015—2017 Standard for pollution control on Polychlorinated Biphenyls (PCBs)-contaminated wastes.
GB 30485—2013 Standard for pollution control on co-processing of solid wastes in cement kiln.
GB 5085.6—2007 Identification standards for hazardous wastes—Identification for toxic substance content.
GB 5085.7—2007 Identification standards for hazardous wastes—General specifications.
GB5085.2—2007 Identification standards for hazardous wastes—Screening test for acute toxicity.
GB 5085.3—2007 Identification standards for hazardous wastes—Identification for extraction toxicity.
GB 5085.1—2007 Identification standards for hazardous wastes—Identification for corrosivity.
GB 5085.4—2007 Identification standards for hazardous wastes—Identification for ignitability.
GB 5085.5—2007 Identification standards for hazardous wastes—Identification for reactivity.
GB 19218—2003 Technical standard for medical waste incinerator.
GB 19217—2003 Technical standard for medical waste transport vehicle.
GB 18598—2001 Standard for pollution control on the security landfill site for hazardous wastes.
GB 18599—2020 Standard for pollution control on the non-hazardous industrial solid waste storage and landfill.
GB 18597—2001 Standard for pollution control on hazardous waste storage.
GB 18484—2020 Standard for pollution control on hazardous waste incineration.
GB 5086.1—1997 Test method standard for leaching toxicity of solid wastes—Roll over leaching procedure.
GB 15562.2—1995 Graphical signs for environmental protection—Solid waste storage (disposal) site.
GB 14585—1993 Regulations for safe management of radioactive wastes from the mining and milling of uranium and thorium ores.
GB 13600—1992 Regulations for disposal of solid low-and intermediate level radioactive wastes in rock cavities.
GB 12711—2018 Standard of safety for low-and intermediate level solid radioactive waste packages.

GB 11928—1989 Regulations for interim storage of low-and intermediate-level radioactive solid wastes.

GB 9132—1988 Regulations for shallow ground disposal of solid low-and intermediate-level radioactive wastes.

GB 16487.8—2017 Environmental protection control standard for imported solid wastes as raw materials—Waste electric motors.

GB 16487.3—2017 Environmental protection control standard for imported solid wastes as raw materials—Wood and wood articles wastes.

GB 16487.10—2017 Environmental protection control standard for imported solid wastes as raw materials—Metal and electrical appliance scraps.

GB 16487.11—2017 Environmental protection control standard for imported solid wastes as raw materials—Vessels and other floating structures for breaking up.

GB 16487.13—2017 Environmental protection control standard for imported solid wastes as raw materials—Compressed piece of scrap automobile.

GB 16487.2—2017 Environmental protection control standard for imported solid wastes as raw materials—Smelt slag.

GB 16487.6—2017 Environmental protection control standard for imported solid wastes as raw materials—Waste and scrap of iron and steel.

GB 16487.7—2017 Environmental protection control standard for imported solid wastes as raw materials—Nonferrous metal scraps.

GB 16487.9—2017 Environmental protection control standard for imported solid wastes as raw materials—Waste wires and cables.

GB 16487.12—2017 Environmental protection control standard for imported solid wastes as raw materials—Waste and scrap of plastics.

GB 16487.4—2017 Environmental protection control standard for imported solid wastes as raw materials—Waste and scrap of paper or paperboard.

GB 14569.1—2011 Performance requirements for low and intermediate level radioactive waste form—Cemented waste form.

GB 16487.1—2005 Environmental protection control standard for imported solid wastes as raw materials—Wastes of bones.

GB 16487.5—2005 Environmental protection control standard for imported solid wastes as raw materials—Waste and scrap of fibres.

GB 19057—2003 Regulation for solid waste treatment and disposal for the destruction of abandoned chemical weapons by Japan in China.

GB 14569.3—1995 Characteristic requirements for solidified waste of low and intermediate level radioactive waste—Bitumen solidified waste.

(2) Recommended Standards

GB/T 34911—2017 Terminology on comprehensive utilization of industrial solid wastes.

GB/T 30760—2014 Technical specification for coprocessing of solid waste in cement kiln.

GB/T 29478—2012 Mobile laboratory hazardous waste management specification.

GB/T 18773—2008 Environmental sanitation standard for incineration of medical treatment wastes.

GB/T 15555.8—1995 Solid waste—Determination of total chromium—Titrimetric method.

GB/T 32326—2015 Assessment guidelines for integrated utilization technology of industrial solid waste.

GB/T 32328—2015 Quality and environment safety evaluation guidelines for integrated utilization product of industrial solid waste.

GB/T 27945.1—2011 The management of hazardous solid wastes from heat treatment salt Part 1: General management.

GB/T 7023—2011 Standard test method for leachability of low-and intermediate level solidified radioactive waste forms.

GB/T 27945.2—2011 The management of hazardous solid wastes from heat treatment salts Part 2: Test method of extractives.

GB/T 27945.3—2011 The management of hazardous solid wastes from heat treatment salts Part 3: Method of innocent treatment.

GB/T 28178—2011 Landfill disposal for very low level radioactive waste.

GB/T 17947—2008 Activity measurements of solid materials considered for recycling re-use, or disposal as non-radioactive waste.

GB/T 4960.8—2008 Glossary of term: nuclear science and technology—Part 8: Radioactive waste management.

GB/T 15950—1995 General requirements for environmental radiation monitoring around near surface disposal site of low-intermediate level radioactive solid waste.

GB/T 15555.3—1995 Solid waste—Determination of arsenic—Silver diethyldithiocarbamate spectrophotometric method.

GB/T 15555.10—1995 Solid waste—Determination of nickel—Dimethylglyoxime spectrophotometric method.

GB/T 15555.1—1995 Solid waste—Determination of total mercury—Cold atomic absorption spectrometry.

GB/T 15555.4—1995 Solid waste—Determination of chromium (Ⅵ)—1, 5-Diphenylcarbohydrazide spectrophotometric method.

GB/T 15555.5—1995 Solid waste—Determination of total chromium—1, 5-Diphenylcarbohydrazide spectrophotometric method.

GB/T 15555.11—1995 Solid waste—Determination of fluoride—Ion selective electrode method.

GB/T 15555.12—1995 Solid waste—Glass electrode test—Method of corrosivity.

GB/T 15555.7—1995 Solid waste—Determination of chromium (Ⅵ)—Titrimetric method.

Epilogue

I have to admit that writing this book took me a lot of effort and all the fragment time I could spare from work and life in the past two years.

I often wrote in two scenarios. One is when my son Xiaocheng was playing table tennis every Saturday in the No.1 Junior Amateur Sports School of Xuhui District, I wrote and waited for him in a café (Friday Patisserie) at the intersection of Yongjia Road and Urumqi South Road for two hours. That is a perfect writing environment with coffee. Another is when I took business trip away from home for three days every month on average, I could go back to the hotel spent two hours quietly writing.

While writing, I was also talking to the publishers. Although my alma mater's East China University of Science and Technology Press once again extended a warm invitation to me, this time, without much hesitation, I chose Chemical Industry Press—this was entirely the intention of my father and mother.

In fact, as early as 1999, my father had published a book titled *Production Process and Operation of Small Ammonia Plants* (ISBN No.: 9787502525330) with Chemical Industry Press. My mother told me that with the publication, the 10,000 RMB manuscript fee (which was a lot of money at that time) was used to support my study pursuit in France… So this time, following my parents' advice, I decided to take over my father's "business" after 20 years, with the same press to renew this destiny.

I would like to thank Ms. Jing Liu, an alumnus of East China University of Science and Technology and an editor of Chemical Industry Press, for her time and efforts spending on the conception, editing and publication of the book. Both of us are students of ECUST, so it is meaningful to have such a cooperation after graduation.

This book is published in English, thanks to the editor of Springer, Mr. Wayne Hu, with whom I had a perfect collaboration for the publication of my previous book in English. Wayne and I both studied in France, so we have a lot in common; he has often discussed with me from the academic perspective of the book, and I have benefited from his various suggestions and comments.

I would also like to thank Baidu Baike, for the writing structure and knowledge in each chapter of this book—this public science database has offered well categorized information of different industries and technologies, from which I selected some easy-to-understand terminology, identified and borrowed some cases for in-depth analysis and non-copyrighted related figures. Under the premise of protecting intellectual property rights, human wisdom and technology should be fully shared. I deeply appreciate it and hope that the results of my efforts can be shared to every reader.

Mr. Jie Zhang of Starbucks (Shanghai) Coffee Company Limited, provided the basic content of the two sections of Chapter 7 on Kitchen Waste and Laboratory Waste based on years of work experience; Dr. Benyi Xiao of the Research Center for Eco-Environmental Sciences, Chinese Academy of Sciences, provided most of the content on Secondary Waste in Chapter 7, and Mr. Hong Wang of SAIC General Motors Corporation Limited, provided references and revisions to the section on Automotive Industry in Chapter 8… The guidance and help from other scholars and colleagues are too numerous to list here, but I feel grateful to them all.

Although the book focuses on waste-related science, technology, and industry applications, however, the book features descriptions of laws and regulations in at least four chapters. "When the rule of law thrives, the country thrives; when the rule of law is strong, the country is strong." Law is the key instrument of governance, and the rule of law is an important support for the national governance system and governance capacity. Since the 18th National Congress of the Communist Party of China, the comprehensive rule of law has been promoted in depth, and the concept of rule of law has become more deeply rooted in people's hearts. The rule of law is of great significance in accelerating the reform of the ecological civilization system and building a beautiful China, also including the realization of the goal of waste-free cities.

Honorably, as this book was about to be completed, the School of Resources and Environmental Engineering of East China University of Science and Technology needed a guest lecturer to teach a graduate course on solid waste and resource recovery. I was invited to participate in preparing this course in English. I could continue to discuss the contents described in this book with the faculty and students of my alma mater. How fun is that!

No harvest can be achieved without the support of the family, especially my wife and children who are with me all the time—and this is the case with this book. I didn't tell my wife about writing the book at all, so that she wouldn't need to sacrifice more of her spare time to support me, and so that I could give her a surprise after the publication. I hope I did it…

This book is also dedicated to all the heroes and warriors who have worked tirelessly and selflessly for the environment, safety and health of human beings, at a critical moment when China is fighting against the COVID-19 outbreak.

Jianming
Early spring in 2020